CRACKING
THE LIFE
CODE

D1157785

This book is dedicated to my unborn child.
Please read this book sooner than later.

35 W 31st Street
New York, NY 10001
(+1) 203 772 8813
help@crackingthelifecode.com

ISBN: 978-1-7376486-0-4 (print)
ISBN: 978-1-7376486-1-1 (ebook)
Ordering Information:
Special discounts are available on quantity purchases by corporations, associations, and others. For details, contact help@crackingthelifecode.com

CONTENTS

CRACKING THE LIFE CODE

Keys to Master Your Mindset, Habits, and Behaviors for Personal Success

BABS FASEESIN

PART 1:

WHAT IS THE LIFE CODE?

Chapter 1

Life Codes Case Study: Matthew and Kari

Matthew Tanner loved his wife Kari. They met on the first day of their sophomore year of college. They'd both signed up for the rhetoric and communication class that all their friends told them was an easy A and a quick way to fulfill one of their general education requirements. He'd been sitting toward the back of the classroom, doodling in his notebook when she came in. Kari was 20 minutes late, and totally flustered. She squeezed past four other students to get to the empty seat, then tripped and landed right in his lap. As soon as their eyes met, it was magic.

For the rest of class, they couldn't keep their eyes off each other. They went out for coffee afterward. She was broke, but he was happy to pay. By the time the next class rolled around two days later, they could barely keep their hands off each other. And it wasn't just an intense physical attraction either. This was so much more. She got him, and like him, she came from a broken home and had a bad relationship with her parents. Kari was the first person who didn't look at him like a weirdo when he talked about his childhood. He trusted her, and even showed her the scars on his back—something he never shared with anyone.

At the end of the semester, they both passed the class, but just barely. Matthew was surprised when it came time to study for the final, only to discover that he'd only taken a total of six pages of notes for the entire quarter. When he asked to borrow hers, she blushingly showed him pages doodled with cute little hearts and the words Mrs. Kari Tanner scribbled in the margins.

Two-years later, they married. It was the happiest day of their lives. Kari began the newlywed life, sleeping in on weekends and doing things around the house with Mathew. She got excited about all the little things, like plating Mathew's dinner and capturing those beautiful moments as a couple to share on social media with her friends. After this initial honeymoon phase, everything quieted down, and Mathew set out to find work. Before either of them had time to think, she told him she was pregnant with twins. The day his sons were born became the new happiest day of his life.

But since then, things started to go downhill little by little, if he was being honest with himself. His nagging mother-in-law moved in for a couple of weeks to help with the children and never left. With so many mouths to feed, he had to work longer hours and began to spend less time with his wife and two boys. He even missed their acting debut in the first-grade play. Feeling guilty, he bought them gifts to make up for the absences. He didn't know what else to do.

Matthew loved Kari, but sometimes she drove him crazy. Like that time he'd found out his department was being downsized at work, and came home only to find out she'd spent thousands of dollars they didn't have to buy instruments for the boys so they could learn to play. While that wasn't a bad thing, they changed their mind about what they wanted to do or be every other minute. Today they wanted to be musicians, and tomorrow they'd want to be firemen.

The money was one thing. But what upset him even more was that she hadn't talked to him about it first. Even after it was done, she *still* hadn't come talk to him. Of course, he became even more upset when she had the audacity to act as if he were the one at fault. He tried to cool down, ask her what was wrong and why she was so upset. But in her usual passive aggressive way, all she would say is *fine*, which he knew from experience was code for *I hate you* and *leave me alone.*

In turn, he decided to oblige her. He called a couple of his friends, but everyone was busy. So instead, he went to a bar by himself. After all, he knew from his own childhood that if he drank at home in his den, he'd turn into an alcoholic. If he went out, he was just being social. Even if he was sitting all by himself.

Matthew and Kari both received bad codes growing up. Matthew's father resorted to violence with his family when he was angry or frustrated. As much as Matthew hated that about his father, those codes were still instilled in him. As he grew up and became an adult, he never replaced those codes with good, healthy ones.

He didn't know how to properly deal with his anger, and never learned to express his emotions in a non-violent way. During childhood, there were other adults in Matthew's life that knew what was happening but never spoke out. This behavior reinforced in his mind that this was normal, and that there wasn't a way out of the cycle. Although he tried to be a better man, the codes ultimately won out when he was pushed too hard.

Kari, on the other hand, was raised in a more emotionally abusive family where her parents didn't talk to one another and used both words and shunning silence to hurt each other. She grew up with codes that told her that it was ok to shut the other person out and not communicate, particularly when she was upset about something. Unfortunately, she didn't try to implement different codes either. She refused every opportunity that came her way to change the cycle and learn healthy communication. And like her parents, she used silence, refused to talk about the problem or help solve it, and saw this as a weapon in her relationship with Matthew.

Matthew and Kari both continued to act out the codes they had been raised with. As much as they might have resented their parents, they never sought out a different way of doing things. They didn't understand that for things to change, they had to undo these negatively learned behaviors. Ultimately, they could only repeat their parents' mistakes. Even worse, they now passed on these bad codes to their twin sons, who were growing up to believe that violence was a normal part of relationships, and that communication wasn't something that needed to be done with your significant other. Without intervention, they will grow up to be just like their parents and the cycle will continue to repeat in future generations.

Whether you realize it or not, everyone lives by a life code. This comprises of a system of beliefs, rules, behaviors, and habits that govern your life. Your life code is made up of the beliefs that have been programmed into you since birth. This is due, in some part, to the way your brain behaves similarly to a computer. In fact, Massachusetts Institute of Technology's (MIT) Mark Harnett's study on neurons revealed that human brain cells could work like minicomputers.[1]

As your brain takes in and analyzes information, it develops a series of responses based on what it figures out. Anytime you learn something new, whether it's a physical action like tying a shoe or a behavioral lesson like saying please and thank you, your brain is coding this information. Once learned and repeated, the behaviors eventually become habit, so much so that they are often done subconsciously. These actions become coded into your brain and are as much a part of you as your genetic code.

For example, when you tie a shoe, you no longer think about the mechanics of it. While it might've given you some problems as a child, you can likely now complete these steps with your eyes closed because your brain has coded the activity. There is now muscle memory in your hands and fingers, and you know exactly what to do. Likewise, when someone holds a door for you or gives you something, you automatically say thank you without having to consciously remind yourself to say it.

Unfortunately, when your brain is taking in information, analyzing it, and forming beliefs, patterns, and habits, it doesn't have a way to determine whether the codes being created are good or bad. When you were a child, you learned from family members, teachers, society, and other children. These experiences and the

---

1   Claire Wilson, "Your brain is like 100 billion mini-computers all working to-gether," *New Scientist*, October 18, 2018, https://www.newscientist.com/article/2182987-your-brain-is-like-100-billion-mini-computers-all-working-together/.

things you were told about the world became the codes in your brain and are the codes that dictate your behaviors and beliefs. The problem is, these may or may not have been the right codes to receive. That's often because these people have broken codes too, and although our family and friends may have good intentions, they cannot give what they don't have. This is a primary reason why codes are often transferred from one generation to the next until one person in the chain realizes the cycle and decides a change needs to be made.

One good way to see how this plays an important role in our lives is to look at education and its overall importance in shaping us as individuals. From very early on, a child will observe how their parents treat education and speak of education. If a parent talks about the importance of learning and going to college, and then demonstrates a desire to keep improving themselves, then the code being passed on to that child is that education and life-long learning are important. A belief will exist that one can and should constantly try to improve themselves. If the child has, on the other hand, a parent who downplays the importance of education or belittles those who pursue it, then the child receives a different code, and may view education has having little value as they progress through life.

This is true in many other areas of a child's life too. Research in child development has established strong connections between parent behaviors and children's attributes.[2] It can play a substantial role in development. The way a child's parents treat each other codes in them beliefs about how a spouse or significant other is to be treated. A coaching client once asked me why she always attracted men with similar traits to her abusive father. Even though she

2   D. Baumrind and A. Black, "Socialization practices associated with dimensions of competence in preschool boys and girls," *Child Development* 38, no. 2 (1967): 291–327, https://doi.org/10.2307/1127295.

disliked her father, for some reason she continued to be attracted to men that reminded her of her father. She knew these men were not good for her but couldn't seem to break the pattern. This is how abuse and negative patterns of behavior regularly perpetuate themselves through families for generations. Children are coded and hardwired to repeat what they have learned and experienced. This is because our mind naturally gravitates towards what's familiar. When children are exposed to these codes, it's normal to see them gravitate towards experiences, choices, and behaviors that reinforce the codes.

This was the case with Matthew and Kari, who both grew up in broken homes where the adults in their life didn't communicate well with each other. While Matthew wanted to be different, he was stuck because he never consciously found a way to break his code. Kari's mother was secretive and passive aggressive, making everyone suffer when she was angry. When provoked, Kari behaved the same way her mother did because she didn't know better.

Both Matthew and Kari had bad codes, and to have a successful marriage they both needed to find better codes and exchange those for the bad ones they'd received growing up. Without changing what was wrong first, they became stuck in the same patterns that troubled both of their families, possibly for generations.

"People never change" is something you might have heard frequently. While it might seem that way, the good news is that change is possible. You don't have to settle for the bad codes that were handed to you. You're not doomed to repeat your parents' and your grandparents' mistakes. It's completely possible to change the codes that have been programmed into you, even if that change won't be easy to come by.

If you're skeptical, think about the people you know. Odds are you have a friend, a mentor, or a colleague who has changed for the better. That person has managed to break free of a bad behavior and changed family patterns. Some of you may be the first or only one to graduate college in your family, or the first to get married. This is done with the effort and understanding that the codes you received are faulty and need to be replaced with new, better codes. This can be done through self-assessment and correction. Of course, it's easier to do if you have friends, teachers, or mentors who can model good code for you and show you the way to do things better. Once you learn to master your life codes and rewrite the ones you need, then it will become possible to begin living an abundant, fulfilled life.

Chapter 2

Learning to Swim When Water Kills

All your observations and experiences help create your life code. According to the Centers for Disease Control's (CDC) developmental milestones, children develop skills such as imitating the behaviors of adults and older children as early as two years of age.[3] This presupposes that a major part of life codes are developed in early childhood and young adult.

As a child, one of my friends drowned in a pool while learning to swim. This experience was quite traumatic, and subsequently my friends and I were prohibited from going into water. I grew up with this fear that water represented danger, and because of this I even avoided going to the beach during young adulthood. While I understood that my parents wanted to protect me from harm, I

---

3   "Child Development: Toddlers (2–3 years of age)," Centers for Disease Control and Prevention, accessed June 14, 2021, https://www.cdc.gov/ncbddd/childdevelopment/positiveparenting/toddlers2.html.t

believe their extreme approach in this instance programmed a bad code in me.

Sometimes learning is direct. Your parent teaches you to be self-sufficient and never ask for help, and when a problem aris-es, you keep everything to yourself. If you're anything like me, perhaps you were told boys are supposed to be brave and not cry when you fall off your bike and skin your knee. These are the types of beliefs that then get directly coded into your being. Moving forward you're liable to act on that belief until you realize that it's wrong, and that nobody is truly self-sufficient. Asking for help when you need it is a strength and not a weakness, and strong men actually do cry. I had to learn that it's okay to show emotions as a man.

Yet, at other times learning can be less direct and more observa-tional. You might notice that your father never asks for help. If he's struggling with something and your mother offers to help him, he gets upset and angry. He doesn't allow anyone to do anything for him, and if it becomes a choice between giving up or asking for help, he gives up. While he never directly told you that asking for help was bad, he demonstrated it for you in numerous ways. So, in this indirect way, the code that you receive is asking for help is bad, and you grow up with that same flaw.

Like the codes you receive from direct and indirect learning, experiences create codes as well. This is a natural part of growth and development that's often very helpful. The first time a child puts their hand too close to a fire, he or she realizes that fire can burn you and is dangerous. That's an important lesson that keeps the child from getting hurt. However, sometimes even a good code can be corrupted.

If a child's only experience with dogs is that one time a dog snapped at him, the code in his or her brain might say that all dogs are bad and should be avoided even though not all dogs are dangerous. This could make parts of life painful and more difficult to deal with than they should be. After all, there's not just the joy of learning that a dog can be a great companion that will be missed. It might make friendships with those who have dogs in their homes difficult. It might also make the child have issues with working in environments where he could encounter a service animal. These are all ways that the codes you have can end up having a lasting impact and affect your life in one way or another.

Chapter 3

Solving the Puzzle of Life

Life is a puzzle that everyone attempts to solve. The faster you can do this, the faster you can get to the place where you're really living your best, fullest, most fulfilling life. Some people seem to get there a lot faster than others, solving it in their early twenties, while others struggle throughout life and are still trying to figure it out in their later years of life. What makes for this extreme difference?

Imagine for a moment that the road to personal fulfillment and success is like a giant jigsaw puzzle. You open the box, dump out all the pieces, and sit there staring at them, wondering where to start. If you have no experience with this and no one to help guide you, you might just pick up pieces and try to put them together without any sense of order or purpose. In this case, you'll quickly become frustrated after hours pass and it seems like you've made little or no progress.

Many people experience this as they get started on their life journey. You don't know what you're doing, and so you just latch on to whatever you can without a real understanding of how to make everything work. You eagerly take the first job offered to you, even if it doesn't match your personality, lifestyle, or career goals. You date whoever agrees to go out with you without putting much thought or effort into figuring out at the start if they will be the right life partner for the years ahead.

When you're first out on your own, you might also be tempted to do things like eschew the healthy habits your parents instilled in you. Instead of getting a reasonable amount of sleep, you stay up late, and your sleep schedule becomes erratic. Instead of eating balanced meals, you eat whatever you want or can afford, regardless of whether it's good for you. You might also surround yourself with friends who are fun but who don't necessarily challenge you to be a better person or to achieve greater things. You participate in activities that, while diverting, have no real value and don't fulfill you on a deeper level.

The point is, when you're young, some floundering is expected. Some of it is even unavoidable. That's because you don't yet have the experience to understand how to do everything the right way. You don't completely understand how the world works yet, and some of us will have a harder time with this than others. That's because they haven't had the right codes programmed into their brains yet.

Like the example of the jigsaw puzzle, given enough time, frustration, and trial and error, eventually you can put it together by yourself with no experience if you don't give up. However, if someone had sat down next to you and told you that there are better strategies to accomplish the task, the experience would've been much easier and less stressful. Suddenly, a problem that might have taken you weeks can now be finished within a day or two.

That's how it is with life too. The picture on the puzzle box is your vision of the life you're trying to achieve. It's your purpose for being—the thing you're trying to bring into existence. At first, each of your efforts should focus on the picture. Then you can begin to examine the different colors, the different sections of your puzzle. Once you complete a section pick another one and try to build as much of it as you can. Keep working on the sections until they take the shape and begin to fit together into a cohesive whole that's allows your vision to come to fruition.

When you're finished, you can stand back and admire what you've created. The hours of toil and work will have not been in vain. Then, and this is truly important, it's time to turn to a grandchild, niece, or nephew, and teach them the good codes that you've learned. This way, they won't flounder as you did when it's time to dump out the puzzle pieces of their life and figure out where to start and what to do.

Of course, the biggest difficulty here lies in the fact that life is far more complicated and messier than your average jigsaw puzzle. You aren't given all the pieces to your perfect life in one, neat package and told to assemble them. Instead, you are given a handful of pieces, some of which might not work for the ultimate picture you want to create. You're also given access to thousands of other pieces that you can choose from in order to complete your puzzle.

These pieces are represented by the skills you learn, habits you form, people you have relationships with, the jobs you can take, the books you read, and the experiences you have. You need to carefully evaluate each of these and ask yourself if these pieces can help you get to where you want to go, and if they're needed to be part of that final picture. Sometimes you'll guess wrong and choose a piece that ultimately doesn't fit with the overall vision and purpose for your life. The good news is, you'll have the opportunity to swap those bad pieces for good ones that can ultimately help you to fulfill your life's purpose.

Chapter 4

Cracking the Code

Have you ever had the experience of putting together a jigsaw puzzle or anything similar only to realize that a piece that seemed to fit wasn't right? It had all the right lines and colors and seemed to lock in place with the others, but ultimately it wasn't the right piece. And unless you moved it, you would never complete the puzzle. This situation can be difficult and extremely frustrating, but it's still important to constantly examine your puzzle to make sure that everything is indeed fitting together as it should. This will allow you to make necessary changes and continue to move forward. It's the same with your life.

Realize though that not all codes lead to success. No matter how much family members and teachers care about you, bad code will still slip in. There is no maliciousness here. Rather, they're simply passing on the bad code that has been instilled in them through their own experiences and observations. And in order to break, erase, and rewrite bad code, you must first acknowledge that the code is flawed. Once you can identify a false belief, a bad habit, or a behavior that holds you back from living life to its fullest, you must acknowledge that it's indeed faulty and needs to be removed.

Creating new empowering codes is a valuable skill to have, but the ability to stop and eliminate your current, bad codes is just as important. Limiting life codes create greater challenges in life. It's like bailing out a boat with a bucket that's still filling with water. Your negative life codes may be drowning your efforts to be successful. But that's the root cause of most bad habits—the desire to feel better in the short term.

To begin to break free of some of some of these limiting life codes you may already have, give this step-by-step process a try:

1. **Consider your goals and list the bad codes that are interfering with reaching these goals.** Consider the far-reaching effects of your limiting life codes. For example, overeating can interfere with your health and appearance as well as your ability to play with your children.

    - *Tip:* You might enlist the help of your partner or close friends. They can probably offer some interesting insight!

2. **Pick one or two bad codes to address at a time.** It's not likely you'll simultaneously be able to drop every bad code you have. Either choose the bad code that's having the greatest impact on your life or choose a code that will be easy to break. Choose to either make a significant change or allow yourself to gain momentum.

3. **Determine the benefit you're gaining from that bad code.** Keep in mind that your negative habits, behavior, and beliefs are providing you with some type of reward. Otherwise, you wouldn't be doing them!

   - *Tip:* Think about how you feel before performing the habit and how you feel afterwards. What do you receive from this action that might not be in your best interest moving forward?

4. **Find another way to get the same benefit.** How can you get the same benefit without harming yourself or limiting your life?

   - *Tip:* List a few alternative behaviors that you believe would be effective substitutes and begin making a positive habit out of the best option.

5. **What happens right before you perform the habit or engage a negative belief?** What are the circumstances that trigger your bad codes?

   - ❖ Is it a certain time of day?
   - ❖ A stressful interaction at work?
   - ❖ Stress in general?
   - ❖ Spending time with a certain friend?
   - ❖ Loneliness?
   - ❖ Fatigue?

6. **When possible, avoid the triggers that are most likely to initiate your negative codes.** Maybe watching TV late at night leads to overeating. If this is the cause, it would make sense to find another activity to keep yourself occupied at night. Do your best to find a way around triggers and bad codes will be easier to overcome.

7. **Install new codes.** This is critical step to your success. Create a new positive code to replace the negative ones. It's not enough to tell yourself that you'll meditate instead of smoking. It's necessary to make a habit of meditating regularly.

   • *Tip:* It can be difficult to think your way past a bad code. Begin by training yourself to avoid the habit and to perform the new codes.

8. **Be patient with yourself.** Remember that changing your life code is a significant undertaking. It will be challenging, so make sure to allow for missteps and understand that backsliding is par for the course. Like anything else worthwhile, it'll take time and patience.

Our lives are largely determined by the number and magnitude of our bad codes. Eliminating these self-imposed anchors is an important skill to develop. Bad codes may provide temporary comfort, which can make them especially difficult to eliminate. Remind yourself of the damage being caused by your negative codes and that the challenge in front of you will make you a better person in the long run.

Another important skill to develop is the ability to deal with discomfort. The ability to handle stress and other emotional discomforts is closely related to your ability to drop bad codes.

New code can be created in several ways:

• *Model the behavior of others.* One of the most effective ways to create new codes is to model behavior from someone who has the code you want to incorporate. Finding a mentor, becoming friends with someone you admire, or even marrying into a family with better codes than the ones you were raised with are all ways that you can learn new codes from other people.

- *Be a seeker of knowledge.* A lot of bad codes stem from ignorance. The way to counter it is to acquire knowledge. Many people shy away from investing money because they were raised with codes that told them that investing is dangerous and only for wealthy people. By researching the topic, you might find that there are many ways to invest with varying degrees of risk. This can also lead to the realization that it's not just a hobby for the rich but rather a vital tool for financial well-being.

- *Be open to new experiences*: It's possible to learn new codes by exposing yourself to new experiences. Life has much to offer when you open yourself to new experiences. Take for instance a person who is traumatized from a childhood experience with a neighbor's dog. Volunteering in an animal shelter might present a different perspective to this negative perception of dogs. This kind of extreme reconditioning is not necessarily for the faint of heart but can quickly change or at least temper someone's perspective.

Keep in mind that identifying a bad code, breaking it, creating good code, and passing on the good code to future generations is a lifetime effort. It's not something you can take care of all at once and then move on. It is a process that will require lots of time and effort.

Sometimes it can seem like your life is planned out for you, but even if your course has been mapped out, you don't have to follow the map. Maybe your parents both have college degrees and work in a particular field. They can have expectations that you'll follow in their footsteps. From the time you were born, they've trained you to do as they have done and are programming you with the codes that they think will help you get there. This can be subtle prodding, or it can be as overt as having your university already picked out for you, with deviation from the plan being unacceptable.

It's not easy to step out of your parents' shadow and be your own person. The expectations of the parents or guardians influence can have a profound impact. However, it's still important as an adult to forge your own path and figure out what's best for you and your own well-being.

Chapter 5

The Three Stages of Life

There are three stages of life, and the effort put in at each stage can significantly impact the years ahead. In my view, our life is broken up into three main stages or parts: morning, afternoon, and night. What's expected of you differs by stage, but generally speaking, you'll spend the first stage building codes, the second creating better codes, and in the third you'll pass along those improved codes to others.

Stage One: Morning

In the early morning, there's a difference to the air, a coolness that only exists in the beginning of the day. Birds sing and the whole world seems to stand in wonder, watching, waiting. The world is full of potential with endless possibilities for the day ahead. There's a sense of wonder, optimism, and hope. As the day begins, there's no telling what wonderful and miraculous things might occur before the sun sets.

Like the beginning of a new day, with the first rays of the morning sun a child is born into the world. Everything is new and bright and loud. The child sees everything with eyes that are not yet jaded. They believe everything they hear without reservation. They feel everything so very deeply because they've not learned how to do otherwise.

This new life is full of opportunity and untapped potential. Each child is born into this world a blank slate, ready to be written upon by life. They spend the first part of their journey absorbing all the information that they can, learning through experience what it means to be part of the world. This is a time of intense learning and growth, and the future is uncharted. In the scope of life, it's the morning that represent these early years of a child.

The morning hours are all about successfully setting yourself up for the rest of your day. It's when you wake, make yourself presentable, eat a breakfast that will provide you with the energy and nutrients you need to begin accomplishing those tasks you have set up for your day. You might notice too that if you skip these steps, it can throw your whole day out of balance. The same is true with the codes you receive as a child.

When you're young, you're waking up to the world around you. As you grow from infancy you quickly become aware that there's more than just you, your parents, and a couple of rooms in your house. You learn that there's a big world beyond your crib, just waiting to be explored. But in order to do so safely and without harm, you need the right combination of knowledge, beliefs, culture, and interpersonal skills.

As you begin to step out into the world, your parents show you important first steps. As a child, they might dress you in clothing appropriate to the temperature and conditions. Many children fight wearing restrictive clothes, but they learn that it's a requirement for going outside and interacting with other people. This is similar to the way children learn that bathing and brushing their teeth are also required to make themselves presentable. Likewise, they're told about the importance of breakfast, how it's the most important meal of the day, and how it'll be used as fuel for the hours ahead.

In fact, there's a whole set of social rules that children come to learn. Some of these rules include learning how to interact with adults who aren't their parents, how to interact with other kids, and what the rules of society are. This is knowledge children aren't born with and need to be taught. In teaching children these things, those around them are instilling the codes that the children will end up living by.

These codes cover every aspect of life. Children listen to what they're told and model what they see. If you train a child to be polite and say please and thank you, then they receive the code that they need to be respectful and polite, and that other people aren't there just to serve them. On the other hand, if you model for a child an entitled attitude or one of complaining about other people, that's what they'll take to heart. Instead, they might be more inclined to grow up with the belief that the world owes them something and have little respect for those around them.

This beginning period of intense learning and modeling generally lasts until the late teen years when the child has an opportunity to experience the world without their parents by their side. For some this begins in high school, while for others it might occur during college or after getting that first job. This time of separation from your parents and having to stand on your own two feet can be exciting, challenging, and even scary.

Think about how this experience was for you. Did you enjoy it? Were you terrified? Did you feel prepared to make that step, or did you flounder and feel completely lost? Perhaps things didn't go as planned, and you or someone you knew was in for a rude awakening. This could stem from a bad code you received early on. Maybe if you didn't do something like a science project or clean your room, your parents would just do it for you. Entering college or the workforce is a distinct transition that marks the dividing line between child and young adult. For some, it's a natural progression. For others it is a harsh reality that goes against everything they've experienced.

Life will test you at every corner, regardless of what types of codes you've received. This can have intense consequences once you're outside the bubble in which you were raised. Some people at this stage flounder and struggle, seeking to find others who will validate the bad codes they received growing up and perhaps rejoice in the comfort of their sympathizers. Others with good codes will stretch their wings. Either way, this is the time to test what kind of codes you have.

To gain further insight into the morning stage of life, it is important to consider ways in which life codes are built and absorbed in the morning stage. Here are some of the ways codes will be developed in these early, morning stages of your life:

- *Preparing for the race*: The morning period of your life is the warm-up for your race. It's when you stretch, make sure that you've taken in whatever nutrients you need to, put on the right attire, and familiarized yourself with what you're supposed to do. Your morning starts at the very beginning in the womb and lasts through childhood. During the morning you're in a constant state of learning and will form the codes that shape the rest of your life. If good codes aren't developed, then life is going to be harder down the road. In this way, it's like trying to run a race without properly stretching first. You're going to end up with leg cramps that might cripple you and extremely hamper your ability to finish at all, let alone do your best.

- *Gathering information:* Children constantly take in information. All their senses are geared toward absorbing as much knowledge as possible. They learn behavior, language, values, and habits that dictate the race they're going to be running. Signals from their family, culture, and society at large provide them with an image of who they are, how they should act, and even what they should be when they grow up. Things that happen that might seem trivial or insignificant can end up having a profound impact much later on. Remember, children model what they see.

- *Learning about emotions:* In this is the stage, you learn a lot about emotions. Ideally, you'll learn a lot of positive emotions, but often many negative ones creep in too. Perhaps the most insidious of all emotions is fear. You don't start off with fear. Instead, you've been programed through a combination of life experiences and observations to have this emotion. When you have an abundance of fear, you see the world with risk and a sense of foreboding and mistrust. You might even learn to sense it in the adults around you and mimic it. That's why it's important as an adult to avoid telegraphing negativity around children, which will be built into their core code and become a normal way of thinking. The same is true with other harmful attitudes, emotions, and behaviors. If you behave recklessly, for example, it will instill in the child the idea that it's ok to behave recklessly too. If you model prejudice, then they will as well. Given that they don't have many life experiences of their own to draw on, they must use yours to help them make decisions and learn about the world and their place in it.

Morning is the time of life where many of your life codes are created. This happens as a natural part of growing up and learning how to live in the world and in society. Since children don't have an inherent sense of what things are supposed to be, they rely on their parents, grandparents, teachers, and other adults to show them. It's crucial that when you have children and grandchildren, that you help them through this phase of their lives by teaching them in such a way that they help to build the right codes. By doing this, you'll save them a lot of time and effort as they grow older.

Stage Two: The Afternoon

Once the morning is over and the sun is high in the sky, it's time to begin the hard work of the day. The rays of the sun are on your face and life is good, powerful, and so much is happening all around you. In the back of your mind, though, you know that the sun can't stay high forever. Sooner or later night will come, so now is the time to celebrate, to dance in the warmth, and to accomplish all you can while you have its life-giving warmth to encourage and sustain you.

When afternoon arrives, so does all the hard work of chasing your dreams and making them happen. It's time to push that little bit extra in order to achieve your dreams. If you're a young Kobe Bryant, you spend endless hours practicing your jump shot with a dream of becoming a great basketball player. Or you work towards creating that tiny business out of your friend's garage that you hope will one day take the world by storm. Maybe you play guitar until your fingers are calloused in the hopes of making it as a musician, or lose endless sleep studying to be a great doctor and save people.

These are all the things done in this second stage of life because this is when you have the time, the energy, the passion, and the opportunity to shape the world around you. Now is when you can create the life that you desire through hard work and dedication. This is the afternoon stage of your life.

The afternoon starts when you transition into the real world. This may be college or the workforce, or whenever you step out onto your own for the first time. While this time will often be met with great rush of excitement, it can also be tempered with fear. Now is when those codes that you received as a child will prove themselves to be helpful or a hindrance. It's also the time when you'll want to rewrite those bad codes you received as quickly as possible before they begin to impact aspects of your career, business, health, and relationships.

Since the afternoon is the time for getting things done, you'll need to start out by learning how to run your race. In this stage, you begin to build your life, your career, your skill set, and learn to fend for yourself. Time becomes crucially important. The energy of youth is yours, and you must put it to good use. This is the time of life when you're at your peak physically and mentally. Great inventors, leaders, and pioneers seize this time, and use their energy and determination to reshape the world around them.

In the afternoon stage of life is when Kobe Bryant became a basketball legend by practicing longer, harder, and with more focus than pretty much anyone else. When he was selected to be part of the U.S. Olympic team, there are stories about how he would often get up in the middle of the night to run, lift weights, and to drill jump shots until he completed eight hundred repetitions *before* the team practice even started.[4]

This is also the time when Jerry Seinfeld became a comedic legend by writing jokes every single day, refusing to stop until he completed his goal.[5] Michael Jackson is said to have practiced his dance steps until his legs gave out.[6] Walt Disney failed in business multiple times but continued to drive harder, pushing himself and those who worked for him to the brink of collapse.[7] Ub Iwerks, one of Disney's chief animators, drew more than 700 drawings a day.[8] The point is, every great star, no matter their field, seizes this time of their life to push harder and focus more intensely, which in turn can yield incredible results.

Of course, you can't maximize your potential, let alone reshape the world, if you don't have the right codes. It's impossible to build anything without the proper tools. After all, how will you know where you're going? How will you understand pacing, or the importance of staying hydrated along the way? How will you keep yourself from being distracted by the other runners? To be successful, you need the right combination of codes to make any meaningful progress in life. The right sets of codes will be your compass, your guide, and your internal motivation. Good codes will tell you

---

4   Tony Manfred, "A Crazy Story About Kobe Bryant Waking Up In The Middle Of The Night To Work Out Before The Olympics," Business Insider, March 5, 2013, https://www.businessinsider.com/kobe-bryant-woke-up-at-4-am-to-practice-before-olympics-2013-3.

5   Jonah Weiner, "Jerry Seinfeld Intends to Die Standing Up," the *New York Times Magazine*, December 20, 2012, https://www.nytimes.com/2012/12/23/magazine/jerry-seinfeld-intends-to-die-standing-up.html.

6   Chris Connelly and Lauren Sher, "Michael Jackson Overexerted Himself in Tour Rehearsal, Insiders Say," ABC News, July 2, 2009, https://abcnews.go.com/Entertainment/MichaelJackson/story?id=7990611&page=1.

7   Eudie Pak, "Walt Disney's Rocky Road to Success," Biography, accessed June 14, 2021, https://www.biography.com/news/walt-disney-failures/.

8   "Ub Iwerks," Walt Disney Archives, accessed June 14, 2021, https://d23.com/walt-disney-legend-ub-iwerks/.

that in order to finish the race you need to stay focused, you need to hydrate consistently, and you can't let yourself be distracted by the pace of others. The question is: What do you do if these codes, and many others you need to succeed, weren't instilled in you as a child?

Maybe you grew up with parents who failed at what they tried to accomplish. Or maybe you were raised in poverty and had to deal with constant uncertainty. Even if your parents loved you, they couldn't offer what you needed to get a good start in life. On the other hand, perhaps they were able to give you a good start, but it was the life they wanted you to live and not the life you now desire. For some, the problem might be that they weren't raised in a loving environment with guardians who modeled good codes. For others, harsh circumstances might have forced you to grow up on the street or bounce from one house to another. Some of you might have parents who suffered from substance abuse or took their rage and frustration out on you. You might have grown up with a deeply damaged sense of right and wrong and been in trouble with the law at an early age because of it. It doesn't matter how bad the codes you were given are. It doesn't matter what you've done with them before now. *All that matters is that you start doing the right thing, right now.* It's up to you to take the first step and break the bad codes you've been given.

To successfully break these codes, you'll find yourself faced with the need to undo much of what you have learned. This requires undoing your current programming and to start over by retraining yourself. Now is the time to learn new codes and unlearn bad ones, and to reinforce or relearn good codes that haven't settled in as deeply as they need to. While you can certainly map out your ideal life and try to figure out your dreams without taking these steps, you'll ultimately struggle unless you're determined to break bad codes and create new behaviors.

The good news is, it's possible to rewire your brain. Even bad codes that seem to be hardwired in can be rewritten. All you need to do is begin to embrace traits like love, humility, respect for others, and tenacity. These behaviors and actions will take you further than you might realize, allowing you to live the life of your dreams even if you aren't naturally ambitious. It's all about rewiring and allowing your brain to learn new, better codes that will better serve you in the future.

A task this monumental can be daunting for sure. But don't waste this time in your life. Know that, as it is in the afternoon, the sun is going down. Time is limited, and therefore, you don't have the luxury to waste it. Push yourself forward, discover your purpose and why you're here on the planet. This focus should be the center of your life, and everything else grows darker as you move away from that.

Realize too that what you do at this stage of life will determine how the rest of your life plays out. If you make good choices and use good codes, then when you retire you can do so in comfort. If you don't make good choices, then the last part of your life may be more of a struggle than you hoped.

In the example of Matthew and Kari, they each had opportunities to break the bad codes they grew up with. Remember that they met in a communications class which, had they paid attention, could have given them the tools needed for a solid relationship. And when they saw examples of happy couples who did communicate with each other, Matthew and Kari both viewed those people as somehow being blessed or naïve. They never took the time to learn from them and figure out what they knew or how they did things differently. If they had, Matthew and Kari would've had the chance to change their bad codes and achieved a happier life together.

When they experienced crisis in their marriage early on, Mathew and Kari had an opportunity at hand. This could have served as the wake-up call they both needed and left them both horrified enough to decide it was time to work together to find a better way. Some couples might use a moment like this to begin counseling and figure out how to better manage their anger and stress and learn to communicate with each other. It's important to remember that it's never too late to change your bad codes. No matter how set in your ways you think you are, there's always time to find a better way to think, feel, communicate, and act.

Work hard to break the codes as early as you can and spend as much time living up to your full potential as possible. The faster and more aggressively you do this, the easier it will be to enjoy the latter stages of your life.

Stage Three: Night

The sun descends, the air begins to chill, and most of the world slows down to prepare for rest. Stillness creeps over the land, and as the light starts to fail, so too may your eyesight. As the sun wanes, so too may your strength. In your heart and mind, you know it's time to slow down and rest. During this final stage, your friends and colleagues are retiring, growing sick, and some even dying. There are those of us that do so with grace, and others who desperately cling to the afternoon, even though it has forsaken them.

Here, you'll need to ask yourself if you're prepared. Have you worked enough, planned well enough, so that you can retire when you choose? Or are you facing a bleak reality of having to continue the daily grind just to keep food in your mouth and a roof over your head? Whether you want to believe it or not, everyone reaches the nighttime stage of their life—some sooner than others.

What you've done before either works for you or against you. If you've received the right code, you can relax and enjoy yourself. You've made it to the end of the course and now is the time to cool down, stretch, and accept whatever medal or award you've earned. Once the hard work is finished, it's time to go have a celebratory meal with friends before getting some rest. This could mean traveling, spending time with grandchildren, or enjoying leisure activities.

However, if you didn't use the code the correct way, you'll find that your race still isn't over. Instead of being finished with your race, you'll need to catch up. If you didn't fix the bad code or maximize your afternoon time the way you should've, then this time of ease and rejoicing can easily turn into a time of more stress and anguish.

If you want to change bad code for future generations, remember that it's at this stage of your life that it's absolutely crucial. When people speak, they speak out of personal experience. When you're around younger generations, it's important that you speak truth and instill in them the codes needed to succeed. This is true generational wealth.

For example, think about a runner that's just finished a marathon and joins up with their friends and family afterward. Rarely is he or she silent. Instead, they explain what it is they experienced along the way, the things that happened to them, and the emotions they felt. They explain how they focused, how they overcame any physical or mental difficulty to reach the finish line, and what happened to other runners who couldn't quite make it.

This is how it should be with your grandchildren or any other child you can help by sharing your wisdom and experiences.

Tell them about your struggles, the lessons you've learned, and the truths that helped you create the life you have. They can learn a great deal about your failures and your triumphs, so the same mistakes won't continue to be made.

Just as a young woman might wear her grandmother's tiara on her wedding day, codes are something to be passed down and used. You have a responsibility to improve yourself throughout the course of your life and to improve the generations that will come after you. This can be accomplished by teaching them how to do things the right way. When you share good codes, strong beliefs, and instill habits that will serve these future generations well, they will be able to pass on even better codes on to those that come after them.

That is because codes, in much the same way as genetic traits or diseases, are passed down in families. Your codes will impact future generations whether you intend it or not. It's your responsibility to make sure the *right* codes are being continued and not the wrong ones. In Africa, it's easy to see the impact these codes have. That's why some families have several generations of doctors or police officers. They teach each younger generation these values and habits, and often expect their children and grandchildren to follow in their footsteps.

Life is meant to be progressive. As the decades and centuries pass, science, technology, medicine, and so many other aspects of society continue to improve. The same should be true with people. Each generation should be an improvement on the previous one.

While many have called the generation that lived through and fought in World War II the "greatest generation,"[9] there's a sad implication that less is expected of the generations that followed. This gap of progression through generations can be avoided if you

---

9   Julia Kagan, "The Greatest Generation," Investopedia, updated April 26, 2020, https://www.investopedia.com/terms/t/the_greatest_generation.asp.

teach your children and grandchildren how to rise up, take hold of the good codes that have been built, improve upon them, and change any bad ones they find along the way. It's then their responsibility to pass on these improved codes.

Nighttime is a fantastic time for teaching. If you've spent your afternoon wisely, then you should have a lot of spare time on your hands. Instead of isolating or focusing just on you, look to your family. Find ways to spend more time with your grandchildren so you can help teach and mold them. One of the most important things you can do is to help them discover their purpose. A person's purpose is identifiable, even when they're a child. Once you learn what to look for, you can help your children and grandchildren uncover theirs so they can maximize the time they spend living for that purpose.

In the end, the goal at this stage is to get a good night's sleep, knowing that you did everything you could possibly do to generate the right code for generations to come. You want your grandchildren and great-grandchildren to learn from your mistakes and failures as well as from your successes. Now is the time to help program them with the codes needed to succeed in life. That is perhaps the greatest accomplishment you can have, and it will provide a truly lasting legacy.

Turn to the workbook section at the back of the book, page 343, for your reflection exercises to help you commit to action.

PART 2:

FINDING AND UNDERSTANDING YOUR PURPOSE

Chapter 1

Find Something Better to Do

Matthew Tanner felt like he'd lost sight of who he was. When he was young, he'd had dreams and aspirations, but now could barely remember them despite having a decent job that was tolerable most of the time. Of course, the constant threat of downsizing didn't help.

Two nights a week for the past month, he'd gone out drinking. Twice he'd gotten a friend to go with him, but for the most part he was drinking alone. Even though he was feeling worse physically, he welcomed the numbness that alcohol brought. The next night when he visited the same local bar, the bartender began to look at Matthew in a way that made him feel uneasy. After handing him a fourth drink, the bartender leaned in to speak with him.

"I know it isn't any business of mine, pal, but don't you have somewhere better to be?"

Matthew thought of the fight he'd had with Kari when he'd gotten home from work earlier. They'd fought about money again, and this time the kids had overheard. He didn't like that, but what could he do about it?

"My wife's not exactly enjoying my company at the moment," he told the nosy bartender.

"Okay, what are you going to do about it?"

Matthew stared at the man. "Why do you care what I do?"

"Look, I'm usually the last guy to judge, but I've seen that look you have in your eyes. You've been coming here a lot and drinking more each time. This never ends well."

Matthew wanted to be angry, but deep down it felt good that someone cared where he was and what he was doing. Still, everything looked hopeless from where he sat.

"My friends are all busy with their families. I hate going to the movies alone. And I can't even imagine what kind of volunteer work I could do," he admitted.

"There's a lot of things you can do. Find something that might make you happy, give you a purpose," the bartender said.

"A purpose?" Matthew said, turning the word around in his mind. He wondered briefly what it would feel like to have a purpose. He tried to shrug it off with a joke.

"I think my purpose is to keep this seat warm."

The bartender shot him a look of pity that he wished he could forget.

Everyone has a purpose. The sooner a person discovers their purpose, the more they can work to fulfill this purpose throughout their life.

Whether or not you've thought about it, you have a purpose. This is the reason you were born. Think of it as the picture that you're trying to make out of your life with your jigsaw pieces. You can think of it as a higher calling, or simply being true to the core of who you really are. Either way, it's what you're called to do for yourself, your family, and society as a whole. It's important to believe that you were put here to do something that only you are uniquely suited to do.

Let's think about that for a moment. There's no other person on the planet who's exactly like you. They might have a similar upbringing, similar beliefs, similar tastes, even similar appearance, but they're not exactly like you. If you want proof of this, look at your fingerprints. A fingerprint is made up of a pattern of loops, whirls, and arches. No two people on the planet have the same set. Not even identical twins have identical fingerprints. And so too is your individual purpose completely your own, unique to you.

As such, it's important not to judge yourself against other people—their purpose will be different than yours. One person's complete jigsaw puzzle might only be the centerpiece for your jigsaw puzzle. Beyond that, the pieces or sections of society's puzzle, and the whole, is not complete without you. We all need to work together to make the world a better place. Everyone has a role to play in that. While we all have individual goals, this should be the shared goal of every individual. By fulfilling your own purpose, you do make the world better.

Imagine a mighty hunter with a quiver filled with arrows. Every arrow is a different size, shape, length, weight, color. When he sees his quarry, he selects the perfect arrow. He knows the physics of how that arrow will fly when aimed and fired correctly. Of course, the hunter must consider distance, wind speed, the size of the prey, and the density of the hide the arrow must pierce. Once he has determined all of this and has selected the perfect arrow, he chooses it from his quiver, and sends it on its way. Once it has found and felled its target, he goes to carefully remove the arrow, clean it, and return it to the quiver.

This is similar to your journey. The Creator is the hunter, and people are the arrows. Whether you realize it or not, you're the perfect arrow to solve a problem that exists in the world. Your race, gender, skills, beliefs, upbringing, location, education, personality, and every other aspect of you was carefully crafted and is required for this singular purpose. When you have fulfilled your purpose, the hunter comes to pick you up, clean you off, and take you home where you can rest and be at peace. This is a good thing for you even though it can cause sorrow for those who are left behind.

Keep in mind that death is not the end—it's simply the journey home. This is why funerals are a celebration of a person's life and all they have accomplished. They're an acknowledgement that a person can now pass on to their reward for a job well done. If there is anything you want to pay significant attention to, it should be finding this one thing you were created to achieve. After all, one of the most important questions you will ever have to answer is, *why am I here?*

Chapter 2

Unlocking Purpose with Interests, Abilities, and Childhood Dreams

By finding your purpose in life, you can turn bad situations into good ones. This can make life more meaningful and give you a reason to bound out of bed in the morning instead of grouching your way to the coffee pot.

I will say that it doesn't have to be as difficult of a process as you might think. This is because you've almost certainly touched on aspects in your life already, even when you were a child.

Remember, you can gain insights into a person's purpose through careful observation of an individual's life from early childhood. A few clues that might provide insights into a person's purpose include what they naturally gravitate toward. As for yourself, look back on the experiences you had as a child and the things you did that made you feel fulfilled. What were they? Do they have a common thread?

It might take a couple of hours of quiet contemplation, but you'll likely find a connection. There's usually a common thread that runs through our life experiences, deepest desires, activities, interests, and aspirations. Even when it seems as though these things are totally unrelated, right in that disjointed, unrelated mess, there's one thing that will likely stand out. Your own experiences might seem like they have no relation to each other, but they almost certainly do. You just have to ponder what thread connects them all. Once you find it, you've likely discovered your purpose, the thing you were born to do.

When you were a child, that purpose might have come more naturally to you and played out in your life in one way or another. As an adult, the sooner you identify your purpose and help others identify theirs, the sooner you can start to fulfill your destiny. Don't go through life like a hamster running on a wheel, failing to take time to reflect on your life's purpose. Since it can be unsettling if you don't know what to do with your life, spend a little time figuring it out. It's important to find your purpose because the cost of never doing so is significant. When you look to your values and preferences, you'll find a life path that appeals to you. All it takes is asking yourself a few pertinent questions.

Consider these ideas to determine your purpose:

- *What am I interested in?* These can be things you like to do, learn about, or think about. Think about what activities cause you to lose track of time and make a list of your 10 favorite activities.
- *What am I naturally good at?* Try to find something that you love and have a natural talent for. What are a few things you do better than the average person? Make another list.

- *What did I want to do when I was a child?* What did you dream about being when you were growing up? Sometimes your first ideas can be your best. Think about your childhood dreams and ask yourself why you were interested in that subject. You might get a few clues.
- *What are my values?* What is most important to you? Is it adventure, helping others, personal development, or overcoming challenges? Your purpose should be aligned with your values.
- *What is my gut telling me?* There's a time for logic and reason. This might not be one of those times. Sometimes, the best choice doesn't necessarily make a lot of sense. Listen to what your soul is trying to tell you and you might get the answer you're looking for.

Chapter 3

My Purpose

For me, my purpose is to inspire others to greatness. It's a true joy to help someone achieve their dreams and to watch their own miracles come to fruition.

I come from a middle-class family in Nigeria. Growing up, my parents were both educated. My mother was a librarian and an entrepreneur while my father was an educator and a businessman. I realized when I examined myself that I must have been given a mindset of success in childhood. At six years old, I went on a kids' television show to recite a poem. How does that fit into my purpose you might ask? Because poems are meant to move and inspire others.

When I was 10 years old, I organized a Christian quiz competition at church. At this point, I began to push others to competition and provide motivation to be better than themselves. At the time, I had no idea what purpose was, but these were my natural progressions in early childhood. By 14 years of age, I began to host young adult conferences. Here you can see I was reaching out, seeking to inspire and educate my peers and those older than me to learn and achieve more.

Throughout my life, this trend continued. In high school I was a prefect—a position of responsibility where I had an opportunity to help my fellow students. In college, I began to teach and engaged in public speaking. I was a leader of the student body and mentored others. And since I was raised in the wilderness, I always kept my primary goal in mind too. I wanted to get my community out of the wilderness and to a place of flourishing.

In my professional career, I became a strategy consultant. I continued to focus on public speaking and writing and did everything possible to inspire my generation. Throughout the years, I've had the privilege of speaking on several business and personal development platforms across 22 countries and four continents, including the National Business Leaders Conference. I was also the convener of the Inspire Africa Tour in 2014—a conference designed to inspire young adults across key cities in Africa to be the best version of themselves. From there, I created crackingthelifecode.com, a platform where people can access information for personal growth and development.

As you can see, inspiring others to greatness has been a driving force in my life. You might think that I'm a rare example of those who find purpose manifesting early in life. But I can assure you, I'm not. Look back at your own childhood. See the things and ideals that you gravitated toward. Were you the one who loved to solve difficult problems? Were you the caregiver for everyone around you? Did you derive joy from uplifting people's spirits with music? Were you the one who connected people to find solutions, or the one people came to for counsel?

Finding your purpose isn't impossible, and if you reflect on these questions, the answer is likely already there waiting for you.

Chapter 4

Living with Purpose

Living with purpose helps to make the tough times easier to deal with, and the good times even better. Think again about the jigsaw puzzle of your life. You can try to put it all together without ever looking at what picture you're trying to form. Eventually you might get there, but it's a whole lot easier and takes a lot less time if you know what picture you're trying to create. This big picture is your purpose. This will help all the pieces come together into their proper place quicker, and with less frustration. You'll be able to cut out distractions and focus on things that align with your purpose. The decision-making process becomes much easier when you look at everything through the lens of your purpose.

Although you may express different aspects at different times, your purpose remains the same over the course of your life. For example, a high school kid may volunteer to read to children at the local library. In college he might study to be a writer and then pursue that as his career. Eventually, he may become a publisher. His purpose has remained the same, to educate through books and share the love of books with others. It's only the expression of that purpose that shifts from reader to writer to publisher.

Sadly, a lot of people actively avoid their purpose. From my experience in working with young adults, I've seen that it's not uncommon to find people who create a pseudo purpose for themselves. This may be because they've found a comfort zone that feels safe, or having continuously tried and failed, they decide to stick with the very first thing they succeed at. While both reasons are valid and understandable, they can hinder people from finding their true purpose in life. This can also deprive people from experiencing the joy, satisfaction, and fulfillment that comes with living in purpose.

You reap twentyfold when you're living in your actual purpose. Living with purpose starts with understanding your own personal system of values and beliefs. Ask yourself what's important to you and what really matters most. When you understand your beliefs, you can begin to live and stick to what's really important in your moral universe. We all have an inbuilt code that can be used to guide the way you make decisions and priorities. It's the bedrock of integrity, and how others will judge you. Living in alignment with your purpose will earn you respect and trust. Perhaps the best gift of living a life of purpose is that you'll relish every moment.

There's no room in life for regret. Everything you do should be part of the bigger adventure, or the puzzle you're putting together. Challenges and setbacks become easier to deal with because you're not letting failure define you. When you're plugged into the present, you'll feel the abundance that exists in your life. Once you're comfortable with your life's purpose, some of the striving and anxiety of life will dissipate. You'll begin to realize how important it is to stay healthy, emotionally and physically. People living with purpose make sure to connect with the people they love, and they don't forget about self-care. Priorities are shaped by purpose, and once you know your life purpose it becomes easier to discover how to achieve your goals. With this clarity, you'll say no to some things and yes to others in a more natural way, allowing you to get ahead much faster.

I've seen many young people who procrastinate because they're comfortable in their current position. They're at point A, even though they know they should be at point C. Point A is their comfort zone, and it can be difficult to step outside of that. But if you want your life to go from ok to great, leaving your comfort zone is a must. While it's true that one person's ok might be another person's great depending on your situation, I believe we each owe it to ourselves to take ownership of our destinies and work towards shaping our lives. Only then will you be living your life in a purposeful way. Remember, it's not enough to find your purpose—you must continue to live within it, and this takes effort and specific tools to achieve success.

The four pillars of success that sustain and support your purpose are **passion**, **platform**, **place**, and **people**.

Chapter 5

How Passion Relates to Purpose, and the Role of Platform

Passion is an important pillar which upholds and furthers your purpose. Passion is what drives you. It's what helps you accomplish your purpose. Imagine you have a car and a destination you need to reach. Passion is the fuel required to help you complete your journey and keeps you going against all odds. It can also make work more fun and enjoyable and provide the mental and emotional energy you need to persevere through rough times and keep hope alive.

In the school of success, purpose precedes passion. Purpose is what gives direction to your passion. Passion without purpose can feel like joyriding. You're simply driving to drive, without a destination in mind. Sometimes joyriding is a waste of time and gas, though it's possible to run into your purpose by simply joyriding.

However, you improve your chances of finding purpose if you start with a destination in mind. Even if you wind up in a different place entirely, it'll be because you chose the new destination. You need to be able to give your passion an outlet, a direction. Channel your passion in the direction of your purpose. To do this, purpose needs to come first to direct passion.

The second pillar that helps to support purpose and allows it to thrive is platform. If passion is the fuel that powers you toward your destination, platform is the road you take to get there. A platform is what helps to showcase your purpose to the world. In my experience, I've seen that most talent, dreams, and purpose need a platform for visibility. After all, of what use is talent when it's not visible to others?

The impact you'll have is limited when purpose is invisible. Before reality television shows, there were many talents that we didn't know or hear about. Many of these talents could have become global icons had they been privileged to grace reality television platforms. There are many famous soccer players who play on professional teams. People know and adore them, and even follow their entire careers. However, they're not necessarily the best soccer players in the world in terms of natural gifts. I can assure if there was a talent scout in some of the remotest parts of the world you would be able to find exceptional soccer players, perhaps some of the best. However, no one knows they're the best, and they have no impact on the game on a global scale because they are not visible to the masses. They don't have the public eye the way others do. In this way, they don't have the same platform.

Platform speaks to visibility. It doesn't matter how powerful your passion is or how significant your purpose is. Without a platform, chances are you'll struggle to make a meaningful impact. When you think of platform, remember that this doesn't have to be a literal stage, but it does need to be a showcase for your passion. You can always go farther in life if you have a platform because it will let you impact others in a more profound way. The platform is the road you take to get to your destination.

One way you can achieve this is to use an existing platform or create your own. Even though it may not seem like it, there are many existing platforms available. Shows like *American Idol* are a great example of a platform created for musicians to take advantage of. Carrie Underwood is an example of someone who used the *American Idol* platform to show the world her passion and talent. She sang for many years before *American Idol*, but this platform gave her the visibility she needed to do bigger and better things. She was then able to get her own show, which might not have been possible without this platform.

My first real job was in banking. Banking is a platform, but I quickly realized it was one I couldn't use for my passion—and that's okay. If one platform doesn't work for you, find another. With all the tools and technology that are available today, it's easier than ever to find a variety of platforms at your disposal. Sites like YouTube and Instagram are easy ways to create an outlet for your voice to be heard by thousands of others with minimal investment on your part.

On the other hand, if you can't find a platform, you create one to showcase your skills and passion. When creating a platform, make it possible for others to fulfill their purpose by using your platform. For example, I searched for a platform where I could help upwardly mobile, young people unlock the potential of their minds. I didn't find the kind of platform I was looking for, so now I'm creating one.

While it might sound easy, creating a platform can be a difficult road. I know it was for me. When I started speaking at events and conferences, I did it for free just to get my name out there. This took time and effort, but it all paid off. Since then, I've been able to connect with and mentor a lot of young people. Even this book you're reading is itself a platform.

As I transitioned from teenager to a young adult, I realized I was the guy people around my neighborhood, school, and church would confide in and seek advice from. And because I genuinely enjoyed helping, each Saturday I began to bring my friends and classmates together for a 30-minute chat about our lives and studies.

During my third year in college, I gathered interested students in my department for a one-hour inspirational session each week. By my final year in college, I was speaking to the entire organization of Christian students at our school. While these experiences occurred in college, it prepared me for the real world. Because I knew I had a deep desire to get my message out to the world, it was important for me to create a platform that allowed me to do so.

I realized that the best way for me to do this was to contact event organizers and religious organizations for opportunities to speak to their audience for free. There is a time I remember driving three hours to speak at an event that started 90 minutes late for free. Instead of being frustrated, I was happy to get my message out. I knew that the more people heard my message, the more likely they'd be to go and tell others.

My goal was to make my audience my evangelists. While that was going on, I also took advantage of Facebook since it was a free platform for me to share my message. Even today, I share my thoughts daily on Facebook, and have quickly maxed out my friends limit in about 18 months. One of the major events that helped me to achieve this type of platform was when I had the honor of inviting the late Dr. Myles Munroe to speak at my Total Life Mastery conference in Africa in 2012. Dr. Munroe was a highly sought-after speaker globally, and at the time, having him speak on my platform gave me immense credibility and social proof. Since then, I've gone on to create several other speaking platforms. This process has taken over a decade, but in the end, it was well worth the effort.

Chapter 6

The Role of Place and People in Finding Purpose

The third and fourth pillars of success are the role of place and people, and how these factors play a major role in finding your purpose. Remember that every aspect of your life is what makes you uniquely suited to solve a problem. This includes place, where you're at both physically and mentally.

In terms of geography, you're more likely to flourish in your natural habitat. A fish swims effortlessly in water, but when a fish is placed on the soil, it will flap for a few minutes before dying. The same is true with most birds. An eagle in the air is majestic, a glory to behold. The same bird dumped in the sea becomes the weakest you've ever seen. Trees and plants need different environments to grow too. Some grow in wetlands and rain forests. Others are built to withstand desert climates and can even flourish there, growing powerful despite the lack of water.

The same is true with people. In order to achieve your purpose and get the most out of your platform, you need to be in the right place. To crack the life code, some of you might need to review what place you're in. If you're feeling strangled by your situation, it might be because you're not in the right place.

Your purpose can often help you determine where you should be. If your purpose is to help bring modern farming techniques to third world countries, you probably shouldn't be living in the middle of New York City. On the other hand, if your purpose is to educate disaffected youth in the inner city by providing mentors, then you probably should be living in New York or another urban area.

It can be easy to find yourself suddenly tied to a place. Whether it's because that's where your entire family lives, you reside in a house that's been passed down for generations, or are used to being around your childhood friends, if you're not living for your purpose, you need to go elsewhere in order to maximize your life.

While many think of place as a physical location, place can also be a state of mind. When you hear people say things like "I'm at a place where…," this is what they're referencing. If you don't have the right mindset, you won't get the most out of life. Real success is not money, but rather having the correct state or place of mind. That's when you can truly maximize your potential.

There's a saying that you shouldn't dress for the job you have but rather for the job you want. This type of thinking is your frame of mind. You can't get to the palace looking, acting, and feeling like a pauper. Instead, you need to put yourself mentally in the place of being a prince. Once you believe that and fully put yourself in that mindset, there are few who will challenge your right to be in the palace.

It's not what you don't have that limits you. Rather, it's what you have that you don't know how to use that limits you. It's not a lack of resources that holds you back—it's a lack of resourcefulness. You see, power and control are all in the mind. Learn to use it and you will see opportunities where others see obstacles.

Another element of place is niche. To find the niche that you're trying to reach, narrow your focus by either location, economic status, or culture. Find your exact niche and you'll find success. Take the field of medicine for instance. This field of study can be a very big space, ranging from neurology to pediatrics. To succeed, you'll need to find that one area that you're called to serve in.

Try to focus on that one thing, that niche that you're trying to reach. Many people become frustrated in their purpose because they're too broad in their focus. Think first of the individual you're trying to reach, then base your efforts on the kind of people that meet that description. Though it can seem narrow and lonely at times, it's important to find your niche.

Other people are the final pillar that support your purpose. Everyone makes a lot out of those who are self-made. While you might engineer your own destiny, there will always be people who helped you achieve success. Even if you've done the bulk of the work, you're not an island. There are people who helped you get to where you are in one way or another. Your parents literally created you, so without them you wouldn't even exist. Beyond family, the person you decide to get married to, the networks you build at school, and the professional relationships you form on the job all play a role in your success.

The bottom line is you need people to get further in life. Whether it's the people who buy your products, pay your wages, make business deals with you, or put in a word for you in the boardroom, you can't always do it alone. Sometimes you might need a person whose platform you can speak on, or to mention your name and speak for you at the table when decisions are being made.

One ugly truth I've learned in life is that certain doors just don't open of their own accord. You're going to need someone to open the door for you to go in. A good boss can help you get noticed, achieve promotions, and ultimately help to shape your career. A happy, satisfied customer can drive business your way, open your eyes to new sales and marketing opportunities, and make joint ventures and projects possible.

A friend or coworker's new business could provide an opportunity for employment or even expand your own skills or business. I knew a singer who would perform at small conventions and local events who got to know the owners of the conventions and venues very well. Using those connections, he was able to go from being a guest at other people's conventions to creating and running his own. Eventually he was able to draw lots of enthusiastic fans and created a whole new business line for himself that helped support him and his family. It was through his interactions with event runners and venue owners that he was able to gain the skills, knowledge, support, and promotion he needed to start his new business and make it a success.

The right people will no doubt make your journey smoother. These people are like fillers for the potholes on the highway to success. You already know that passion is your car's fuel, and the platform is the road. Realize that the road will always have potholes, and people are the ones who will help you smooth them over, so you don't get stuck. It's people who literally pave the way for your success.

That's why people who are great at networking always achieve more in life than those who aren't. Build relationships and networks. Assemble a group of people you can trust. Find a mentor who has already gone ahead of you and can help you avoid some of the pitfalls. You always need somebody. As a personal goal, I am building my network of friends from every critical field of life, from medicine to plumbing, so that I'll have a reliable friend in all professions.

Another saying that's worth noting is *your network is your net worth*. This speaks to the importance of people. When you're just starting, you might have moved cities, had a break from the work-force, or might not be sure where to begin to build an active net-work. If you're feeling lost and not sure where to start, try these simple tips to connect with the right people and create a new circle of professional relationships:

- *Start with who you already know.* Even if you're starting from scratch, you'll be surprised at how many contacts you al-ready have. Sit down and make a list of all your colleagues and clients, friends, neighbors and college professors. Think of what connections you might be able to make. Start to build your LinkedIn network with people you know, and it'll gradually increase over time. Participate by liking and sharing posts and articles. Follow industries, influencers, and organizations that interest you. Before you know it, people will be sending you invitations to connect.

- *Commit to connect.* Make one of your first goals to reach out and build your network. This can range from following up with contacts from meetings and conferences, checking in with LinkedIn connections, or starting up conversations with old colleagues and clients. Always keep an eye out for professional courses and conferences where you can make new contacts.

- *Expand your social circle.* If you're new in town, make new friends and professional connections by joining a book club or a sports team, sign up to learn ceramics, or find a writing group. Check social media for expat groups who don't just meet online, but who organize all sorts of social occasions. Making contacts will not only make you feel less lonely but can hook you into all kinds of local opportunities.

If you find that you're not living in your purpose, plan to start by making small, gradual changes that will get you there. Don't be too hard on yourself, or despair if you feel that you're a long way away from where you want to be. Sometimes the circuitous route that you take to get there will end up providing you with skills and opportunities you might not otherwise have had. Even after you're living in your purpose and find you've strayed, don't be discouraged. Just work on getting yourself back into alignment.

It's never too late to start fulfilling your purpose. Unfortunately, some people don't try until shortly before they die. It's best to start fulfilling your purpose as early as possible to completely exhaust all possibilities in this life.

To help you get started on your way, a realistic self-assessment will need to be the next step in your journey.

Turn to the workbook section at the back of the book, page 347, for your reflection exercises to help you commit to action.

PART 3:

THE WHEEL OF LIFE AND THE IMPORTANCE OF REALISTIC SELF-ASSESSMENT

Chapter 1

Life Codes Case Study:
Back on Track

Kari Tanner sat in the doctor's office, scared to death. The doctor ordered some extra bloodwork, and he was frowning over the results. She hadn't told Matthew about it. What was the point? They never talked anymore. All they did was fight.

The doctor looked up at her but didn't speak.

"Am I sick?" she blurted out.

"No, but you're going to be if you keep going like this," he said.

"What do you mean?"

"Your blood pressure is high. So is your cholesterol. You're about 15 pounds overweight, but what concerns me more than that is you have pretty bad muscle tone. How much sleep are you getting a night?"

"Um, it varies. Some nights I don't sleep well and with the kids." She drifted off, realizing he wanted actual numbers. "I don't know, maybe five hours a night."

He shook his head.

"On a scale of one to ten, what would you say your stress levels are?"

She could feel herself getting defensive. She didn't know what he was looking for or why he was asking. She thought of how frazzled she'd been lately. She'd managed to forget two dentist appointments, and most days she missed lunch, napping instead to make up for not sleeping at night.

"I guess an average amount," she stammered, not wanting to admit that most of the time it felt like at least an eight, if not a 10.

"When was the last time you took a vacation?"

She burst out laughing before she could stop herself. It was a hard, bitter laugh that sprung from years of arguing about money and time off with her husband.

"It's been a while," she admitted finally. "Why are you asking this?"

"You're showing a lot of wear and tear on your body that is usually triggered by high stress, bad diet, irregular sleep, and a general lack of balance in your life."

"Balance?" she asked.

"Yes. The human body isn't designed to be in one mode, nonstop. You need dependable sleep and regular rest and relaxation. Most of my patients that end up in the condition you're currently in get there because they aren't taking care of themselves."

Kari laughed again before she could stop herself. Taking care of herself? What a joke! She was so busy taking care of their incredibly active and demanding kids, and when that was done, she had to use what energy she had left to take care of her husband. What time for herself could the doctor possibly think she had?

"I'd like to help you," the doctor said solemnly. "If you don't start to change your lifestyle, in a couple of years you're going to end up with any number of health problems, including diabetes and heart issues."

Kari felt like she'd been slapped in the face. Her father had died a slow, lingering death of diabetes, and she'd swore that would never happen to her.

"I barely eat any sugar," she protested.

"It's not just about sugar," the doctor said. "It's about keeping your body in balance."

"What do I do?" she asked, with fear racing through her mind.

"I'm going to give you something. It's a self-evaluation tool. I want you to take some time and evaluate your life and see where it is out of balance. Then, once you figure that out, I can give you some strategies to try and help you get through some of it. I can also recommend someone to help with the other parts. Will you at least try?"

She nodded her head slowly, the specter of her father haunting her.

In order to truly fulfill your purpose and live your best life, you need to make sure that you're addressing every area of your life and not just focusing on one or two. It's not enough to just have a fulfilling career, you must also have good health and strong relationships. To achieve balance, you can use a tool called the wheel of life to help you figure out where you're at now and where you want to be in the years ahead.

Scientists have developed many different tools to assess personal well-being, ranging from relatively simple questions about positive emotions to complex assessments of satisfaction with different life domains. One tool that I believe both successfully addresses the complex nature of well-being and comes in a practitioner-friendly format is the wheel of life created by Paul J. Meyer, founder of Success Motivation Inc.[10]

The wheel of life is a coaching and diagnostic tool used by many people to help quantify their satisfaction with the different areas of their life. People tend to view their life as one thing, whether it's good or bad. However, there are several different elements of life, and not all of them are likely to agree with each other. The wheel of life is a visual representation of the different aspects of life that we need to focus on when talking about success, happiness, and growth.

Like any wheel, it has sections, and these sections represent the different areas of your life that are important. The wheel of life encompasses your career and business, health and wellness, finances, relationships, personal growth and development, and spirituality.

10   "Industry Pioneer," Paul J Meyer, accessed June 17, 2021, https://pauljmeyer.com/the-legacy/industry-pioneer/.

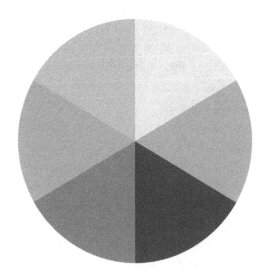

Career & Business

Spirituality

Personal Growth & Development

Relationships

Finances

Health & Wellness

When you ignore any one of these areas your life will be out of balance. Many people, unfortunately, are living their life this way. They sacrifice their health to work 60 hours a week or more. Relationships are torn apart because of problems with finances. Personal growth and spirituality take a back seat to everything else that seems to be more pressing.

But what good is working endless hours to get ahead in your career if you destroy your health along the way? You've heard the expression that if you haven't got your health, you haven't got anything. Yet millions of people go through life ignoring basic nutrition, exercise, and rest requirements. Many end up dying in what should be the prime of their life. Your body is the vehicle for your purpose. If you don't take care of your vehicle, it's going to fail you much sooner than it should.

Think about all the maintenance vehicles require. You have to change the oil, rotate the tires, get the engine tuned, and do small repairs consistently in order to keep it running smoothly. Those people who do this successfully often can get 200,000 miles or more of dependable service out of a vehicle. Those who don't are often lucky if the car or truck doesn't have a major breakdown before 75,000 miles. Your body is the same way. You need to keep it properly fed, fit, balanced, and in tune. You need to stop and take care of small problems before they become big ones if you expect it to serve you well into the nighttime of your life.

Relationships are another aspect of the wheel that often get pushed to the side. Many people put marriage or having children on hold until they reach a certain point of financial or job security. What's the point of having all the money and career success in the world if you can't share your life with people you love? Relationships enrich you more than any bank balance can. On the flip side, it can be problematic to bring children into a situation where the bills aren't getting paid and there's no clear path forward for the family.

Of course, each of these areas of your life are affected by your life codes, both the ones you were programmed with and the ones you acquired along the way. Oftentimes, it's these bad codes that get in the way. Bad codes tell you things like, *I'll rest when I'm dead,* or *there'll be time to think about family, retirement, or health later,* and *I don't need to learn anything new to accomplish what I want.*

In order to live life to its fullest and to be your best, you need to pay attention to all these areas. It doesn't work to say you'll focus on a couple now and get around to the others later. Whether it's one year or one day, being out of balance hurts your life and gets in the way of you fulfilling your purpose.

Chapter 2

A Realistic Look
in the Mirror

The wheel provides you the opportunity to look carefully and methodically at every aspect of your life. If you ask yourself how you're doing on your life's journey, it would be easy to give yourself an overall score and not realize that there are some areas of your life that are working better for you than others.

Say you're reasonably satisfied with the way your life is going. You might give yourself a B or B minus. This doesn't take into account the fact that while you might be doing well with your career or finances, you might be failing in other areas such as relationships or health. That's why it's important to look at the whole, as well as each of the different areas that make up your life to see what can be improved upon.

People have the tendency to evaluate themselves based on only one or two factors. This can cause a lot of confusion, struggle, and unhappiness. You might be making a lot of money but find that you're miserable. You'll ask yourself why, and perhaps try to bully yourself into feeling better because you've achieved success monetarily, reminding yourself how many people would love to be in your shoes. Still, you might feel depression, a lack of fulfillment, unease, or ongoing frustration without understanding why.

But when you look at every aspect of your life, things start to become clearer. Sure, maybe you do have a lot of money and you can buy expensive things. It's entirely possible to be unhappy despite this because other areas of your life aren't doing so well. If you're health is poor, this can certainly lead to depression even if everything else seems to be going well for you. After all, what good is having money if you don't have the health to enjoy it? Relationships could be another aspect of your life that could be a mess, too. Maybe you don't have a loving, committed partner with whom to share your good fortune. Even worse, maybe you have the wrong partner who makes every moment with them seem like a chore.

In order to be truly happy and fulfilled, you need to attend to every area of your life. Your wheel needs to be balanced, and this isn't a one-time effort. The wheel needs to be constantly balanced because it's revolving, and it's your responsibility to keep it going.

For every area on the wheel, you need to routinely sit down and take stock. What are you happy with? What are you unhappy with? What steps do you need to take to change that? While there are six separate areas of your life that need to be examined, don't think that they're completely unrelated to each other. All the spokes on the wheel are interconnected. When one is changed, the others will be impacted.

As you begin to improve one area of your life it can often lead to discoveries about other areas. You might have thought that your romantic relationship was a problem because you don't see eye-to-eye with your partner. What you might find as you look closer at your relationship is that your finances are a disaster, and that this is what you argue about most of the time. Fix the finances and it might help fix problems with the relationship.

If you find that you're having problems keeping up with your work, take a look at your health habits. It could be that you're not getting enough sleep, and that in turn makes it hard for you to stay focused and sharp at work. Perhaps the problem is you need more exercise, which helps build endurance and can make you feel more energetic overall. It could be that those constant fights with your spouse also keep you up at night and affect your sleep, therefore negatively impacting the quality or quantity of your work.

While it's important to do an assessment on each part of the wheel, realize that you might not truly understand what the root problems are until you start to push the wheel and make changes, even if they're tiny ones. Only then will you see if everything on your wheel is working together or not.

It's important to live in your purpose and maximize the time you spend doing this, particularly during the afternoon of your life when you're shaping your existence. In all likelihood, you'll have some good codes, some codes that need reinforcing, and some codes that need rewriting to achieve true success. But in order to do that, you need to do some realistic self-assessment. Some people may naturally love analyzing their life in depth while others don't. Regardless of which type of person you are, self-assessment is vitally important for growth. After all, if you don't know what's wrong, how can you begin to fix it?

Self-assessment is part of the process needed to move your wheel of life and keep yourself on track. This will help you to reach your goals and ensure your life isn't falling out of balance. The most important thing to remember though is to be truthful with yourself, both about where you are and where you want to be. The assessment needs to be realistic and honest, which can be painful to do. However, how you got to where you are now is far less important than what you're going to do from this moment forward to get where you want to be.

Keep in mind that this can be a challenge if you love your life and think it's going well. For the successful, it can sometimes be hard to find weaknesses. Nevertheless, everyone has weaknesses, no matter how far you've progressed. If you're still breathing, there's still room for you to improve.

As you begin an honest self-assessment, it's important to ask yourself a series of questions and evaluate your life based on these three metrics: satisfaction, contribution, and growth potential.

Chapter 3

Satisfaction, Contribution, and Growth Potential

You might be able to tell everyone around you that everything is fine, and that you're happy with every aspect of your life. However, you can't lie to your Creator, and lying to yourself won't be easy either. Of course, you can try, but the truth will find a way of working its way free. The truth is, unless you decide to get real and honest with yourself, then you'll never get where it is you want to be.

Start by examining every aspect of your life. What are some of the pressure points? Do you like certain aspects of your job, but feel discouraged or frustrated by others? Do certain times of the year put more of a burden on you in the workplace than others? Is your boss someone who acts like a friend until things go wrong, then he throws you under the bus?

Discover what the untold truths are of your situation. Determine if your relationship with your spouse runs smoothly, or if it derails if you don't handle all the chores at home after you've already put in a full day's work. Look at your health see if it seems to be suffering lately. Is it because you don't have the time, money, or energy to spend taking care of yourself? If the whole family gets sick, are you the one who must take care of everyone else, even if you are in the worst shape? Making these determinations can go a long way toward uncovering those aspects of your life that need the most work.

Sometimes it can be hard to take care of yourself, particularly if you're used to taking care of other people. This self-assessment is not for other people to see and evaluate, it's a tool for yourself. And since no one else is looking, don't be afraid to be honest, even if the truth isn't pretty.

It's not disloyal to admit to friction in relationships or the workplace. In fact, having the courage to be honest with yourself about your feelings and needs could be the one thing that saves your marriage, or helps you get a promotion at work. Many marriages are destroyed because one or both people can't be honest about what they want and need, or about what's working and what's not.

The same can be true about your work situation. Have the courage to admit that you're upset to yourself, then figure out what you can do about the situation. Is there something you need to change so you'll be the first up for a promotion? Do you need to talk to your boss and make your desires on the topic clearer? If your boss doesn't realize that you want to advance, then he might assume you're happy where you are, and promote someone else instead. It may also be time to look for a new job outside of the organization, or even pursue a different type of work opportunity that fuels instead of hinders your creativity.

So many times, people go through life coping with things that are ok, or just deal with things that aren't. You weren't meant to live like that. In order to fulfill your purpose, you need to reach above and beyond. It's not greed or ingratitude to want to live your best life and strive for great instead of just ok. Being clear about how you feel about your career, health, finances, relationships, spirituality, and personal growth is the first step to being able to get to a place that makes you excited to be alive. Only then, when you're at your best, will you be able to help others the most.

The second element you must analyze when doing a self-assessment is the contribution you're making to those around you. Life is meant to be a balance of give-and-take. Success is measured by both. You have a responsibility to make the world better, not just for you but also for the generations that come after you.

Now is the time to assess your contribution to the world. Most people will find satisfaction through contribution to other people or by uplifting society. Remember, you have a purpose. You're unique and have a specific role to play in making the world a better place. It's time to get honest about that. How are you doing? Interestingly enough, once you truly feel that you're contributing to society in a positive way, it can actually help relieve stress. So, it's good for everyone.

As with satisfaction, it's important to evaluate the contribution you're making in each area of your life. Make sure to figure out how you're doing in your career, relationships, finances, health, spirituality, and personal growth, and how each of these areas contribute to others.

The final element you need to examine in your self-assessment is growth potential. This means you need to measure your overall potential and determine what it will take to continue to progress your life. Figure out where you'll be in another 10 to 20 years.

If you don't like the answer, then you know that something must change. The point of this assessment is to figure out which elements of your life aren't working for you. It might seem like you're doing fine at the age of 30. But working a 60-hour week, barely sleeping, and not making enough money to really put aside savings might catch up to you in 10 years if you stay on your current path. This may cause you to sacrifice your health and have no long-term savings plan for when you retire. While it's true that you might have a big house and a nice car, those things cost more money to maintain. So, you'll be running faster and harder in your race just to keep up, even in the later years of your life. In the bigger picture, this is not a good plan. When you look at your life and your future, words like flourishing, motivated, and inspired should jump to the forefront.

As you do the assessment, ask yourself whether you're making progress on your goals. If not, why? There's clearly something that's not working for you and needs to be addressed. Keep in mind that progress is subjective and can differ between people. It might look and feel different depending on your reasons.

What's the reason you get up in the morning? Many people think that they're doing everything to give their kids a better life, or that they're trying to achieve a certain level of success and retire early. Instead of simply saying these things, look at your purpose. What is it you're meant to do and accomplish? When you look at your purpose, it becomes easier to assess how you're doing and what your true growth potential is. Go back to the blueprint before you make your assessment.

When thought of in these terms, it becomes easier to see whether you're on track and progressing toward achieving your purpose. Again, like with satisfaction and contribution, you need to address each area of your life individually. What's the potential for your finances, relationships, career, spirituality, health, and personal growth?

You can't ignore any one area of your life and expect it not to impact you in some way or another. If you don't pay attention to your spouse, how long will it take before the relationship starts to fray around the edges? If you're not actively trying to grow an area of your life, then it's probably withering away and getting worse.

When it comes to health, it's true that everyone dies eventually. But the amount of effort you put in can help determine how long you live. Even more important, it can help improve the *quality* of your life, particularly during those later stages.

Stop now and take stock of where you are. Give your life a long, hard look. Don't be afraid to be honest. After all, that's the only way you're going to get anywhere with this process. As you begin this assessment, it's fine to start with any area of the wheel you choose. If you're unsure where to begin, choose the area that takes up the largest chunk of your day. For most, this will be your career and business, but feel free to choose the area of the wheel that's the best starting point for you.

Turn to the workbook section at the back of the book, page 355, for your reflection exercises to help you commit to action.

PART 4:

CRACKING YOUR CAREER AND BUSINESS CODES

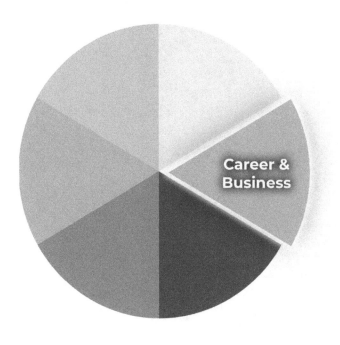

Career & Business

Chapter 1

How You Spend Your Day

Matthew Tanner stared numbly at the packet of papers in his hand. He'd survived three rounds of layoffs at his company, only this time he hadn't been so lucky. His severance packet was what the HR person had cheerfully called *generous*. She could afford to be cheerful, because she still had a job.

It took him five minutes to clean out his desk. Now he sat in his car, staring at the papers, wondering what he was going to do next. He'd worked for the same company since graduating from college. It was the first job offer he'd had, and he'd jumped at it eagerly, desperate to start getting paid after he and Kari got married.

Part of him wondered why he was so upset. He hated the job, if he was honest with himself. The work wasn't fulfilling, and he'd only had three raises the entire time he'd been there. The thing was, he wasn't ready to go home and face Kari, so he drove back to the bar instead.

The bartender frowned when he walked in and took his customary seat.

"What are you doing here so early?" the big man asked.

"I got laid off."

"Sorry, man."

He ordered his usual and began to drink.

A minute later, he blurted out, "What am I going to do?"

"Anything you want," the bartender said.

Matthew rolled his eyes.

"I'm serious. Maybe it's the universe telling you that it's time to rethink your life choices."

"Right, like I'm going to take career advice from a bartender," he snapped.

He regretted it an instant later. After all, this man was his access to the alcohol that numbed the pain.

To Matthew's surprise, he didn't get upset. Instead, he just smiled. "Maybe you should take career advice from a small business owner doing what he loves."

It took a moment for his words to sink in, and then Matthew looked at him in surprise.

"You own this place?"

"Yup. I used to work as a stockbroker. I quit seven years ago and bought this place."

"Lost your shirt in the market?"

"No, I was pulling down seven figures a year. It wasn't satisfying, though."

"How could that much money not be satisfying?" Matthew asked, thinking how meager his own salary had been in comparison.

"Money isn't everything, and no amount of money can compensate for a job you hate."

"So, why a bar?"

"I like interacting with people. I like seeing them have fun. I also like helping people who need it."

"Like me," Matthew said.

"I've been watching you for a while."

"And what conclusions have you come to?"

"You're not happy."

"Well, duh."

"But you can be. Honestly, I think you losing your job was a gift, because now you can figure out what you really want to do with your life."

"Back to that whole purpose thing again?" Matthew asked, remembering their last conversation.

"Ideally, yes."

"Yeah, but how will finding my purpose help me pay the mortgage?"

"It might take a while to find your purpose, and for your work to align with that. But you can find work that will help you in the meantime that won't slowly kill you like the last job was doing."

Matthew shook his head.

"Look, do yourself a favor. Take the rest of the week and spend it thinking about what you love doing. Don't spend it searching for the next mindless job, wallowing in pity, and getting drunk every day."

"Careful, you could make a lot of money over me wallowing in booze," Matthew said.

"Trust me, I don't need to make money off your wallowing."

Matthew finished his drink and stood up.

"Okay. I'll think about it," he said.

"Really?" the bartender asked with a smile.

Matthew shrugged. "What else have I got to do?"

When you were a child, it's likely that your parents, teachers, and other adults talked to you about your career. "What do you want to be when you grow up?" is a commonly heard question for most children. You're coded to understand that work is important and choosing a career is a big deal. Many children dream of being doctors, firemen, astronauts, and other careers that they perceive as being exciting or important.

Well-meaning adults often push children toward specific careers. Lots of parents want their children to have good paying jobs, and careers in medicine and law are often put on a pedestal. Others value education and push their children to be teachers and educators. More practical occupations are valued by others, because working in construction or as mechanic doesn't require as much in the way of formal education as other careers.

Unfortunately, some children aren't given much of a choice in their future career because they grow up in a family that owns their own business. For these children, sometimes there's very little questioning about what the child wants. It's assumed that they'll work in the family business regardless of their own desires. Some might even be expected to start their own company, just like a parent or grandparent did before them.

Keep in mind that there's a difference between a career and a business. A career is a job, and you're part of a bigger picture that has hundreds of thousands of other people working toward a shared goal. With a career, you're contributing to a pool in a professional space and hopefully will make money, though it's possible to have a career you don't generate income from.

A business, on the other hand, is the platform you build for other people to contribute to. You lead with the vision and are responsible for building the groundwork of the platform, directing the affairs of the vision. Business is about income, product, services, and flow of cash within the supply and demand space.

I have a career as a strategy consultant. But I also have multiple businesses that have nothing to do with my career and aren't even related. This is something I learned from my mother. In her career she was a librarian, but she also built several businesses, including a clothing company and a restaurant. None of those had anything to do with her job as a librarian. She took the skills she learned in her job and applied them to her businesses, just as I have.

Whether you have a career, a business, or both, it's important to try and enhance what you're doing so that you're maximizing your potential. Since a huge part of your life is devoted to career and business, it's important to find fulfillment in them. If you're in the afternoon time of your life, you need to maximize your career and business as much as possible with the time you have.

Chapter 2

Your Finite Resource

Whether you realize it or not, work takes up a huge percentage of your time, energy, and thoughts. Most people spend at least 50% of their waking hours either at work, commuting to work, or thinking about work.[11] For many, that number may be even higher, with some devoting up to 80% of their waking lives to work in some way. Sleep becomes their only refuge, and even then, they might be dogged by dreams of work.

Without a doubt, work takes up a significant part of your life, and most people don't stop to question this balance. After all, many people are raised to believe that building a career is a sign of responsibility. For these people, automatically sacrificing half or more of your waking hours is sensible, regardless of the cost to other areas of your life. Many are raised with the belief that they

---

11   "American Time Use Survey – 2019," Bureau of Labor Statistics (BLS), June 25, 2020, https://www.bls.gov/news.release/pdf/atus.pdf.

must work hard to get ahead and will sacrifice everything into the process. These codes and others related to work are hardwired into you from a young age. Growing up, you likely saw one or both parents spending time away from you at work. Even when they were with you, they were probably either talking about work or thinking about it, and that's if they hadn't brought some home with them. This sends a clear signal to children that work is important, which equates having a good job with being valued.

After high school or college, most people are inclined to jump straight into the workforce and take a job that doesn't pay very well. Because they don't yet have the skills necessary to succeed, long hours at work may be required. Those long hours can burn lead to burn out, and after a few years, a new job will be sought because they're unfulfilled and never reach a place of satisfaction with their career.

It's true that no one has infinite time. Everyone gets 24 hours a day until they die. Some will live many years, others only for a few. Time is the most valuable commodity we have in life. One easy way to determine what direction your life is headed is to evaluate where most of your time is being spent. Whatever job you are committing your time indirectly consumes the corresponding value of your life. This means that in terms of hours spent, your wheel of life might more closely resemble one of these:

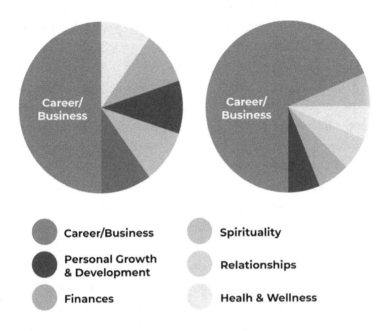

This is why it's important to constantly evaluate and reevaluate your work. Ask yourself if this is what you should be committing your time to. And *commitment* is the key word. After all, you most likely spend more time with your job than your spouse. What makes this even more alarming is the fact that quite a number of people I've interacted with are not happy with their career.

There are a staggering number of people who devote their life to something they aren't passionate about. Over the course of my career, I've had the opportunity to conduct employee engagement surveys for hundreds of organizations in markets like the Middle East, Asia, Europe, Africa, and North America. The goal of these surveys was to determine how engaged employees are with the organizations they work for. The average results revealed that just about 50% of the respondents were engaged. A 2020 global employee experience trends report by Qualtrics revealed that 53% of employees worldwide are engaged in their work, with the United States leading other countries at 55%.[12] If employee engagement is an indication of job satisfaction, then we can conclude that almost half of the workforce is not quite satisfied with their current employment. In 2017, the Gallup Sharecare wellbeing index showed 38.5% of people surveyed expressed unhappiness in their lives.[13] That's the highest in over a decade.

The saddest part of these statistics is the fact that if you're giving that much of yourself, your time, and your life, to something that you're dissatisfied with, it's going to affect the other areas of your life as well.

You've most likely seen the changes that can come over a friend or loved one when they are unhappy at work. It can make them irritable and difficult to be around even when they're home. They might also frequently spend more money than they should to buy things that make themselves feel better. That's because when depression sets in, people let their sleep, exercise, and healthy eating habits slide. All of this can turn even the most good-natured person into a toxic one who is no fun to be around.

The state of your career can affect the state of your mind, and ultimately affect the state of your well-being. This becomes even more painful if the job you've chosen has nothing to do with your purpose.

12   "2020 Global Employee Experience Trends," Qualtrics, accessed June 17, 2021, https://www.qualtrics.com/ebooks-guides/2020-global-employee-experience-trends-report/.

13   "2017 State Well-Being Rankings," Gallup Sharecare Well-Being Index, 2017, https://wellbeingindex.sharecare.com/wp-content/uploads/2018/02/Gallup-Sharecare-State-of-American-Well-Being_2017-State-Rankings_FINAL.pdf.

Chapter 3

What You're Worth

Money is an exchange of time for value. Therefore, money is more than just an exchange for your time, it's an exchange for a portion of your life. You're putting a price on your own life, giving your employer a piece of your life in exchange for what they're willing to pay you.

Which begs the question: How much is your life worth?

That's a sobering thought, isn't it? It makes the idea of compensation a little more intense, certainly worth more consideration than you might have otherwise given. What you get paid is an indication of your value to the organization, or at least so it seems. For most, getting more pay equals giving up more of your life.

Money can become a status symbol. People are valued not by who they are or what they can do, but by how much they make.

This is bad code that needs to be changed, especially when you perceive your value and the value of others in this way.

Of course, very little in life stays the same. Eventually you begin to desire more money to afford the things like a car or a house. But how do you do that? To get more money, you'll need to keep giving up more of your life. Let's put it this way. If another person owns 80% of your time, do you really own your life? At the very most, you're leasing the few hours of your day not owned by your employer.

When negotiating with an employer, there are things you can ask for that will benefit you without requesting more money up front. Instead, think about the additional benefits you can receive as compensation. Getting medical and dental insurance is a must for many jobs. But what about vision and life insurance, a 401(k), and employee stock options (ESOP)? Vacation time is another area to look at. If they're willing to give you an extra week off a year, take it (and then actually take it). This helps to reduce some of the pressure and stress that can build up over time.

Other non-monetary perks can also be requested and include all those things benefits are great perks for you but can cause push-back because they cost the employer money. Look for things that will add value to your life but won't be an obvious cost to them. Working from home is a big one here. It saves you time commuting and gas money, which means you'll be spending more time with your family and saving some money in the process. Even if you only get to work from home once a week, it can be a huge benefit. Offering to work a modified schedule such as four 10-hour days instead of five eight-hour days can free up an entire day in your schedule.

There are other perks you can ask for that will help as well. If parking is an issue at your company, try to get an assigned space, preferably close to the building. If the commute traffic is a nightmare, ask if you can adjust your hours either earlier or later so you can miss the traffic. Find out if the company holds tickets to games, theater performances, or other events that you'd like to attend. Asking to bring your well-behaved dog to work can save you from having to hire someone to walk him while you're away at work.

Once you've been with a company for a while, you can start to push for other changes. Try to convince the company to get involved with a charity or outreach program that's important to you. Lots of companies are looking for ways to give back to the community or to improve their image. They can get a lot of publicity this way as well. Find ways to help direct your company toward projects and initiatives that align with your goals and life purpose.

Something I often say is, "I work for much more than money. I live for much more than bread." I try to live by this. When you're getting value, even if it's compensation that isn't monetary, then the picture starts to shift. When you live your life for a higher purpose, *your purpose*, it becomes about more than the creature comforts. When you start to think of it in these terms, it can change your entire perspective on compensation. You will start to see your job as something that can help you acquire the tools you need and a way to build a network so that you can eventually work in alignment with your purpose.

Chapter 4

Keeping Life Fresh

When I graduated college, I knew I wanted a lucrative job, and one that would allow me to progress in the world. At the time, banking was prestigious and lucrative, and since I wanted a job in business, I focused on getting into banking and finance. However, my excitement landing a banking job soon fizzled when I began to experience a hostile work environment.

It didn't take long before I began to hate Mondays. I was even depressed on Sunday evenings just thinking about the work week ahead. Although the pay was great, I was miserable. The job just didn't seem to give me any satisfaction, and knowing myself, I knew I couldn't survive a job that made me so unhappy.

Sometimes work can make you angry, depressed, or bored because what you're doing is not aligning with your purpose or fulfilling on a personal level. It's possible to have problems at work even if the job aligns with your purpose. Toxic work environments with depressed, rude, or hostile coworkers can make any job a nightmare. Lack of decent pay, no room for growth, and unsympathetic bosses can also make what should be a great job a terrible one. Fortunately, you do have alternatives.

Here are some things you can try:

- *Ask for what you want.* If you're not happy where you are and there are one or two things like better compensation, promotion, or working on a different team that could make a real change in your satisfaction level, ask for them. Like they say, you don't know until you ask. It's possible your boss will be happy to accommodate you so that the company doesn't lose your talent. If they're unwilling to accommodate your requests, then you can consider pursuing other avenues available to you.
- *Find a job at a competitor.* If you like the type of job you're doing, but have problems with the workplace, coworkers, or the pay, take a look at the competition. Oftentimes, you can find a job working for a rival company that might provide the perks and the environment you're looking for.
- *Start your own company.* While you should always be on the lookout for how you can create your own platform, I will caution you that starting a company is not easy. With the benefit of being on both sides, (as an employee and an entrepreneur), I can safely say if you thought the hours were bad at your old job, then be prepared for them to get a whole lot worse. Working for yourself does provide more freedom but it also comes with a ton of responsibilities along with endless workdays.
- *Start a new career.* It's never too late to do something new. When I got physically sick from my banking job, I began to

research alternative careers in the business field. I found out about consulting and made the switch. I was fortunate to make this move early in my career. However, you can start a new career at any time. After all, famed painter Grandma Moses didn't devote herself to painting until she was 78 years old.[14] If she can start a career at that age, then you can start a new career right now. Just remember to choose something that will help you align with your purpose.

14   "Grandma Moses (Anna Mary Robertson Moses)," National Museum of Women in the Arts, accessed June 17, 2021, https://nmwa.org/art/artists/grandma-moses-anna-mary-robertson-moses/.

Chapter 5

Align with Your Purpose & Tools for Success

The ultimate goal is to align your work and business with your purpose. If you work in line with your purpose, work can be fun. It doesn't make work less difficult, but at least you're happy to be doing the work because it's in line with your purpose.

If possible, choose a career aligned with your purpose to reduce frustration. With your career, do what you can to learn skills, develop tools, and gain discipline from what you're doing. These will all be of service to you later in life.

Unfortunately, not a lot of people have the luxury of doing something in the line of their purpose or passion. A career should always be thought of as a lever, tool, or platform to help you achieve a greater goal. Until you see your career as a tool to help you achieve something bigger, you will continually remain frustrated.

This is why a self-assessment is needed to help you discover how your career is beneficial to you and how you can achieve something bigger. When I started my career, I didn't pay attention to this as much as I should've. But as I progressed, I've learned to place value on my skills. As a practice, when I attend job interviews, I usually find a way to ask the interviewer why I should consider an offer from their company. It's a way to flip that popular question, "Why should we hire you?" This is because I understand the value I bring to the table, and I would like to make an informed decision. It's important to me to know why one company thinks I should work for them over their competition. I once asked the CEO of a leading advertising agency this question. At the time, I was considering an offer from three different agencies. He confirmed he hadn't heard that in an interview, and he practically sold the agency to me. Remember, you're going to be giving this employer a percentage of your life. It's impossible for that organization to pay you what your true value is for your time. Step back and see all the ways a job can help you achieve your larger goals.

When you go to work, you learn a skill and build a profession. Those are important. A career is a tool that helps you fulfill something bigger, which can be your purpose. Look at it from this point of view and you'll be less frustrated. In the beginning, my knowledge of business was limited to the few textbooks I read. However, after landing a job in business consulting, I was exposed to several business tools and strategy models that I would never have had access to without a career in this field.

A career can provide useful tools that you can use to help you progress along a path toward fulfilling your purpose. You'll receive hands on training, gain knowledge of best-in-class tools and technology, and sharpen your skills in the process. It's possible to also acquire meaningful experiences and intangibles that even more important. A career often gives you the fundamentals and the foundation you'll need on the path to something greater. In addition, you'll have the benefit of building professional and personal relationships, developing personal skills, and be exposed to the people you need to serve. With the right career, you'll be able to break bad codes and rewrite them. It can also open your mind to codes you didn't know existed, but that you'll need on your journey.

Working for a company is a fantastic opportunity to increase your skill set and your interpersonal communication. Many people get into a position at a company and end up with tunnel vision. They only pay attention to their job and only interact with those they're likely to see throughout the course of the day. This is as bad as going to college and refusing to take your general education classes or talk to anyone besides your roommate.

You need to take advantage of every opportunity around you. Talk to one of your coworkers and ask them about their job. Most people love it when someone takes the time to ask about them and what they do. If they use special software or equipment that you don't, ask them to teach you something about it. You never know when that knowledge will be useful. If it's possible, ask to shadow people who do different things than you on your lunchbreak. This will allow you to learn more about how the entire business works and get to know the different aspects of it. Listen in on a sales call when you can or offer to help prepare for a meeting. Not only does this help bolster your resume, but it also gives you a better understanding of how businesses function in general. The more you know about that before trying to start up your own business, the better.

The more you know about how your company runs the more valuable an employee you will be. Don't shy away from getting practical hands-on experience wherever possible. If a coworker is out sick or needs to go on maternity leave, step up and volunteer to handle some of their responsibilities while they're gone. When you see a need in the office that's not being met, volunteer to figure out how to take care of it. You'll not only gain skills but also the respect of your colleagues and supervisors.

Chapter 6

Cracking the Code
Case Study

Victoria, like many people, would often get nervous when she had to do something new, particularly in a work situation. She didn't want to look foolish or incompetent and was afraid she'd embarrass herself. In fact, she would become so incapacitated by fear that she would sometimes just give up rather than try at all.

When she ended up landing an administrative assistant position in an unconventional environment, the job required her to figure out how to do things she'd never done before. One of those things she'd been tasked with was to present a status report to management on all the projects her team was working on every couple of days. With this news she became extremely agitated and thought about quitting.

For once, she decided to stick it out for a little while. She asked questions whenever she could, feeling bad if someone had to show her how to do something more than once on a slide presentation. Even though she worried that people would think she wasn't any good at her job, she kept trying and learning as she went, picking up a lot of new skills in a very short period of time. Victoria even took public speaking classes online and practiced presenting to her husband over the weekend.

After she'd been on the job for six weeks, she was called into her supervisor's office. Victoria dreaded the interaction, wondering what she'd done wrong or if they'd finally tired of dealing with her learning curve. To her surprise, she was given a raise. It turned out her bosses and coworkers had all noticed and appreciated how much she was learning, realizing how hard she kept trying despite the obstacles in her way.

Leaving the office that day, Victoria was stunned and excited. She'd set to work breaking her bad codes—the codes that told her that asking for help was a sign of weakness, and that trying new things where she risked failure was bad. The new codes told her that experimenting was ok, even if she failed, and that asking for help right away when she needed it was the smart thing to do.

Over the next several months, Victoria used these new codes as her guideline and made incredible strides in her job skills. She even started to volunteer to take on projects, learning some basic coding to create a company website when she realized that the company needed someone to tackle the project. She began to branch out into graphic design and marketing as well when a need presented itself.

At the next annual evaluation of all the employees, Victoria was rewarded for her boldness. She received the largest raise of anyone working for the company, nearly double the other top performers.

Armed with her new set of tools, eventually she decided to leave the company and go to work for herself. Once she did, everything that she learned came into play once again. She designed her own website, handled her own marketing, interfaced with the media for advertising, and created her own logo and company design. None of these skills were demanded of her in her role as an administrative assistant, but by breaking her bad codes, being open to learning other areas of the business, and stepping up to help address issues, she had gained valuable skills that helped her launch her own business.

There's a lot to be learned working for a company, no matter its size. Some people scoff at the perceived limitations of working under bosses, dealing with set hours, or recurring deadlines. But quitting because you have an issue with a structured environment and creating your own business won't solve this problem. Instead, take the opportunity to learn how to structure your life so that when it is time to create your own business, you'll be ready.

One of the other important tools that you can gain from working for a company is self-knowledge. Before you have experience working you might have a vague idea of what you would like out of a job. Then again, you might not. Even more common is to get into a company and realize that the things you thought you would enjoy about the job are instead the things that are dragging you down. This was my experience when I had a short stint in banking out of college. It was a respectable and lucrative profession, but I quickly realized it was not good for me.

Repetitiveness is a good example of one of those things that people often change their minds about. Retail, fast food, assembly line work, shipping and receiving, the list goes on. If you've ever worked in any of these career fields, there is a chance you've encountered some form of boredom. This boredom could be coming from completing repetitive tasks the job requires. Doing these tasks over and over can often cause people to feel constricted and frustrated.

However, some people think that having a job with a high degree of repetition is good, because they can learn something once and then just keep doing it without the stress of having to figure out something new. They think it will also give them a chance to clock out mentally and just do the job by rote. Oftentimes, people who make these assumptions will quickly discover that the repetition bores them and find themselves climbing the walls, wishing for creativity and variety in their work.

Others might think that they want as much creativity and freedom as possible in their working environment only to come to find that freedom comes with a different type of stress. If they're not good at managing their own time, meeting deadlines, or being creative on demand, then they might find themselves happier with a job that is more predictable and doesn't require as much decision making or the spontaneous acts of creation.

I had a coaching client who once expressed deep dissatisfaction in her career. At the time, she had just been promoted into senior management at one of the leading consumer packaged goods companies. Her frustration quickly degenerated into depression as her daily tasks required her to sit in meetings and at her desk for long hours. Having coached her for a while, I knew her personality was the always-on-the-go type. Before her promotion, she was a field director, and oversaw several markets within North American. Needless to say, the change in responsibility that came with her promotion created a sharp change that took a severe toll on her mental health.

During one of my coaching calls with her, I sought to find what was most important to her in that stage of life. She was clear about wanting the freedom to physically move around, and her new role didn't afford her that opportunity. We began to work on a plan for her to launch her own market activation company, and over 19 months she did indeed launch her new business. While she was still working, she started to look forward to the weekends so she could work on her business, which allowed her to move around a lot.

I've seen teachers who decline promotions because they find great joy in being in the classroom, realizing that moving into management or curriculum development might be a recipe for disaster. Instead, you should try to choose a job in line with your lifestyle preferences. This is where self-assessment can really help you. Are you an introvert or an extrovert? Do you love travel or prefer to stay at home? Do you need a job that gives you scheduled time off every year? Are you the kind of person that likes to stay until tasks are done, or do you clock out exactly on time, watching the last couple of minutes run down on the clock first?

The more you know and can learn about yourself, the easier it will be to find a job that truly suits you. There'll always be some trial and error, but a little preparation and thought can help save you from countless jobs that aren't worth giving your life to. For instance, if you're an introvert, it's not likely you will be happy working at a job that requires you to constantly be outgoing and reaching out to people. Whether or not you like travel can be a consideration in taking some types of jobs as well. If you have an incredible desire to travel, you could be a traveling nurse. On the other hand, if you don't like a fast-paced environment you shouldn't be an ER nurse. These are some examples of how knowing yourself and what you want can help you choose a job more fitted to your personality. Keep in mind that if you need a job that taps into your creativity, this can sometimes be hard to find in established organizations, and you might do better in a start-up. The point is, there are always considerations you'll have to make, but knowing yourself and the environments you thrive in is a key step in the process.

Chapter 7

The Power of Networks

One of the crucial elements needed to fulfill your purpose, as discussed earlier, is people. A career can help you network and find people that can help you achieve success. Networking will expose you to different types of people and different cultures to help broaden your horizons and can even provide you with the opportunity to interact with the same people you're called to reach out to. It's important to remember that in the race of life, although you're running, you're not in competition with the people around you. The only competition that exists is with yourself. Therefore, if you can use the help or expertise of those around you, ask for it.

Throughout your life, you will need many mentors for many different things. Each area of your life could have multiple mentors. Some you will have at the same time, while others will come at different times throughout your life. When I launched my first e-commerce business, I depended heavily on my knowledge and experience as a strategist. While my business consulting experiences were valuable, they were limited. One would imagine that as someone whose profession is to help companies achieve business success, building a business of my own would be an easy win. I wish it worked that way in real life.

Eventually, I was able to build a business that generated half a million in revenue within 18 months of operations, but it had zero profits. I struggled through the first few years of the business and was ultimately unsuccessful monetarily. However, there were very important lessons to be learned from this experience. It is safer, easier, and quicker to achieve business success when you have a valuable mentor who truly cares about your success. When it comes to your career and your business, mentors are crucial. They'll help you along your path and provide the advice and wisdom you need in order to be successful.

It's important to assemble a strong group of mentors over the course of your life. One person can't be your mentor in all things. Instead, you need to find experts who have traveled the path before you. They're the ones who will help you avoid pitfalls and find opportunities you might otherwise be overlooking. I have at least one mentor for all the different areas of my life. When I run into career challenges, I reach out to my career mentors. The same goes for any challenges I encounter in business, spirituality, and relationships, among others.

Seven years after my first failed attempt at e-commerce, I launched another e-commerce business with the guidance and help of my mentors, and they were able to show me the secrets of e-commerce supply chain, recommending exceptional suppliers from their networks that could give me valuable advice. This time, the journey was much easier, smother, and quicker. Though I still had challenges that needed to be overcome, the major ones were taken care of by the guidance I received from my mentors.

The value of mentors cannot be overstated. However, you must choose your advisors carefully, otherwise you could wind up in worse situation. Always look to leaders who have something to teach you and possess traits that you wish to emulate. Many people make the mistake of surrounding themselves with either those who are at the same place in life or with friends who might be fun but don't bring value to the relationship. Studies show that you model yourself heavily off those who are closest to you and those people you spend the most time with.[15]

This is referred to as social proximity effect. Humans are social creatures, and we're all highly influenced by the people around us each day. This is why it's crucial to surround yourself with people that are doing better than you in some area of life—especially in the aspects of your life you're currently working on. This way you'll strive to live up to their example and it will push you to grow and achieve more. Peers can help keep you firmly in place, but keep in mind that some can drag you down.

This is why it's important not to seek out a mentor just because they're the most accessible to you. Instead, seek out masters of their profession and leaders in their field regardless of the degree of accessibility. Develop a plan, put in the work, and reach out to them in the most professional way possible. Most successful people are willing to share their knowledge with others because they don't feel threatened by doing so. Instead, they've learned the value of passing on good codes to those coming up behind them. Even if they don't have the time or ability to establish a long-term mentoring relationship with you, try to get what you can out of

---

15   "Proximity and the Mere Exposure Effect in Social Psychology," Neuroscience, July 13, 2018, https://www.neuroscience.org.uk/proximity-mere-exposure-effect-social-psychology/.

them. Invite someone you admire out for coffee or a meal and use it to pick their brain. You'll be surprised at how much good advice a leader in their field can impart in just half an hour. It took me eight years and 71 attempts to finally get the attention of the late Dr. Myles Munroe, who later became a mentor. I was determined to connect with him, and so I made several efforts including flying to conferences wherever he was speaking.

If you're thinking you don't know anyone who fits the description of who you're looking for, that's not an issue. With modern technology all the world's thought leaders, experts, and pioneers are at your fingertips. All you need to do is a little research and you can easily find the people who are leading the field that you want to be in. Start by reading some of what they've written. A good way to learn how a person thinks is to read their books or articles. If it speaks to you, go ahead and reach out. Your mentors don't have to live in the same town as you. They can live halfway around the world, and you can still easily communicate.

What matters is the knowledge they have and your willingness to ask them to impart it on you. Keep in mind that some leaders are almost unreachable, so be realistic in your choice. I love a lot of things about Bill Gates, but realistically, I'm not sure it's a good idea to reach out to Bill for mentoring. However, I have read just about everything he's written and have followed him closely from a distance and believe he has influenced me significantly.

Remember that mentors don't just have to be related to business, as you can have a mentor for each aspect of your life. This can include a spiritual mentor, a relationship mentor, and mentors for every other area of the wheel of life. You might even consider multiple mentors who specialize in slightly different fields. For instance, in business you can have a legal mentor, a marketing mentor, a sales mentor, a financial mentor, and so on. If there's something you need to do, it's never a bad idea to get the advice of someone who's significantly better or more experienced at it than you.

The key, though, is that once you find a good mentor, listen and do what they suggest. It does you no good to have one of the greatest mentors in the world if you won't take their advice. A thousand wise people can tell you that you need to choose A, but if you ultimately choose B then you've wasted their time as well as your own. Sometimes their advice can be challenging, and it should be. After all, success takes hard work, and greater success takes more hard work. Sometimes you must change your entire way of thinking or doing things. A mentor will help you understand what bad codes you've been working with, but, ultimately, it's up to you to do the work to change them.

That said, remember that it's also important to be true to yourself. Other people aren't in your shoes and don't share the exact same thought processes, beliefs, and instincts that you do. If you feel in your heart that you need to go a certain way, and that way differs from the advice your mentors are giving, then you have a decision to make. When you're blazing a trail, sometimes you have to go against conventional wisdom and be willing to take that first step off the beaten path and into the wilderness. However, this should be a purposeful, informed choice. Don't cast aside lightly the advice given to you by those who's with the wisdom and knowledge you have sought out.

Once you have achieved success in an area of life that you were looking for, remember that the circle always continues. When you have learned something important, make sure to pass it on to people that you encounter who need to hear what you have to say. It's never a waste of time to help the next generations, rather consider it your responsibility to do so.

Whether you're working in an office building, volunteering to coach Little League, or attending religious events, it's important to keep in mind the people you encounter in your daily life can potentially become strategic partners. Always be on the lookout for people you can partner with. When creating and running a business, there are numerous opportunities to work with others. No business operates in a vacuum. It needs workers, customers, suppliers, and others in order to function. That's just to cover the basics. Then there are opportunities to branch out, co-create, cross-promote, and work with other businesses to help support each other and share your combined client pool.

One good place to start is to look at who you already do business with. Sometimes promotion opportunities are right under your nose. If you have a restaurant, look at your food suppliers. Do you buy a specific brand of something because of its superior quality? Try reaching out and seeing if you can market yourself as an official supplier of their product. If you're just buying whatever is cheapest on the market, stop and think. Do you know someone from your community that makes that product? If so, you can probably strike a deal with them, which could provide them more sales, give you a discount, and provide promotional opportunities for both of you.

Sometimes these opportunities are not obvious, so it can be very beneficial if you think outside the box when brainstorming good partnerships. I know a famous writer who enjoys finding small, family-owned restaurants with great food and partnering with them for promotion. She lends her name and likeness to a food item or to advertisement inside the store, giving it her stamp of approval. Then she promotes it on social media to her readers and their friends, which helps to drive diners to the restaurant. In return, she gets the publicity and the opportunity to promote her work to the restaurant's patrons who might not already be reading her books. It's a fun experience that helps both the restaurant and the writer. Writers and restaurants are not in the same business, yet with some creative thinking, these two can find ways to promote each other.

Often, it's enough just to float the idea of working together to someone you know who has a thriving business. Chances are, they're on the lookout for ways they can increase their visibility too and might be willing to work with you to figure out what you can do together. Sometimes it will be as simple as a joint-sponsorship opportunity. Other times, it might lead to something bigger, like a joint business venture.

There will be times when you need expert help, but you can't afford to pay for it. That's when it's time to get creative. What can you offer someone else in exchange for the help you need? Bartering is one of those areas where you can really see networking at its finest. Everyone needs something, and if you can find something you have or can do then you might be able to make a trade.

One of the areas where you see this happen frequently is at conventions, fairs, and shows that have an area where merchants are selling their products. Oftentimes one merchant will find something being sold by another and offer to trade for it. This also works for other industries as well. I know of a lawyer who ended up trading time spent reviewing and refining a contract in exchange for home repairs.

This idea of bartering or haggling can be difficult if you were raised with codes that say that it's not alright to do so. Some cultures thrive on this while others teach that you pay the price quoted without even bothering to ask for a discount. If you have the codes that tell you that it's demeaning or wrong to try and barter for goods or negotiate a better price, it's worth trying to break them. What's wrong is to go without goods and services that you need when you could acquire them through bartering. If an individual or a company tells you no, then that's fine. Move on to someone who might be more willing to work with you. If you need something and can't spend the money, try to barter and see where it gets you. You have nothing to lose and everything to gain.

Chapter 8

Aligning Your Business with Your Purpose

Over the years, I have come to realize that sometimes, we may not be able to land the job of our dreams, but we can turn our dreams into our jobs. Either by personal choice or necessity, we sometimes find ourselves building a business or working for ourselves. I know some of you reading this book have started a business, either out of necessity or passion. It's important to understand that your business plays a significant role in the big picture of your life. A frustrated businessman can easily become an unloving husband.

Since I began writing this book, I've done a lot of soul-searching, not only the words that I've written here, but also because of the feedback, emails, and reading comments in various groups and forums. I've realized for a long while that I've been very fortunate and blessed to have an entrepreneurial spirit and a stubbornness that refuses to allow me to quit. Early in my entrepreneurial journey, I decided that the mantra *failure is your friend* would drive me when things got tough.

It came in handy when I went four days without food in my belly because I couldn't afford a two-dollar sandwich. By the fourth day, I began to have blurred vision when I stopped by a pizza place on the corner of 34th Street and 5th Avenue in Manhattan, New York. I asked to speak to the manager and explained to him that I was a graduate student at the business school just a few blocks away, and that I'd not eaten for four days. I was so hungry that I was barely audible but managed to ask him for a slice of pizza. I left my driver's license with him as a guarantee that I would come back to pay him. Carlos, the pizza store owner, invited me to the back room and gave me 20 slices of pizza and a big bottle of Sprite. Normally, I don't eat a lot of pizza, but on that day, I may have broken the world record of pizza eaten in one sitting.

Unfortunately, I've met many people who have wanted, maybe desperately needed, to earn income from the comfort of their home. They want to do what they're passionate about, but they've let a little adversity convince them that they weren't smart enough or worthy enough and quit before they found success. Have you ever wondered why some business leaders like Bill Gates read a lot, while others like Richard Branson read very little? How do some people like Mark Zuckerberg become so incredibly financially wealthy, perform great academically, and go to great schools like Harvard, while others like Henry Ford and John D. Rockefeller didn't even graduate high school? The truth is what really matters in persistence. The dictionary defines persistence as firm continuance in a course of action in spite of difficulty or opposition.[16] History is full of examples of incredible demonstrations of persistence. Sara Blakely, the youngest self-made female billionaire according to Forbes,[17] Oprah Winfrey, and Michael Jordan are a few such examples.

Persistence is where success comes from. Keep it going no matter what. There's only one guaranteed way to fail very quickly, and that's to give up on your dreams and passions. When you throw in the towel, you surrender your dreams to the wicked hands of life's frigid conditions, and before you know it, you're paying somebody else who didn't give up on their dream. This is the same reason people who aren't as wise and don't have the experience, degrees, and networks than you sometimes have great success just by mastering the art of staying true to their dreams no matter what.

Once you give up, your chance of success drops to zero. This applies to every area of life. I know this because I've quit a few times in my lifetime too. I quit swimming class, music in college, and even when I tried to get into a top business school like Harvard after being rejected a few times. I had moments where I regretted my decision to quit some of the things I really wanted.

Therefore, it's just as crucial to align your business with your purpose as it is to align a job or career with your purpose. The good news is, you have the opportunity to drive in the direction you want to go. Entrepreneurs tend to be big dreamers. While others might not understand our pie-in-the-sky dreams, we wouldn't feel like us without them. You're in business for yourself because you want to change your life, financially and otherwise. You know that you're going to make it big someday, and may repeat this

16   "persistence," Lexico by Oxford English Dictionary, accessed June 18, 2021, https://www.lexico.com/en/definition/persistence.

17   Clare O'Connor, "Undercover Billionaire: Sara Blakely Joins The Rich List Thanks To Spanx," *Forbes*, March 7, 2012, https://www.forbes.com/sites/clareoconnor/2012/03/07/undercover-billionaire-sara-blakely-joins-the-rich-list-thanks-to-spanx/?sh=7032cf8ad736.

belief to your spouse, parents, and kids. But maybe there's always something getting in your way that causes you to ask yourself, *why hasn't it happened yet?*

You might think things like:

If I could buy *this* product, my life is totally going to change.

If I could get ahold of *this* tool, my marketing will all come together.

If I could get rid of *this* problem in my life, I could have made it big already!

If I had more money, I could really succeed in earning a good income online.

If I had more time, I could make more money online.

These are thoughts you likely repeat to yourself to mask what's really going on. Do you, deep down, think things are going to change on their own? Can you really see yourself becoming one of the ones who make it big with your dream?

If you've been at this for a while and you're still dreaming instead of doing, then you might be allowing the code of scarcity mindset to hold you back. Part of the problem is rooted in negative codes like the mindset issues that we've talked about earlier in this book. For example, you might say, if only I get ahold of *this* tool, my marketing will all come together. Then we see the bright shiny object tool smack dab in the center of the road, taking us off track, and distracting us from what we know our focus and goal should be.

Most people have a scarcity mindset. They think of all sorts of "if only's" and use them as excuses and a reason to procrastinate. On the other hand, abundance thinkers who operate with the right code have a mindset that looks at all possibilities and opportunities, and loves the fact that scarcity thinkers are so easy to compete against. You must decide which of these you will be.

The scarcity and abundance mindsets affect all areas of your life, not just business.

Having the code of scarcity mindset about life and money affects your work and business. You subconsciously won't allow yourself to take the right steps toward achieving your business goals if you have a scarcity mindset and will self-sabotage without even understanding why.

In addition to networking and finding mentors, there are other things you can do to help your business thrive as you work to fulfill your purpose. Applying for grants is one such way and are readily available in areas you might not realize. Applying for a grant can help give your company the funding it needs to expand and reach more people. Grants aren't just available for education or arts like many people think and are available for many business-related ventures. In addition to helping financially, this can also help bring you strategic partners, mentors, or new technology that your company needs.

Hiring people whose purpose align with or compliment yours is another area you should concentrate on. When you have your own business, particularly when it's expanding, you need to find people to work for you. In addition to the slew of typical job interview questions you might ask, try to get a sense of an applicant's purpose. If you can find a way to help them fulfill their purpose while they work to help you fulfill yours, then you'll create a situation in which both of you are happy and doing what you're meant to do.

Not everyone is born to be a salesman. If you need a salesman but can't find one whose purpose would be fulfilled in that function, find something that they can also do that's in line with their purpose. Maybe their passion lies in creating fantastic websites, driving traffic to your business through social media, or even rearranging inventory so that it's easier to access and more attractive for customers. If you have a goal or calling for your business, find people who are pulled in that same direction. If one of your business focuses is on sustainability, find people with a passion for that.

Also don't forget the importance of giving back to your community. This will create a sense of personal fulfillment while also showing goodwill toward your neighbors and potential customers. And the good news is, you don't have to be a big company or spend lots of money to make a big impact locally. Hosting a fundraiser, supporting a local charity, or even just showing up once a year to provide free ice cream for the kids and parents at a little league game can make quite an impact. Look for ways to actively engage your client base in a way that'll make everyone happy. This is one way to get new customers and ensure the loyalty of existing ones.

Incentive programs are great for both employees and customers, can give you an opportunity to win loyalty and share your core values. There are lots of companies that can help you set up a program, or you can design one of your own. It's all about not being afraid to try something new. Too many businesses and business owners get stuck in a rut. Don't let that happen to you. Variety is the spice of life, and you might find that when you have the courage to take a risk and tweak things, you'll end up appealing more to your customers while also making things better for your business partners, and yourself. Like with many things in business, this might require you to look at the codes you have if you feel resistance to the idea of change along the way.

Chapter 9

Letting Go of Negative Codes

This area of your life is very fertile soil for negative codes to be formed and grow. Society teaches you that a job should be the most important aspect of your life and form your identity. It teaches you that all other considerations, including health and relationships, should be secondary. You might have learned to value people based on what they earn and have a low self-esteem, because you've been taught to think of yourself as slow, unskilled, or unsociable based on what family, teachers, and employers have told you.

These are codes that need to be changed. But before you can, you need to understand exactly what's wrong and then figure out how negative codes are reinforcing or creating these problems for you. The first step to changing what's wrong in your life is self-assessment. Once you figure out what's holding you back, then you can begin to move forward.

Look at this list and see if there are any patterns you can recognize in your own life:

- Do you tend to procrastinate?
- Are you confused about which business model you should choose?
- Do you spend most of your work time chatting on forums and social media sites, or attending webinars?
- Do you rarely follow anything through to completion?
- Do you tend to sabotage opportunities after you have any kind of success?
- Do you believe it's hard to earn money, perhaps so hard that you shouldn't even try?

You might feel like there's something wrong with you, or that everything would change if only you could find a magic button. Well, the good news is there's nothing wrong with you, and you can absolutely develop positive codes in place of a negative code. Some other good news is that there really is a magic button, and it's called mindset.

Keep in mind that the stress and frustration of your career and business can take a physical toll on your health. Taking care of some, if not all, of these challenges can help to rewrite those bad codes that exist in your career and business and allow you to maintain your health.

Below are a few career affirmations I like to use that can help you on your journey:

- **I will take action for my career dreams today.** I know that when I combine my exceptional abilities with massive action, I can truly achieve limitless results. I will avoid waiting for things to happen and make them happen instead.

- **I will achieve each of my career goals, no matter how big they are.** Nothing can stop me because I'm relentless in pursuing them. I know the Creator has my back. This belief gives me great confidence as I pursue my goals and seek to access incredible opportunities. My career is what I make of it, and today I will make it a happy and satisfying experience.
- **I am laser-focused to get what I want, because what I focus on will become a reality.** I control all my thoughts and use them to push me toward achieving my professional goals. My thoughts lead to my feelings, which lead to my actions, which lead to my reality. I affirm that I will climb the corporate ladder with integrity and confidence.
- **I affirm that this will be my best year yet**. I will hit all my goals. I will attract the promotion that I desire and deserve. I will have a career of success.
- **I am excited to see all the good things happening in my career.** I will keep pushing and striving until I reach the success that I desire, and make my dreams come true.

Turn to the workbook section at the back of the book, page 369, for your reflection exercises to help you commit to action.

PART 5:

CRACKING YOUR HEALTH AND WELLNESS CODES

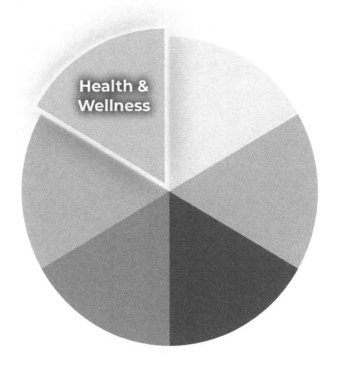

Health & Wellness

Chapter 1

Kari and the Role of Health

Kari left the doctor's office and didn't want to go home. If she did, she knew she'd just end up falling asleep on the couch again. More than anything she was tired, more tired than she liked to think about. She patted the slight pooch of her stomach and thought about what the doctor said about having poor muscle tone. Was that why it was getting harder and harder to do things she'd always be able to do before?

With creaking knees and panting breath as she went down the staircase, she'd told herself it was just part of the aging process. But was she wrong?

There was a café half a block from the doctor's office, and she decided to have lunch there to sit and think a while. She began to walk, head down, trying not to think of the things that had happened to her dad in the last few years of his life.

"Kari, hi!"

She looked up, startled to hear someone calling her.

Linda, one of the other mothers from her boys' school, was locking the door of a yoga studio. She was wearing loose workout clothes.

"Hi Linda, what are you doing here?" Kari asked.

"I'm just closing up for lunch."

"That's right, I forgot you own a yoga studio," Kari said.

"Yup. Where are you headed?"

"The café."

"What a coincidence. I am, too. Do you want to have lunch together?"

Kari wasn't really in the mood to talk to anyone, but as she stood there staring at Linda something in the back of her mind urged her to accept the offer.

"Ok, sure."

Five minutes later, they were seated at a table. They chatted about kids and school for a few minutes before Linda gave her a sympathetic look.

"What's wrong, Kari?"

Kari was used to being private about her troubles. She'd learned that from her mom. She was about to brush off the question with one of her standard replies but stopped again.

"What do you know about balance?" she blurted out.

Linda chuckled. "I'm a yoga instructor, so I'd say quite a lot."

Kari smiled. "Sorry, I meant, balance in life."

"Well, the body is life. And I can tell you from experience when you take care of your body, it can help your balance and take care of the rest of you," Linda said.

Kari nodded, although she didn't really understand.

"What's going on?" Linda asked.

"My doctor said that I'm not balanced. I'm not sleeping well, and my body isn't doing well because of it."

Linda nodded sympathetically. "I used to have those problems. I used to have the worst insomnia. I'd worry about everything. I binge ate when I worried, and I worked so hard that I never took time off for anything."

"How did you get over that?"

"A friend of mine drug me to her yoga class. After a couple of sessions, I found that I felt better and started sleeping better. Once I slept better, I started to feel clear headed and was able to make smarter decisions about everything in my life."

"Really?"

"Absolutely. I've got an idea. Why don't you come to my 11 a.m. class tomorrow, and afterward we'll have lunch again?"

Kari found herself nodding. She didn't know exactly what she needed to find balance and get healthy, but this might be the universe trying to tell her what the first step should be.

Every sound mind deserves a sound body. All your talent, skill, and knowledge are being carried around by your body. If your body is weak, everything else can fall apart or be severely affected. That's why it's critical that you take care of your health. While not everyone is blessed with a perfect-looking body or even a healthy one, it's your duty to do your best to try and keep it operating as best as is possible. With changing schedules, increased responsibilities, and very demanding daily routines, it's easy to forget to attend to our physical and mental health needs.

Health cannot be secondary to wealth building. Most people focus on their career or business at the expense of their health, particularly when they're younger in the morning and early to mid-afternoon stages of their lives. This, however, is a huge mistake. For what use is wealth if you don't have health? Some people think they can commit 70% to a career or business and 30% to health, but this is not the case. The two need to be equal, and without one the other becomes meaningless. In fact, if I had to choose, I'd rather be healthy and poor than unhealthy and rich. You know why? You can always find a way to get money, but if your health is gone there's nothing you can do to regain what you've lost.

This means more than just being able to do the things you want to do. Without health, you can't truly excel. Part of you will have to focus on taking care of your ailing body and be consumed with worry over how much longer it will be before your health begins to decline. Plus, when your body isn't strong, you won't have enough energy, stamina, or strength to accomplish your goals. It's also crucial for emotional stability, growth, and all-around soundness. If one area of your life isn't doing well, it's bound to negatively impact all the others.

This is not a topic I take lightly. My concern for my health and the health of everyone I coach isn't just academic. It comes from seeing firsthand what ignoring your health to pursue other things can do to a strong, vibrant person. Take my mother, for instance. She was an amazing woman who worked as a librarian at a university and ran several of her own businesses all at the same time. Each day she was up at four in the morning to work on her businesses before getting my brothers and I up and ready for school. Once we were out the door, she'd go to her job at the university. When she came home, she cooked dinner and continued working at her businesses, going to bed long after the rest of us. She made sure we were active in church, participating every Sunday, and she never missed a choir practice. My mother did all of this to be the best mother, wife, sister, and daughter that she could be. But after she succeeded in raising great boys and helping her other family members, she succeeded at something else too. She succeeded at damaging her health by her early forties.

She put everything and everyone else before herself. When you do that, as you advance in age, the body can't function effectively because of the amount of stress it's been under. That much stress and neglect prematurely ages and wears you out to the point of exhaustion. And before you know it, you can no longer enjoy what you've achieved, and your body gives out. One of the most heart-wrenching experiences of my life was my inability to help my mom physically as I watched her go from a happy, ambitious mother, wife, daughter, sister and cousin to a very sad, frail, and deflated woman when her health eventually went downhill. This is the punishment for ignoring health in pursuit of everything else. A loss of joy, frustration, the inability to maximize your life, and even dying young are all consequences. That's why it's important to always put your health first.

Four areas that are important to focus on when it comes to your health are mindfulness, rest and relaxation, exercise, and eating right. To make things right, my mother was forced to make lifestyle changes while prioritizing rest relaxation, and diet, and although her health is not fully restored, she has managed her health much better for the last 15 years and is showing many improvements.

Chapter 2

Mindfulness and Case Studies

If you've ever played around with a fitness tracker, you've likely heard about mindfulness. Mindfulness is being in the present moment and fully aware of your body, thoughts, and emotions without casting judgment on them. These days that can be tough to do, and you'll need to unplug and breathe to make it happen. It's also important to be intentional about taking a break. Sometimes you need to turn off your phone and make time for hobbies and interests, or even to just sit and focus on nothing. Sometimes your body and mind need time to relax and get in tune. While this might sound easy, it can be a real challenge—especially in today's modern business world. Often our mind is constantly running to the next meeting, the next call, and what you'll do tomorrow, the next week, or the next year. It's easy to spend so much time focusing on the future that you miss out on the present.

That's dangerous for several reasons. First, you risk missing out on what your body might be trying to tell you. When the body breaks down, it rarely does so without warning. Often it spends weeks, sometimes even years, trying to tell you that something is wrong. If you're not paying attention, you can miss the signals. And even if a few of them do make it through, people tend to put off having their health checked out because they feel fine or they're just feeling the aches and pains of getting older, when, in reality, this couldn't be further from the truth. In fact, this type of procrastination can lead to serious medical complications and even premature death.

The human body is an incredible machine and can function for a long time on limited sleep, bad food, and huge amounts of stress. However, this doesn't happen in a vacuum. Everything takes its toll. When the body needs a break to rest and recharge, it starts sending signals. Many people have found out the hard way that if they ignore the signals to slow down and rest, their body will find a way to put them flat on their backs, often in a hospital bed.

Cracking the Code Case Study

Ginger was very driven. She worked hard to take care of her family as both the primary bread winner and the homemaker. Sometimes she worked 18 hours a day, including weekends. Even though she was able to do it for a while, eventually it all began to catch up with her, and Ginger started to have stomach pains along with some intestinal distress. She put it down to stress and eating the wrong types of foods and tried to ignore the discomfort and inconvenience as best she could. This went on for months.

Then one afternoon, the pain increased so much that it felt like her entire ribcage was being crushed, and she began to vomit. That was when her husband chose to act, ignoring her protests that she would be okay in a few minutes. He took her to the hospital, and early the next morning, a surgeon removed her gallbladder. It had gone completely gangrenous and was just hours away from exploding and killing her.

Had Ginger's husband not acted when he did, she would have died. Her gallbladder didn't get into that kind of shape overnight, though. Her health had been declining for at least a year, but because she was so busy working, she hadn't paid any attention to what her body tried to tell her. If she had, she would've realized that her symptoms were very similar to a friend of hers, who'd had her gallbladder removed too.

You would have thought this close call would have impacted Ginger. Unfortunately, as soon as she was released from the hospital, she went right back to her breakneck pace, convinced that if she slowed down or took a vacation that everything she'd worked for would collapse. Ten years later, she ended up right back in the emergency room, having successfully ignored a new set of signs and symptoms. After having surgery to aid another damaged organ, she vowed to stop ignoring her body. Now, whenever she begins to receive signals that she needs a break, she stops as quickly as she can and takes at least a day to rest. It's far from ideal, but she's learning to pay more attention to what's happening in the present.

Part of Ginger's problem stemmed from the bad codes she received growing up. Her father also worked insane hours to support his family and rarely took a sick day. Whenever there was something wrong with him, he'd downplay it and pretend that he was fine even if it was clear that he wasn't. From him, Ginger learned that health was secondary to business, and that medical issues should be ignored or at least downplayed. It was this kind of thinking that nearly got her killed.

Ginger had to work hard to replace the bad code with a good code. The good code tells her that if she doesn't take care of her health, she won't be able to take care of anything else, including work and her family. She knew she needed to stop and rest when she was tired, and that pulling all-nighters was not a badge of courage. Instead, she vowed to seek medical help at the first signs of trouble, and to get annual check-ups. This fundamental change wasn't easy, but as she found out, it was necessary in order to survive.

Another hazard of not being mindful is that you miss out on enjoying the present. You blink and your children are grown before you even have a chance to teach them what you wanted to. Before you know it, you'll have let all those years pass by, realizing you never got to do things like taking them on that camping trip, going to see a baseball game, visit Disney World, or even just getting to know them as people.

Have you ever tried to enjoy a holiday or a vacation with your family, and found yourself instead thinking about work? You end up missing out on fully enjoying the time you've set aside for those people who are most important to you because you're not really with them. Yet, you're not really working either. You're stuck in limbo, and not really accomplishing anything.

Cracking the Code Case Study

Paul had an incredibly demanding job in the computer industry. He worked 16-hour days, had a one-hour commute each way, and was on call 24/7. Most weekends he had to go into the office because they needed him. He barely got to see his wife and daughter and knew that was a problem.

Growing up, his own family hadn't spent much time together, and certainly not the kind of quality time he was looking to spend with his. He knew that he had to make a change if he wanted to really get to know his daughter and be able to connect with his wife in a meaningful way.

It took him a few years to work it out, but he finally managed to take an extended vacation with his family once a year to a location free of all distractions from work. For three to four weeks, he would be 100% present with his wife and daughter, living completely in the moment. Little did he know, it was those trips that ended up saving him from an early grave. He also made sure that he and his daughter had a close, loving relationship even though they didn't see much of each other during a normal week at home.

The third problem with not being mindful is you may miss out on creative breakthroughs. Your mind is constantly working, no matter what you're doing. Even while you're asleep, your subconscious is hard at work to come up with solutions to whatever problems you've been thinking about. Sometimes, though, you can get so busy thinking about things that you don't stop to listen to yourself. When you silence the constant chatter of lists and schedules and trivial thoughts that run through your head, you will have an opportunity to hear what's important.

Did you ever have the experience of trying to think of a name or something you've just forgotten, and you can't for the life of you come up with it? Have you noticed that sometimes, hours later when you're doing something completely different, that the name pops into your head? That's because you posed a question: What's the name of this person or place? While your active thoughts have moved on from that, your subconscious is still working to answer the question. It's searching through your memories to come up with the answer, and then it just blurts it out once it's discovered.

The subconscious mind constantly has things to say, but how often do you hear it? By learning to silence the active part of your mind, you give your subconscious an opportunity to communicate more clearly and effectively. This is when inspiration strikes and you're more likely to receive the answer you're looking for.

Many people also discover that it's when they silence the active mind that they can hear another voice—whether it's God or the universe—attempting to talk to them and provide help or comfort. This is why so many spiritual people take time to meditate and silence their thoughts so that they can more clearly hear what God, or the universe, is trying to tell them.

Mindfulness can also provide other benefits. You can learn to better regulate your emotions this way. Mindfulness, time, and exercise are great tools to relax after a stressful day. To incorporate mindful practices into your life, try including meditation, journaling, and technology-free quiet time into your life. You'll be surprised at how big of an impact it can have.

But while it might sound easy, mindfulness can be a difficult thing to get used to. A great way to start is to set aside 10 minutes a day to meditate. Meditation is the practice of learning to be still, relax physically, and calm your mind. You might be thinking that sounds nice, or that it's easier said than done. While it's true that it might take a few attempts before you see the benefits, the practice can be quite profound.

Just remember, it's important to start slow and increase the time as you get used to it. For me, meditation was particularly challenging in the beginning. My personality and lifestyle are the opposite of meditative activities. While meditation encourages stillness and calm, my go-getter personality made being still very difficult for me. Because I work in a fast-paced industry, my mind is constantly trying to figure out the next million-dollar idea. When I tried meditation for the first time, I had my eyes closed for less than five seconds before I said out loud, "No, this is not for me."

And that was it. I dropped the idea of meditating. But around 14 months later, I organized a weekend retreat for 15 young professionals. On the first day of the retreat, one of the participants suggested a great idea. "How about a meditation challenge this weekend?" Of course, I said it was a great idea, but I knew I was going to struggle, and I didn't want my participants to see me in that vulnerable of a state. So, I stayed up that night to trying my best to meditate, failing once again. But what I did end up learning was that I needed to ease myself into it slowly. Although I still struggled with the meditation challenge during the weekend retreat, it was the beginning of my meditation journey. Meditation has now become an integral part of my life.

Keep in mind that meditation does not have to be a religious activity. It's simply a way to connect more closely to your body and mind. Studies by the National Center for Complementary and Integrative Health (NCCIH) have shown that meditation can help with several ailments including high blood pressure,[18] irritable bowel syndrome ,[19] ulcerative colitis,[20] insomnia,[21] anxiety, stress, and some psychological disorders like depression.[22] A 2011 study conducted by the NCCIH found that eight weeks of mindfulness meditation in a group of women reduced the severity of irritable bowel syndrome symptoms.[23] Another NCCIH study in 2009 found that Transcendental Meditation not only lowered blood pressure for those at risk of high blood pressure but also helped reduce anxiety, depression, and anger, and increased participants' coping abilities.[24] More studies are being done to determine how meditation can be used to reduce pain and fight other illnesses.

Your body and mind will send signals when something is wrong. If you're running too fast and are too distracted to pay attention, early warning signals can go unnoticed and the potential for catastrophic injury or illness rises. This is one of the reasons it's important to take time to listen to what your mind and body are trying to tell you. Meditation is one way to do this.

18   Carly M. Goldstein et al, "Current perspectives on the use of meditation to reduce blood pressure," *International Journal of Hypertension* (2012), www.doi. org/10.1155/2012/578397.

19   Susan A. Gaylord et al, "Mindfulness training reduces the severity of irritable bowel syndrome in women: results of a randomized controlled trial," *American Journal of Gastroenterology* 106, no. 9 (2011), www.doi.org/10.1038/ajg.2011.184.

20   Jedel S. Hoffman et al, "A randomized controlled trial of mindfulness-bases stress reduction to prevent flare-up in patients with inactive colitis," *Digestion* 89, no. 2 (2014), www.doi.org/10.1159/000356316.

21   Jason C. Ong et al, "A randomized controlled trial of mindfulness meditation for chronic insomnia," *Sleep* 37, no. 9 (2014), www.doi.org/10.5665/sleep.4010.

22   Kevin W. Chen et al, "Meditative therapies for reducing anxiety: a systematic review and meta-analysis of randomized controlled trials," *Depression and Anxiety* 29, no. 7 (2012), www.doi.org/10.1002/da.21964.

23   Gaylord et al, "Mindfulness training."

24   Elias Dakwar and Frances R. Levin, "The emerging role of meditation in addressing psychiatric illness, with a focus on substance use disorders," *Harvard Review of Psychiatry* 17, no. 4 (2009), www.doi.org/10.1080/10673220903149135.

The first step you'll need to figure out to begin practicing meditation is to choose a place where you'll meditate. Ideally this should be somewhere quiet and free of distractions. Sometimes this in itself can be a challenge. If you don't work in a place where you can lock your office door and tell people not to disturb you for 15 minutes, then you'll need to find an alternative. You can try sitting in your car in the parking lot or find an unused conference room. One woman I knew would sit in the bathroom at her workplace because she knew she could usually hide out and be undisturbed for a few minutes.

At home, it can sometimes be even harder to find quiet, private space. If you have a busy home and it's not possible or appropriate to establish your own space for a period of quiet time, then look outside the home. Maybe you can go to the porch or in the yard. You might be able to take a walk to a nearby park. I know a man who during busy holiday times would volunteer to drive relatives to the store and then sit in the car and wait for them. It was the only way he could get 15 minutes to himself, but he made it work.

One thing that can really help is to be as comfortable as possible. Being physically at ease when meditating will help free you from distractions and get into the zone a bit easier. Again, this might be next to impossible given your circumstances, but if you can, wear comfortable clothes, slip off your shoes, and sit or lie in a comfortable place. If you're experiencing a lot of physical discomfort, including pain or hunger, it can be even harder to calm your mind. These obstacles can be as much of a distraction as a needy coworker or a crying baby. But do what you can to minimalize physical discomfort so that your mind won't get distracted by and obsess on any one thing. Again, this might take some creative thinking on your part, but neckties can be loosened, and car seats can be reclined if that makes things easier. It's okay if you can't get

100% comfortable, just do what you reasonably can with the time and space you have.

Another thing you can do to make things easier is to give your brain something else to focus on. The mind is on a constant mission to fill itself with input, and it looks for stimuli everywhere. Anyone who's ever spent a sleepless night knows how hard it can be to shut down errant thoughts. That's why it's important to give your mind something to focus on. Fortunately, there are many options.

One of the easiest things to focus on while meditating is your breathing. Inhale slowly through your nose, then exhale slowly through your mouth. Counting as you breathe can help to establish a steady rhythm. Focusing on your breathing can also help to calm down your nervous system. What's more is that it sends extra oxygen to your brain, which helps it perform better. Most people don't breathe correctly, often taking too many short breaths which puts stress on the entire body and builds anxiety.[25] This is why long, deep breaths have a noticeable calming effect. Practicing this type of breathing is something you should strive to do multiple times a day, not just when you're meditating.

For some people relaxing sounds like a rainstorm or ocean waves can help to clear their mind when they're trying to meditate. There are many audio tracks and apps that you can find that will give you access to these soundscapes. If you choose, you can get these natural sounds overlayed with soothing music. There are also music tracks that can help get your mind into a focused, centered place. A quick search on your favorite digital music store will help you find something that appeals to you.

---

25   Terry Gross, "How the 'Lost Art' of Breathing Can Impact Sleep and Resilience," NPR, May 27, 2020, https://www.npr.org/sections/health-shots/2020/05/27/862963172/how-the-lost-art-of-breathing-can-impact-sleep-and-resilience .

Spoken word meditations are another option you might want to investigate. These fall into two types of categories. The first is a guided meditation by someone with a pleasing voice. Again, music stores and apps offer several options depending on what appeals to you. Alternatively, you can record yourself speaking slowly and clearly with positive affirmations that you write out. These should be things you want to focus on. You can praise your positive qualities, remind yourself that you're doing a good job, describe your favorite peaceful place, or paint a picture with words of how you want your life to be in the future. The possibilities here are only limited by your imagination.

While it might seem counterintuitive, technology can be used to your advantage. There are a ton of websites and phone apps out there designed to help you meditate. If you're using any kind of fitness tracking device or software, it probably already has meditation information and assistance available to you. Don't be afraid to try out some of the many options until you find something that speaks to you.

Remember too that you should give yourself permission to have this time for yourself. As unfortunate as it is, busy people often feel guilty taking time for themselves, even if it's vital to their health and well-being. Be intentional about setting this time aside. Remind yourself that it's important, and literally give yourself permission to take this time. This will help you get rid of those nagging feelings of guilt and frustration as you meditate. It can also help silence the voice that reminds you of all the things you need to do, and keep this voice from reminding you of all those things you need to do *now* instead of later.

Ready to get started? Here comes the hard part. You need to let your mind drift. Don't try to force it to do anything in particular. The mind is so busy all the time reminding you of a hundred little things, so this can be difficult in practice. The goal here is to let that all fade away and not focus on anything. Focus only on your breathing or the audio you're listening to. This will give your subconscious an opportunity to speak up and make connections you've never had before. You might feel more creative or inspired. This is also the time when your body has an opportunity to let you know if there's something wrong.

If at first the meditation doesn't come easy, try again. Initially you might find it difficult to clear your mind. After all, you've spent a lifetime training your brain to constantly race ahead, always anticipating the next thing you have to do, worrying about some problem that needs to be addressed, or rehashing a conversation that didn't go the way you wanted it to. Without discipline, your mind will be everywhere but the present.

But with practice, it does get easier. Meditation is one of those things that you need to do consistently for several days before you relax and really notice the benefits. As you clear your mind of all the busy thoughts, you'll find that you feel better too. You might even find that your subconscious tries to talk to you about an issue with your health or find a solution to a work problem you've been trying to figure out. If this happens frequently, keep a piece of paper and a pen nearby so you can jot down what comes to you once the session is over.

Writing down your thoughts by hand has additional benefits for your brain too. First, the stimulation that comes from combining words with fine motor skills integrates both hemispheres of the brain, challenging you on several levels simultaneously. Second, you process your thoughts better, and imprint what's important from your memory. Journaling is the practice of writing down what you're thinking and feeling. People process information in different ways. An important part of processing is talking something through. Regardless of whether or not you have someone in your life that you can honestly talk through everything with, journaling is crucial. It is literally talking things through with *yourself*. The act of writing things down in this way has tremendous benefits.

Have you ever heard that the only way to get some thoughts out of your mind is to get them onto paper? The simple act of journaling and getting thoughts on paper can be very therapeutic. You'll start to make connections you never would have made before. I've seen firsthand the incredible benefit of journaling, especially when I suffered heartbreak when I was engaged to be married, exactly 21 days before the wedding day.

As you might guess, all the planning had been finalized, and my bride to be called off the wedding abruptly without any clear explanation. She wouldn't answer my calls or speak to me. Six months later, I found out she had a baby, and it was impossible that it could be my child. This shocking experience shattered me deeply. Processing the experience was difficult, and I would drive long hours to an unknown destination while I wallowed in my thoughts.

I had almost no information to work with. Why would my bride-to-be cheat on me, and why didn't I see this coming? What did I do wrong? So many questions with very few answers. As time went by, I began to process things a little differently. I began to get the thoughts in my head out and put them on paper. After two years of journaling, I had 1,700 pages of words about this specific situation.

Journaling played a significant role in my healing and recovery and can be an incredibly useful exercise. For instance, there may be a memory from your childhood that consistently nags at you. You may not really understand why, which is all the more reason to investigate, reflect, and consider how that memory affects your life today. In addition to focusing on events that stand out in your life, reflect on your life as a whole. Consider your childhood, young adulthood, and adult life to this point. Why do you think you tend to fall into the same habits and patterns?

Sometimes you have worries, concerns, or even to do list items that keep ambushing you throughout the day. By taking the time to acknowledge and address these thoughts, you can keep them from continuously recurring at inopportune times, interrupting your current task.

Journaling can also help to sort through complex emotions or brainstorm solutions to a challenge you're facing. Sometimes your thoughts are nebulous and half-formed, and because of that they can be troublesome. By putting them down in in written word, it'll be easier to understand what you're thinking or worrying about. Once you've articulated these thoughts, you can then address these properly. With a clear mind, you can choose to either dismiss them as baseless fears or address the issue. Anytime you can't get your mind to be still or release stress, consider writing it down. This makes everything feel more real, and therefore easier to address in one way or another.

While journaling, it's helpful to record a list of things you're grateful for. Doing this first thing in the morning or the last thing before you go to bed can work over time to radically shift your attitudes and emotions. Focusing on what you're grateful for can calm your mind, put you into a positive, problem-solving state, help you relax and rest, and make your day a little brighter.[26] Another benefit to keeping a gratitude journal is that it helps you express gratitude toward friends, relatives, partners, employees,

---

26   "Giving thanks can make you happier," Harvard Health Publishing, November 22, 2011, https://www.health.harvard.edu/healthbeat/giving-thanks-can-make-you-happier.

bosses, and coworkers. Expressing this will make the other person happier and strengthen the bond between you. Strong bonds help you maintain emotional health, which contributes greatly to physical health as well.

Whether you're trying to accomplish great things or are just trapped in the quagmire of everyday minutia, it can be hard to see the forest for the trees. That's why it's important to track your progress in the form of daily victories. Not only will this help mindfulness, but it'll also provide encouragement on your journey. It can be easy to take small victories for granted, or even miss them altogether. Being intentional about marking them will give you a sense of accomplishment, and serve as proof that you're building toward something, which in turn can help keep you focused and motivated.

Just like anything having to do with your health, consistency is key. If you only journal occasionally, gains might only be marginally helpful. This is similar to only exercising once in a while or eating healthy once a week. What you're really doing when journaling is training your mind to think through problems and look at the world in a positive, problem solving way. You can't train your mind in a haphazard way because it won't learn the new behaviors. Do what you can to make a journaling habit easy on yourself. Pick a certain time of day, and if possible, choose a dedicated place to be when you do it. Being in that place at that time of day will trigger your mind that it's time to do the activity, and will make the entire process faster, easier, and more autonomic.

It's also a good idea to be mindful about choosing what you're going to write about. Some people prefer typing and have no problem storing their journal as a computer file. Others need the physical contact with pen and paper. Do what makes you feel most comfortable and happy so that the task is easier on you.

CRACKING THE LIFE CODE

While you're journaling, don't forget to disconnect from the outside world so you can focus solely on your thoughts.

A key component to mindfulness is to unplug from the rest of the world. There are a million opportunities to be distracted, and most of them relate to the accessibility of information and entertainment. Smart phones, computers, e-readers, and TVs all vie for your time and attention. The problem is, they're a constant buzz of distraction for your mind. Have you ever realized that you didn't get everything done on your to do list for the day but did manage to spend a great deal of time responding to social media alerts or looking at a dozen emails from your coworker with pictures of cats, humorous stories, and the latest email hoax? When you stop to realize how much time people waste with these devices, it's horrifying. Even worse, they're stealing time from truly important things like work, family, and relaxation.

If you want to connect more with your family, ban all electronic devices at the dinner table. This will enable everyone to talk and interact with each other instead of staring at their phone or the TV. Spend time focusing on each individual instead. In fact, this is a good thing to do for lunch dates and important business meetings as well. It helps you be truly in the moment. When you are, not only does the other person feel valued and allow connections to be more easily formed, but you can also pick up on non-verbal cues they're sending you. Body language makes up a huge percentage of a conversation, and if your head is down, you're missing half of what the other person is trying to communicate.

Paul, the computer guy who focused on his family during the annual vacation, knew that screens of any kind killed communication, connection, and the special moments he was trying to create with his family. Even though the family spent hours each day at home on computers or had the TV on in the background, while on vacation they unplugged completely. There was no TV watching and no computers. This time spent together meant everyone was present, in the moment, and really spending it with each other instead of staring at the nearest screen.

A study by GWI, the leading audience targeting company for the global marketing industry, has shown that the average adult spends about two hours and twenty-two minutes a day on social networking and messaging platforms.[27] What could you do with an extra two hours in your day? You could make more sales, spend more time with your kids, get a hobby, or even focus on improving your future. The possibilities are endless, but not if you're letting social media rob you of those two hours every day.

The problem with social media is that it's insidious. You get alerts on your phone and in your email. You log on for a minute to post something or check something out, and suddenly you're scrolling through your newsfeed and liking motivational quotes and pictures of cats posted by people you don't even know. Five minutes here, 15 minutes there—it all adds up.

Be intentional about your social media usage. Turn off your alerts so you don't get notified every time someone likes a post or uploads a photo. Then, pick a specific time of the day when you will go online and check your social media. Set a timer and give yourself a specific amount of time, maybe 15 or 30 minutes only.

For busy professionals who pride themselves on always being on the job, this probably sounds horrifying. However, it's a relationship saver when it comes to being able to spend quality time with friends and family. It also forces others, including those you work with, to respect your boundaries and give you the downtime your brain and your non-work relationships so desperately need. Don't worry about emergencies. There's a way set up most smart-

---

27   "Connecting the dots," GWI, 2021, https://www.gwi.com/reports/ trends-2021.

phones so that certain people like parents, children, spouse can get through even when your phone is on *do not disturb* mode. You can even set it up so that anyone can get through if they call multiple times in a row with an actual emergency.

This might require some breaking of old codes on your part to get started. Many people have a hard time setting hours where they won't answer the telephone. This is not a new problem. It's been around for generations. Often a family crisis or a special anniversary dinner might come second to whoever is on the other end of that ringing phone. A lot of people lose a lot of sleep because their spouse receives work calls all night long. Millions of romantic moments have been sidelined because a boss, or a mom, or even a telemarketer called at the wrong time. Many people are interrupt driven, meaning that no matter what they're doing in that moment, they'll drop everything to deal with whatever is interrupting them.

This is a code that needs to be broken. Most of the time a ringing phone is not the end of the world, and certainly not the most important thing in the world. It's ok to let it go to voicemail, or to not answer a text or email immediately. Obviously, there are some personal and work issues that require a timely response, but this is where discretion comes in. It's important to teach yourself to not be a slave to your mobile device. Then it's even more important to turn around and teach it to the younger generation, most of whom are already hopelessly addicted to their phone.

Make a conscious decision how often you watch streaming services too, as platforms like YouTube put a world of entertainment and information at our disposal wherever you go. Whether it's on TV, your computer, or your phone, control how much time you spend streaming, binging, or vegging out. Much like social media, entertainment can be a trap.

I'm not saying you have to give it all up. But you need to decide for yourself how many hours a day you're willing to sacrifice to something that doesn't create a bond, build your business, or provide personal satisfaction. Whatever your magic number is, stick with it. While it might mean you have to choose carefully what shows you continue to watch, remember that your time is a valuable commodity.

Chapter 3

Strategically Taking It Easy

Are you sleeping well at night? If you are, count yourself lucky. According to Centers for Disease Control and Prevention's (CDC) Morbidity and Mortality report, one in three Americans aren't getting anywhere near enough sleep.[28] As many as 70 million Americans suffer from chronic sleep problems. [29] Between those two statistics, good sleep seems more than a little difficult to come by. Every living creature needs time to let the body and mind rest in order to recharge. Cats are masters of this particular attribute and sleep up to 18 hours a day.[30] They need to do this in order to compensate for the amount of energy spent when they're

28   "1 in 3 adults don't get enough sleep," Centers for Disease Control (CDC), February 18, 2016, https://www.cdc.gov/media/releases/2016/p0215-enough-sleep.html.

29   "Sleep and Sleep Disorders: About Our Program," CDC, updated June 5, 2015, https://www.cdc.gov/sleep/about_us.html.

30   "An Age-Old Mystery: Why Do Cats Sleep So Much?" Oakland Veterinary Referral Services, September 6, 2017, https://www.ovrs.com/blog/cats-sleep/.

awake either hunting for food or play hunting if they're well-fed pets. Cats expend great amounts of energy in bursts, and then must rest quite a bit to recharge for the next effort. People could learn a lot from their pets in this regard.

It may seem obvious that sleep is beneficial. Even without fully grasping what sleep does for us, we know that going without sleep for too long makes us feel terrible, and that getting a good night's sleep can make us feel ready to take on the world. Human adults optimally need about seven to nine hours of solid sleep a night to function at their peak.[31] Unfortunately, about a third of Americans aren't getting enough sleep.[32] They pound caffeine to get themselves started in the morning and perhaps rely on it at other points during the day.

Most people think that caffeine addiction and sleepiness are the only downsides to not getting enough rest. The reality is much grimmer. Sleep deprivation causes severe problems and puts people at risk for certain diseases. Not getting enough sleep can prematurely age your skin, cause cognitive problems, kill sex drive, cause people to be forgetful, increase weight gain, lead to depression, and impair judgement. Lack of sleep also leads to increased risk of high blood pressure, strokes, diabetes, heart disease, and heart attacks.[33]

Kari found out the hard way that her insomnia was triggering ripple effects with her own health. Crashing on the couch wasn't a viable alternative for getting a decent night's sleep. When the doctor told her that she risked severe health issues, it really scared her. She didn't want to go down the same path as her father. Even though she didn't entirely understand immediately what the doc-

31   Taylor Jones, "How Much Sleep Do You Really Need?" Healthline, updated December 8, 2020, https://www.healthline.com/nutrition/how-much-sleep-you-need.

32   "1 in 3 adults don't get enough sleep," CDC.

33   Alex Dimitriu, "Sleep Deprivation," Sleep Foundation, updated November 4, 2020, https://www.sleepfoundation.org/sleep-deprivation.

tor was trying to tell her about balance, she did understand what he was saying about the impact that lack of sleep could have on her body and vowed to make a change.

When the human body gets the rest it requires, it improves your mood, eases stress, lowers your risk for serious health problems, allows you to get along better with others, and enhances your ability to think clearly and make good decisions.[34]

While few people can argue against the mountain of evidence about how much sleep is required, many people still ignore the fact that the mind needs just as much of an opportunity to rest as the body does. While the brain does rest some at night, it's also still busy processing data from the day before and preparing you for the day ahead. So, while the body might be at rest for seven hours, the brain is not. As you sleep, your brain forges connections, pairing new information with old, and makes creative leaps you might not be consciously ready for just yet.[35] As your brain cycles toward sleep mode, it sends certain signals to the rest of your body that it's time to rest and recharge. It tells your body to repair cells, to stop digestion, and to rest. The mind requires relaxation as well. Too much cortisol, the hormone linked to stress, can do some serious brain damage over time.[36] This is why it's so important to take the time to shut down your mind.

Most people have a lot of repetition in their daily routine. The same is true whether they're students stuck in a pattern of classes, studying, and exams, or are workers doing the same task day after

---

34   "Get Enough Sleep," U.S. Department of Health and Human Services, https://health.gov/myhealthfinder/topics/everyday-healthy-living/mental-health-and-relationships/get-enough-sleep.

35   Tom Stafford, "How sleep makes your mind more creative," BBC, December 4, 2013, https://www.bbc.com/future/article/20131205-how-sleep-makes-you-more-creative.

36   "Chronic stress puts your health at risk," Mayo Clinic, March 19, 2019, https://www.mayoclinic.org/healthy-lifestyle/stress-management/in-depth/stress/art-20046037.

day. Very few people have a day-to-day life that isn't somewhat repetitious. The brain gets into a rut as time wears on.

Have you ever driven home, gotten there, and realized you remember nothing about the drive? That's because your brain is so accustomed to the route that it didn't need to expend much conscious energy to follow it. The pattern is burned in. This is also why sometimes you get in the car to go somewhere new and find yourself accidentally driving somewhere else, passing your exit on the freeway, or realizing you're halfway home without having stopped at the store. (This is also where a little more practice with mindfulness can come in handy).

Like ruts in a road, the more you grind in the same routine, the deeper the ruts will become, until one day they're dangerous potholes that pose a hazard. The mind needs to be constantly challenged and exposed to new stimuli so that it doesn't start to wither. This is where relaxation becomes crucial.

Relaxation doesn't have to be a sedentary activity, either. Some people go white water rafting to relax. Relaxation can look different for different people, but the important thing is that the activity is outside of your normal routine. You might need to do more outdoor physical activity to feel refreshed, like you've let mind and body do something to heal and recharge. Or you might need to curl up on the couch with a good book and let yourself drift away into someone else's life to feel like you've had the break that you need. There are several things to keep in mind when figuring out how to get yourself the rest and relaxation you need.

Even if you're stuck with a routine, there's no reason you can't change up elements of it. This helps keep your mind healthy. If you drive to work every day, take a different route one day a week. If you eat out every Thursday because that's the only day you can get a babysitter, eat at a new restaurant and order something you've never had before. Go ahead and dress up like you're going to the opera or a wedding, or the most important date of your life while you're at it. If alone time with your spouse is limited to certain hours, fine, but remember it doesn't have to be in the same room. Bring in homemade cookies or store-bought bagels for your coworkers even when it's not someone's birthday.

There are a lot of different ways to mix things up even if you're stuck in what seems like an unbreakable weekly routine. Trying new recipes, new foods, or even just changing what kind of cheese you have on your sandwich at lunch can help keep your brain engagement. After all, introducing new flavors, driving routes, and wardrobe options stimulate different areas of your brain that often are stuck in the same rut that you're in.

Start by making a change today. What's one thing you can do in a different way? If you want to give your brain a real thrill, figure out how to do something different that has an extra benefit. For example, taking the stairs down to your car at quitting time instead of the elevator has the added benefit of getting you exercise. Eating your lunch outside of the deli instead of inside provides fresh air and sunshine, which is important for your vitamin D intake. Drinking mint tea with dinner instead of iced tea can help your digestion, while drinking green tea can help with bloating and weight loss.[37]

Once you've conquered something today, start looking at what you can do throughout the week to add a fresh twist to all the normal, mundane tasks you do. Then take the time to be mindful about the results, writing them down in your journal. Did the tea work? Are you getting stronger taking the stairs, or did it give the parking lot an extra five minutes to clear out, so you didn't have

---

37   Allie Flinn, "11 Teas to Help Reduce Bloating," Byrdie, updated October 20, 2020, https://www.byrdie.com/best-teas-for-bloating-5080839.

to battle the normal line of cars? Did you find that new restaurant because you chose to drive to work a different way?

This is your opportunity to impact your code at a very basic level. Habits, like the route you take to drive from point A to point B, get encoded in your brain. By changing simple codes like this, it makes your brain more receptive in general to seeing and considering other ways to do things.

Besides what it can do for your mental and physical health, changing things up like this can also lead you to new connections. Maybe you've never met a future love interest because he's always eating outside at that deli while you're eating inside, and by changing things up you provide yourself an opportunity to meet him. Maybe the waiter at that new restaurant turns out to be looking for a job and you know he has the right personality for an opening at your company. You might even notice that next door to that restaurant is a bakery that can make your wedding cake for a couple hundred dollars cheaper than the bakery where your sister had hers done. Life is all about connections, both the ones you make and the ones you miss. Sometimes, altering your routine even in the slightest way can make all the difference in the world.

When you have the ability to alter your schedule or add something to it, try doing something completely new. This is a great opportunity to start a new project, a side job, or even a hobby. Whatever you do, remember to pick an activity that stretches your mind and gives you an opportunity to grow. If you enjoy reading an hour or two a day, try writing a book of your own for an hour or two once a week. Take a cooking class to learn how to cook a new type of cuisine. If you're an art lover, take a painting class so you can try your hand at creating your own masterpiece. Plan a trip to a foreign country, down to the last detail, and then learn the language. The possibilities are endless and can add a tremendous amount of value to your life.

Consider choosing a hobby or activity with a physical element too, as taking up ballroom dancing, yoga, or joining a bowling league helps your body physically as well as mentally. Remember that these opportunities also give you the chance to meet and network with new people.

When is the last time you exercised your brain? Ok, maybe you can't exercise your brain quite as easily as you can the rest of your body. After all, the cerebrum is not good at sit-ups, and your frontal lobe can't exactly be sent out for an invigorating jog around the block. On the other hand, there are things you can actively do to maintain your brain health. While you might not realize it, the brain is capable of more than you know. There's a lot of untapped potential locked within your own head, and the brain gets bored if it's constantly doing the same thing repeatedly if you never mix things up.

Keeping it stimulated and building connections is important. That's why it's good to present your brain with challenges and build cognitive skills. You can encourage brain plasticity when forced to think critically and draw conclusions. Engaging in exercises designed to challenge your mind forces you to hone your cognitive skills. A game of chess, sudoku puzzle, and other logic exercises and brainteasers are all good ways to make this happen. There are even apps for your phone designed to keep your mind moving. Fortunately, the opportunities are plentiful. Puzzles are one of the easiest ways to do this, as you're presenting your brain with a riddle to solve that will help to build neuropathways and keep your mind agile and fit. You don't have to do something overly complex to keep your mind interested and stimulated either, although over time you'll likely find yourself seeking out more challenging options.

Games are a great way to stimulate and challenge the brain while connecting with other people, which makes them a double win. Try something with just your significant other, like planning scavenger hunts for each other around the house. You can include the entire family in these types of games, too.

Hosting a game night for friends and family is always a good idea too. You can play teambuilding games with people at work. For a little more of a challenge, take a group to an *escape room*. These are recreation companies that provide experiences where you and a group of people are shut inside a room and follow a storyline, using objects in the room in specific ways to help you escape. There's usually an hour time limit and the ticking clock element adds to the suspense. The opportunity to really think outside the box and work together to escape can be as fun and stimulating as it is challenging.

Another great side effect of games and challenges with family, friends, or coworkers is that in addition to quality time spent together, you're also building trust and improving your communication skills. To add a physical boost to the activity, try an outdoor group activity like an obstacle course, mini golf, or a paintball campaign.

You'll be surprised at the benefit that comes of trying something you never have before. In a study by Johns Hopkins researchers, it was found that people who engage in multiple activities showed a much lower risk of developing cognitive problems. It further revealed that each addition of activity results in lowering the risk of cognitive problems by 8-11%.[38] Why not take a class, or try a creative outlet that's always intrigued you but that you've never

38   M. C. Carlson et al, "Lifestyle Activities and Memory: Variety May Be the Spice of Life. The Women's Health and Aging Study II," *Journal of the International Neuropsychological Society* 18, no. 2 (2012), 286-294, https://www.doi.org/10.1017/S135561771100169X.

taken the time to experience firsthand? Learn a new language, or even just find a series of webinars or TED Talks online to inspire you. Throw yourself into something new and reap the benefits of being a lifelong learner. When I discovered this idea, I made a deliberate effort to learn a new skill or pick up a new hobby each year. Over the past decade I have acquired several new skills, from videography to podcasting, playing ping pong to food plating and photography.

Many studies have proven that being in nature has restorative properties that help heal mind and body.[39] Camping and fishing trips have long been associated with having a grounding, restorative effect. They also provide great bonding opportunities for the individuals involved. You don't have to go away for a couple of days in the middle of the woods or a remote lake to get the benefits of being in nature. All you have to do is go outside to your own backyard.

Memory performance and attention span improve by as much as 20% just by moving things outdoors.[40] Even if you can't go outside, you can bring nature to you by growing plants indoors, which makes for an oxygen-rich environment and helps to calm your mind. In the workplace it has been proven that the calming influence of plants improves people's accuracy in performing tasks. Flowers and ornamental plants reduce stress and depression, improve concentration, promote happiness, and make people feel more relaxed. It's even been shown that the presence of flowers in hospital rooms accelerates the healing process. Even having a view of gardens outside the window helps, too!

---

39   "Health and well-being benefits of plants," Texas A&M Agrilife Extension, accessed June 20, 2021, https://ellisonchair.tamu.edu/health-and-well-being-benefits-of-plants/.

40   "Going out—even in the cold—improves memory, attention," Michigan News, December 16, 2008, https://news.umich.edu/going-outsideeven-in-the-coldim-proves-memory-attention/.

The list of benefits to spending time in environments with plants and flowers is extensive. Studies have shown that people who do are more compassionate and therefore have stronger relationships.[41] Improved outlook, higher energy, and good mental health are also associated with exposure. Being around plants helps people concentrate better in the home and workplace. Studies show that tasks performed while under the calming influence of nature are performed better and with greater accuracy, yielding a higher quality result.[42] Moreover, being outside in a natural environment can improve memory performance and attention span. Children who are around plants have been found to improve learning, focus and engagement especially for children with attention deficit disorder (ADD).[43]

In fact, the impact of nature on people doesn't just operate on the individual level, but also on the community level. Neighborhoods with beautiful parks tend to have higher levels of community involvement and lower levels of crime. It also improves people's perception of the quality of life in the area.[44]

Whether your idea of a relaxing vacation is a scenic tour of the national parks or a culinary tour of Italy, make sure you're taking your vacation time. A great number of Americans don't use their

41   "Health and well-being benefits of plants," Texas A&M AgriLife Extension, accessed June 20, 2021, https://ellisonchair.tamu.edu/health-and-well-being-benefits-of-plants/.

42   Danielle F. Shanahan, Richard A. Fuller, Robert Bush, Brenda B. Lin, Kevin J. Gaston, "The Health Benefits of Urban Nature: How Much Do We Need?" *BioScience* 65, no. 5 (May 2015), https://doi.org/10.1093/biosci/biv032.

43   Tara Parker-Pope, "A 'Dose of Nature' for Attention Problems," the *New York Times*, October 17, 2008, https://well.blogs.nytimes.com/2008/10/17/a-dose-of-nature-for-attention-problems/.

44   Mardelle Shepley et al, "The Impact of Green Space on Violent Crime in Urban Environments: An Evidence Synthesis," *International Journal of Environmental Research and Public Health* 16 (2019), https://www.doi.org/ 10.3390/ijerph16245119.

vacation time, or only use a fraction of it.[45] This is a dangerous trend that leads to burnout. Interestingly, according to a study done by the Center for Economic and Policy Research, America is the only country out of the thirty-six in the Organization for Economic Cooperation and Development that doesn't mandate paid vacation or paid holidays.[46] Therefore, not every worker gets paid time off, which can make taking a vacation difficult. However, a large portion of the workers that do get paid time off aren't taking it.

Many of the ones who do make the effort to take a vacation can't seem to leave work completely behind. This is a huge problem, as the mind and body need downtime. If you look at the history of humankind, there has always been downtime. For tens of thousands of years people hunted, farmed, and preserved food the best they could, knowing that during certain times of the year they wouldn't be able to. Winter for many people was a time for hunkering down and surviving. While there was great loss of life and hardship during this time, there was also a cessation of the year's normal work. In modern life, things don't stop when winter sets in, but our minds and bodies haven't necessarily gotten the memo yet.

All things in life have rhythms and perform on cycles. There's a time of growing, blooming, flourishing, fading, and finally hibernation. A great many plants participate in the yearly ritual, as do a great many animals. That natural cycle has been disrupted in modern society. It's become easy to continue working day after day without regard for the passing of time. It's ironic that the same

45   Hannah Sampson, "What does America have against vacation?" the *Washington Post*, August 28, 2019, https://www.washingtonpost.com/travel/2019/08/28/what-does-america-have-against-vacation/.

46   Rebecca Ray et al, "No-Vacation Nation Revisited," Center for Economic Policy and Research, May 2013, https://cepr.net/documents/no-vacation-update-2014-04.pdf.

society that makes sure children get regularly scheduled breaks from school doesn't defend as fiercely the need for adults to get regularly scheduled breaks from work.

Vacationing is a time to recharge mentally and physically and shouldn't be forsaken. When you let go of all the things that are normally pulling at your attention to get clarity, it becomes a multi-day form of meditation. Many great entrepreneurs and visionaries have had some of their biggest breakthroughs while on vacation. By taking the mind and body out of their normal routine, you provide the opportunity for new thoughts to occur.

Remember too that you don't have to spend two weeks and thousands of dollars to get this done. Even if you only have a week and no money, you can still make a great staycation that will fulfill your most basic needs. The most important thing is to disconnect as much as possible from ordinary life. If you can afford to stay at a hotel down the street or go visit family two hours away, do it. If you can't, then try pitching a tent in the backyard, sleeping in the guest room, or find another way to shake up your home routine.

Make it a point to go out and enjoy things you don't normally. Many museums are affordable or free, and there are a ton of concerts, festivals, fairs, and other events happening almost every weekend of the year within a couple hours driving distance of most places. You can plan your vacation out just as painstakingly as you would a vacation to another country if you seek out opportunities take advantage of. Or, if you work at a job that requires you to constantly micromanage things, throw a list of possibilities in a hat and draw at random just to give your mind a rest from normality.

I have a client whose job requires her to make hundreds of decisions every day. By the end of each day, she suffers from decision making burnout. Unfortunately, she's expected to continue making decisions at home in the evening. As this decision-making burnout continued, I suggested the idea of a vacation. However, my recommendation was to consider a vacation that required her to make the least amount of decision. We agreed that an all-inclusive cruise was her best choice because she enjoys cruises and they'll give her a set time for meals and an evening show. While on vacation she wants to make as few decisions as possible to rest her brain. In fact, she's so dedicated to not making decisions while on vacation that she takes full advantage of one of the unique features of a cruise. At every meal, she simply orders everything on the menu. That way, she doesn't have to decide what to have. She samples dishes in the order in which they arrive until she's full.

Isolation has also proven to be very damaging to the brain.[47] The longer you go without stimulating conversation, the more likely you are to experience ill effects. Over time, if you go too long without meaningful conversation, your brain itself begins to grow smaller, losing actual mass. This is why it's so important to get out and socialize, especially with people who come from a different background than you and hold opinions that may not coincide with yours. Once you're there, talk about the important stuff, allowing yourself to be challenged. If you can keep an open mind, you'll be amazed at how much you learn and just how exciting conversations can become.

Whatever form of relaxation you choose, it's important to commit to it. Put relaxation on your *to do* list. Seriously. It's important to make time for it in your schedule on a daily, weekly, and annual basis. Do something different to refresh yourself each day. Let your weekend, whenever it falls during the week, be a time where you can do something different that makes you happy. Lastly, don't forgo vacations and the opportunity to really get

---

47   Amy Novoteny, "The risks of social isolation," *American Psychological Association* 50, no. 5 (2019), https://www.apa.org/monitor/2019/05/ce-corner-isolation.

outside your normal life. When you do, you'll find it refreshes your creativity and your perspective. Remember, everything goes in cycles. Rest and relaxation are just as important to your mental and physical health as consistent exercise.

Chapter 4

You Gotta Move

Most people exercise to become healthier and feel better. But have you ever considered that exercise benefits more than just your body? In fact, exercise impacts your mental health in more ways than you can possibly imagine.[48] For your body, it's important to get your heart pumping and your muscles moving to keep your body strong, limber, and healthy. The same is true with your muscles and your mind. Doing so brings fresh supplies of oxygen to your blood, which carries it to all your muscles, including your mind. Human bodies weren't designed to sit in a chair all day. They were designed to be up and moving. If you don't get a certain amount of exercise, it becomes harder for you to move your joints and to keep all your organs in top shape.

---

48   Ashish Sharma et al, "Exercise for Mental Health," *Primary Care Companion to the Journal of Clinical Psychiatry* 8, no. 2 (2006), https://www.doi.org/10.4088/pcc.v08n0208a.

As my mother's health began to deteriorate, I saw how easily people can go from being mobile to becoming completely immobile. That was when I started to take exercise more seriously. I had no idea how unfit I was until I signed up for a gym membership. It was almost impossible to imagine I played soccer from early childhood through college. My professional life had impacted my physical fitness negatively, and I hadn't even realized it.

Today, I live a very active lifestyle. I exercise 12 hours a week, and over the years I have conditioned my mind, body, and muscles. Over many years of consistent effort, I have watched my body transform into a more solid physique. Exercise has many benefits on top of this, including releasing feel-good hormones called endorphins. It also provides mental alertness, increases your metabolism, and improves the efficiency of how you use oxygen.

Many people think that it takes too much time or expensive equipment to work out properly. That's not true. You can exercise in five-minute increments. There are stretches you can do at your desk at work, and many items around your home you can use as free weights. The important thing is to just do *something* to help yourself get started.

Stretching, strength training, and cardio exercise all play a part in building muscle, increasing stamina, and maintaining balance and flexibility, particularly as you age. It's important to choose a regimen that's easy for you to follow but that ideally combines some form of all three during your week. The benefits will speak for themselves.

When it comes to stretching, many people realize that it's necessary before exercising to warm up muscles and prevent injury. Stretching has a great deal more to offer, though. As people age, they lose flexibility and balance. Stretching can counter this, allowing people to stay limber and give them greater range of motion. It also improves posture and can help heal back pain.

Stretching has also been shown to help relieve stress.[49] When the mind is stressed, the muscles in the body tense up. By helping to loosen the muscles, you ease the burden on the body. If you practice mindfulness exercises while stretching, then you're relieving stress for mind and body simultaneously.

Strength training is another important part of fitness. While most people think of strength training as lifting weights, but other exercises such as push-ups, pull-ups, squats, abdominal crunches, and even jumping jacks land in this category as well. Aside from increased muscle and physical strength, these types of workouts offer many benefits that include boosting metabolism and increasing stamina.

For those suffering from osteoporosis, osteoarthritis, and muscle spasms, strength training increases bone density. Improved lung capacity, blood circulation, and heart health are other benefits to consider.[50]

When you get into weightlifting, you can see some dramatic results in both how you look and feel. Building muscle mass is important to combat natural losses as you age. Take the time to consult a fitness expert or coach before starting your own regimen to learn the proper technique and prevent injury.

Cardiovascular or aerobic exercise is anything that gets your heart pumping for prolong periods of time. This includes brisk walking, swimming, biking, running, or playing your favorite sport. Experts often recommend that people get 75 minutes of

49   Justine Cosman, "The Amazing Benefits of Stretching," Whole Body Health Physical Therapy, February 27, 2017, https://www.wholebodyhealth-pt.com/wbhptblog/the-amazing-benefits-of-stretching.

50   "Strength training: Get stronger, leaner, healthier," Mayo Clinic, May 15, 2021, https://www.mayoclinic.org/healthy-lifestyle/fitness/in-depth/strength-training/art-20046670.

vigorous or 150 minutes of moderate aerobic exercise a week.[51] While there are many ways to get your cardio done indoors, getting outdoors for your exercise allows you to receive the additional health benefit of vitamin D from the sun. If you can exercise in a park or area with plants and flowers, you can also receive those health benefits as well.

Aside from improving overall cardiovascular health and keeping fit, there are numerous health benefits to this type of exercise. It helps lower blood sugar, reduce asthma symptoms, reduce chronic pain, improve cognitive performance, and can increase balance and agility. A lot of research has been done on ways to maximize health, and the fat-burning benefits of aerobic exercise is one way to do it. It's been found that doing rigorous activity for short bursts of a few seconds alternating with longer stretches of moderate activity repetitively revs up your system and gives you a more impactful workout in a shorter amount of time.

Using a fitness app or device can be very helpful in tracking your progress. Many of these even have built in alarms that remind you to get up and move every hour, helping to negate the problem of spending hours in a chair or at a computer while working.

It can also be helpful to choose someone to either workout with or compete against. There are apps which allow you to set daily goals (such as exercising for a set amount of time, meditating, getting enough sleep, drinking water, etc.) and then share those with a partner. The two of you can then encourage each other or engage in friendly competition. Having someone you're working with or trying to beat can be a great motivator and make you more likely to exercise.

---

51   Edward Laskowski, "How much should the average adult exercise every day?" Mayo Clinic, April 27, 2019, https://www.mayoclinic.org/healthy-lifestyle/fitness/expert-answers/exercise/faq-20057916.

Exercise gets the body in shape and helps to release stress. Stress and the damage caused by it leads to so many diseases and organ failure that the list seems endless. By helping you to relax and releasing endorphins that make you feel good and can calm you down, exercise can be a big benefit. There are so many benefits to exercise that it's often mentioned in the same breath as the equally important need to eat a healthy diet.

Chapter 5

Fueling Yourself

Another key to health is to be mindful of the things that you consume. In this world of processed food, GMOs, pesticides, and preservatives, it's easy to put a lot of unhealthy, even toxic, things into your body.[52] All of these chemicals build up and can cause the body and mind to become more and more sluggish and unhealthy. Here, mindfulness can also play a large part. It's easy to grab fast food for its convenience, or to order something because it sounds good while not really paying attention to how nutritious it is. When you aren't paying attention, you're more likely to make poor food choices that won't help you in the long run. When you're not mindful, you don't pay as much attention to *what* you

---

52   Claire McCarthy, "Common food additives and chemicals harmful to children," Harvard Health Publishing, July 24, 2018, https://www.health.harvard.edu/blog/common-food-additives-and-chemicals-harmful-to-children-2018072414326.

eat, *how* much you eat, and even *when* you eat. This is a mistake, as all three of these play a huge part in your health.

The first thing you need to take control of is what you eat. Nutrition is an important element in keeping your body healthy. The closer your diet is to the things produced by nature, the easier it is for you to be well. The more your diet is filled with artificially produced foods, the harder it is for you to be well. When my grandmother died at 105, she was still tending to her garden. She was healthy and strong enough to do that every day. Everything she ate came from that garden. I cannot remember ever seeing her buy groceries from a store or market. She grew all of her vegetables and fruits. No artificial thing entered her body—and look at the long life she was able to experience.

Four things that are important to stick to are to make sure you know what's in your food, choose based on nutrition not convenience, learn how your body interacts with foods (particularly if you have any allergies), and drink plenty of water. Doing this can have a huge impact on your health.

Ideally, things that have labels to read should make up a very small portion of your diet. However, since not everyone can eat directly from their own garden for every meal like my grandmother, you need to do some investigative work. Not all packaged foods are alike. Not all brands are alike. You want to watch out for added sugar, food coloring, and chemicals you can't pronounce the names of. If something is artificial, then it shouldn't be going into your body. Also, if an item has more than five ingredients, be concerned. At this point, it's starting to steer away from what's natural.

Don't just trust what you read on the front packaging. Words like *low fat* and *sugar free* don't necessarily mean that something is healthy. In fact, depending on what they did to the food to make it low fat or sugar free, it can make the item even worse than the full fat, sugar-filled item sitting next to it.

Fast and easy are what most people are looking for. However, saving a little time or energy at the expense of your health is a bad trade. There are always healthy or, at least, healthier choices that you can make. Make sure to skip the fries, no matter how delicious they are.

There are many quick, portable meals and snacks you can either make or pick up at the grocery store. Deli sections often have items such as ready-made hardboiled eggs which can save you time and effort. Opt for fresh-made bread that isn't packed with preservatives, and get lots of fresh vegetables when ordering one of their deli sandwiches.

Spend a few hours each week and make lunches and dinners for several days. You can prepare and cook these meals ahead of time and then store them in the freezer for easy reheating later. This is a great way to make sure that at the end of a long day you have something healthy that you can pop in the microwave or oven to reheat. It's quick, easy, and you don't have to make much of a decision. What's even better is that it's a much healthier meal than you would likely have managed to make or order. While many people do this with dinners, you can also do it with lunches if you have access to a microwave at work. This can save you the cost and hassle of having to run out to get something, which won't be half as healthy as what you cooked for yourself at home.

Do yourself a favor and do some research. According to a publication of Harvard Medical School, superfoods like berries, beets, and dark chocolate can help lower blood pressure.[53] Other foods like apples, ginger, and peppermint help with digestion. Probiotics

---

53   "Beating high blood pressure with food," Harvard Health Publishing, August 23, 2019, www.health.harvard.edu/newsletter_article/beating-high-blood-pressure-with-food.

have been the subject of a lot of discussion lately, and you can find any number of items in the dairy section to help you with your gut health.

When people think about food allergies, they think about dramatic reactions like hives, swelling, or trouble breathing. Other signs of allergies include nausea, stomach pain, itchy eyes, rapid heartrate, and sneezing. The most common foods that people are allergic to are things like peanuts, tree nuts, milk, eggs, shellfish, fish, wheat, and soybeans.[54]

More common than allergies are food intolerances, which affect a great many more people. An intolerance means that you have a problem digesting a particular food either when eaten frequently or in large portions. Some of the symptoms are similar to food allergies and can include cramps, nausea, headaches, heartburn, fatigue, joint pain, difficulty sleeping, and irritability, or nervousness, among others.

If you suspect you have a food intolerance, you can try doing an elimination diet. With this type of diet, you'll eliminate the most common food irritants and slowly reintroduce them into your diet one at a time to identify the one(s) you're having a bad reaction to. You can find plenty of resources online to help with each step of the process.

You probably know that soda and caffeine are bad for you and tough on your system. They also cause dehydration, which can cause a cascade of health problems and even contribute to dangerous spikes in your blood sugar. Whether or not you manage to avoid these beverages, it's important to drink plenty of water. A reasonable goal is to drink 64 ounces of water each day to stay hydrated for your overall health. Depending on a number of factors, you might require more or less than that, but it's a good initial

---

54   Helen West, "The 8 Most Common Food Allergies," Healthline, January 25, 2017, https://www.healthline.com/nutrition/common-food-allergies.

goal.[55] Water can also help keep your blood sugar stable if you overeat certain types of foods.

While you should practice mindfulness when choosing what to eat, you should also be mindful of what you're doing when you eat. Good habits are a great practice, particularly if having dinner with family. Instead of just shoving down food while watching TV or using your mobile devices, try discussing what you're eating. Attempt to engage all five of your senses while you eat. The French are famous for plating food in an elegant manner. The idea is that food is first experienced with the eyes. While you might not have the time or inclination to plate your food in the same way, you can still engage your senses when interacting with your food.

Try this exercise with a raisin. Hold it first in your hand and stare at it. Think about what it looks like, including how its appearance differs from that of the grape it once was. Notice the color, the lines, the texture. Feel it against your fingertips. Notice the stickiness, the sugar of the fruit coming out. Smell the raisin and focus on that for a moment. When you finally put it in your mouth, savor not only the flavor, but also pay attention to the texture. How does it feel when you bite into it? You can even engage your sense of hearing. How does it sound when you chew it? Is it different than the sound of other foods?

This much detail isn't required with every bite but do spend more time contemplating the look and the taste of the things you eat. You will get more pleasure out of food, and it will start to impact the choices you make when at a grocery store or restaurant. There are other added benefits as well. By slowing down and giving yourself a chance to digest better, you'll also be able to more easily notice when your body is signaling that it's full.

55 "Water: How much should you drink every day?" Mayo Clinic, October 14, 2020, https://www.mayoclinic.org/healthy-lifestyle/nutrition-and-healthy-eating/in-depth/water/art-20044256.

When people aren't mindful and in the moment, they tend to eat food quickly, and when they do overeating is common. It takes several minutes for the body to signal that it's full, so when you're shoving food down your throat while you're busy with that next thing, you don't have time to receive that signal. It's possible to eat two or even three times more than what you actually should be consuming When the food tastes good, overindulging becomes even easier to do.

It's not just about how much you eat overall but also about how many different types of food you consume. Even if you eat a smaller meal, stopping just before you get full, if it's all fat and sugar then you shouldn't be patting yourself on the back. The truth is you need good fats, protein, and carbohydrates. Whether you need to focus more on protein, need an equal balance of all three, or want to avoid carbs as much as possible, you still need to balance each of these at every meal. Do some research and consult your doctor to find out what ratios are best for you.

For those who are overweight, have diabetes, or have a family history of diabetes, blood sugar is crucially important to keep steady and under control. When you're trying to regulate blood sugar, the question isn't how much you're eating. The question is, how many carbs are you eating? The recommended amount is about 60 grams of carbs per meal and 20 grams of carbs per snack, with at least two hours in between snacks and meals to allow blood sugar levels to reset.[56]

There are many apps out there that can help you log your food and provide nutritional information to help figure out how many calories, carbs, protein, and even ingredients you're consuming.

---

56   "Carb Counting," Centers for Disease Control and Prevention (CDC), updated September 19, 2019, https://www.cdc.gov/diabetes/managing/eat-well/diabetes-and-carbohydrates.html.

Doing this simple exercise helps keep you on task and enables you to make active, healthy choices. Again, mindfulness is key here.

The body needs food at predictable intervals to maintain its natural rhythm. In this hectic world it might seem like breakfast is the only meal with timing you can control. You need to do what you can to make lunchtime and dinnertime as predictable as possible. If you don't, it plays havoc with your body's blood sugar, which over time can lead to serious diseases. More simply put, if you don't watch what and when you eat now, you might eventually have to figure those things out in minute detail every day.

A lot of people discuss how many meals are optimal for healthy living. Some recommend three with one or two snacks in between, while others recommend five smaller meals spaced out throughout the day. Whichever you choose, consistency is the most important thing. When you're traveling, particularly for work, this can be difficult. Learn to travel with small, portable snacks or protein bars that you can use to substitute for a meal in a pinch. Even if you just eat something small, you should never skip meals. The one exception is if you're fasting.

Unless you have a condition that prohibits it, it's important to participate in some form of fasting on a regular basis. This allows your digestive system to rest and reset. Fast when you can to let the body clean out built-up toxins. Your digestive system is the hardest working system in your body. It's important to give your digestive system a break and allow it to reset occasionally.

In addition to detoxing, studies have shown that fasting has several other health benefits.[57] It can aid in weight loss, lower blood pressure, increase levels of good cholesterol, and produce more anti-aging hormones. It can also help treat several ailments

57   Stephen Anton and Christiaan Leeuwenburgh, "Fasting or caloric restriction for Healthy Aging," *Experimental Gerontology* 48, no. 10 (October 2013), https://doi.org/10.1016/j.exger.2013.04.011.

such as pancreatitis, rheumatoid arthritis, and epilepsy. There are many more health benefits to fasting too. If you are considering it, discuss it with your doctor before starting to find a method that works for you.

Many people participate in fasting for purposes other than physical health. Many do so in order to clear their mind or focus on a particular thought or problem. Fasting has long been associated with prayer and spiritual reflection as well. In this way, fasting contributes to the overall health of both body and soul.

No matter what, you shouldn't take your health for granted. How well you take care of your body determines the quality, and sometimes even the length, of your afternoon and nighttime periods of life. It can determine how vital you are during those times. If you want to spend the nighttime of your life enjoying the fruits of your labors, then you need to make sure that you take care of yourself through the first two stages. No matter what your age, it is time to start taking care of yourself. Physical and mental health should be on the top of your priority list. When you make time to be mindful, get the proper rest and relaxation, exercise well, and eat the right things, you're preparing yourself for a long and prosperous life.

Try some of these healthy affirmations to change your bad codes to good ones:

- **I have a healthy body and a sound mind.**
- **Today, I affirm that I am healthy in my body, mind and spirit**. I have a sound mind and a vibrant spirit. I choose to appreciate the opportunity to enjoy new levels of energy and well-being.
- **I attract healthy, empowering energy and I affirm that my healthy, natural glow shines brighter.** When I com-

bine my positive mental energy with my inner strength, I truly experience endless possibilities.

- **I love my body.** I am grateful for the health in my body and mind. I appreciate my body and honor my body by trusting the signals it sends to me. I manifest perfect health by making smart choices. Every part of my body functions with ease. My system operates naturally as I balance life between work, rest, and play.
- **I affirm that this is my best year yet.** I hit all my goals. I attract the promotion that I desire and deserve. I am a career success.

Turn to the workbook section at the back of the book, page 385, for your reflection exercises to help you commit to action.

PART 6:

CRACKING YOUR FINANCES CODE

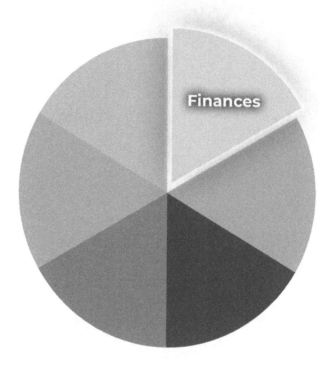

Chapter 1

The Currency of Living

Matthew took a deep breath before he went into the house. He wasn't looking forward to a confrontation with Kari, and he had no idea how she was going to react when she found out he'd been laid off.

He found her in the living room, curled up in a chair reading a yoga pamphlet. He recognized the woman on the front cover.

"Is she one of the moms from school?" he asked.

Kari nodded brightly. "Yes, Linda. She owns her own yoga studio." She hesitated for a moment. "She's invited me to try a class tomorrow."

"I don't think we should spend the money," he said.

"Oh, but it's a free introduction class."

Matthew stared at his wife. Yoga would probably be good for her. He knew a guy at his work who raved about what it done for his wife. Correction, a guy at his former work.

He sat down heavily. It was then that Kari seemed to realize something was wrong.

"You're home early," she said. She took a noticeable whiff and scowled, clearly smelling the alcohol on his breath.

"I got laid off," he said.

"Oh no!"

"Yeah. We're going to have to make some changes around here."

"Wait, changes?"

"Yeah. We need to cut down on costs ASAP."

"Um, okay. I can buy the cheaper hot dog buns and get generic condiments. I can pick up some stuff from the dollar store," she said. She could feel fear nibbling at the edges of her mind. Her family had been dirt poor and going back there terrified her.

He shook his head. "I'm not just talking about a few bucks on groceries. We need to make some real changes."

"Didn't they give you a severance package?" she asked.

"Yes, but it has to last until I can find a new job that pays the same."

"What are we going to do?" she asked, eyes wide.

"Well, first thing I think we need to do is take a good, hard look at everything we spend money on."

"And then?"

"And then we make a budget and stick to it."

Next to your career, money is what can determine if you'll maximize life or not. Financial literacy and financial freedom are popular topics because they're crucial in order to fulfill your mandate, flourish, and live your best life possible. With financial success, it's not only about the quantity of money made, but also concerns the management of the money you make. Being the master of your money is an empowering feeling, similar to that of mastering your emotions. Once you've experienced it, you'll never want to go back.

Mastering money is coming to realize that you're in control of every area of your finances. It's difficult to turn around a bad situation overnight. Habits, codes, and values help the process and make it easier to turn things around when something goes wrong. If there's a problem, though, it's important to start immediately trying to fix it before the problem compounds itself. Until you realize that money is a tool, you serve money while money uses you. Ideally, the opposite will be true. Unfortunately, many people give away their entire lives for money.

A lot of people are unwilling to discuss money topics. As uncomfortable as it might seem, having a shaky financial state can severely affect your well-being in ways that will make the discomfort of the current discussion dwarf by comparison. Emotional well-being is directly related to finances.

Money is one of the biggest relationship issues in marriage. You don't just need a spouse who has mastered emotion, but a spouse who has also mastered money. Ask the other person about their credit scores while you're dating. While this might seem odd for some, credit scores are a way to evaluate financial skill. If you're joining your life with another person, it's important to know what financial baggage they're bringing to the equation.

A coaching client once shared this with me. She was expecting a big tax refund one year and made plans on what she was going to do with the money. However, things fell apart for her because the government seized the refund due to her husband's unpaid student loans. His bad financial choices ended up causing her a lot of anguish and put the marriage in jeopardy. For many, poor financial skills can ruin even the strongest relationship. They can also negatively impact your career if you're behind on child support or need to get a security clearance. Organizations that trust their employees with the company cards often do their due diligence to ascertain how responsible they are handling money.

How you feel about and deal with money likely relates to the codes that were instilled in you as a child. I was fortunate. When I was very little my father took me to the bank and showed me how to fill out a deposit booklet. He also showed me the other services the bank offered. I'm not sure I fully grasped everything he was trying to tell me because of my age, but every time he had to go to the bank, my father would take me and have me watch what he did. He taught me what the different numbers on a check were (routing and account) and showed me how to balance a checkbook.

Codes like prioritization and self-control should be programmed early so they can be useful later in life. Those codes are filled with what you need to build a healthy financial life and solid financial skills. If it's possible, don't wait until you're an adult to acquire these.

Some equate money with success. Money by itself is not success, but a symbol of success. A lot of people who are unable to attain success in the real sense sometimes get emotional comfort out of holding onto symbols of success. That's why people hold on so tightly to material things, especially in the overly materialistic world we live in today.

The sooner we shift our focus from the symbols of success to actual success, the more meaningful our journey gets. Success is not tangible like money, cars, or properties. Real success is a state of mind. Those who are poor in pocket but rich in their mind can transfer the richness from their mind to their pocket. The reverse is also true. When a person is poor in their mind it doesn't matter how much they have in their pocket, as a poor mind cannot manage a rich purse, and will almost always ruin it.

As always, when inspecting this area of your life there's some hard questions you'll need to ask and answer. How satisfied are you with your finances? What's the contribution you're making? Is there room for continuous growth?

It's important to be mindful about your finances and to keep on top of them. When looking at this area of your life, examine how you make money, manage money, and multiply money in order to see where improvements can be made.

Chapter 2

Making Money

Money is what makes the world go around. Without money, it's difficult to survive in the modern world. Making money is also what helps society function. Everyone pulls their weight and the taxes that the government takes help pay for things like highways that everyone uses.

Some kids grow up so aware and motivated by money that they get jobs at an early age to pay for activities and items that they want. Other kids grow up assuming that things will just be handed to them throughout their life. How a child feels about making money depends a lot on the codes they were raised with. You'll want to review the money codes instilled in you. Did you hear statements such as these a lot around you?

- Earning money is too hard, I am too old to become wealthy.
- The taxes will kill me.
- Good people don't care about money.
- People like me never get ahead.

- I don't deserve it.
- Why try when the system is made to keep us poor?

If you did, it's going to take some work to change the way you think. Your money codes form the foundation for your abundance mindset. Money codes at this level affect your ability to create and manage money too.

Some kids grow up with a paranoia about money running out, or a belief that to survive you will have to work several jobs, and that it may still be impossible to make ends meet. Other children get a head start by being born into a family where money already exists, and the parents are open about how they come by it. As those kids start out in life, they have the opportunity to tap into resources, both in the form of financial support from their parents and the codes they received that help to capitalize on the opportunities that come their way. Kari grew up in a family where money was scarce, but her mother wasn't allowed to have a job. She was expected to take care of the household and that was it. Matthew and Kari have a similar arrangement, where he works, and she takes care of the kids and the home. It never occurred to her before he got laid off that contributing financially might be a good thing—not just for her, but also for the family.

When you're starting out in life, in order to master your finances, you need to build capacity to make money. You can do this several ways, ranging from formal education, to getting a job or starting your own business.

For many people, the route to take is to go to college and study for a particular career field. Depending on what you want to do for a career and what you study, formal education may or may not give you the skills needed to get started and find your first job. Unfortunately, some undergraduate degrees don't qualify you for many career options starting out. Some careers also require you to go to graduate school, and perhaps work internships before you can be hired to work in your field.

As an alternative, community colleges and even some high schools can help you learn a marketable trade or skill that can help you land your first job in chosen fields. If you want to be a mechanic, a skilled laborer, or work with computers, this can be an ideal fit. It requires less formal education, costs less, and provides more hands-on learning.

If school isn't your thing, you're never too young to start your own business. There are teenagers who started their own business who are now millionaires. Mikaila Ulmer made millions by the time she was 11,[58] and was sparked by an idea for a company after being stung by bees when she was four.[59] She began her own business called Me & the Bees (lemonade and other products) and has been doing very well for herself ever since. When they were 10 and 11 years of age, Isabel and Caroline Bercaw created a multi-million-dollar bath bomb business.[60] There of course are many more examples of successful entrepreneurs who started young without formal education.

If you have a great idea, can provide a solution to a problem, or have a true passion for something, this might be where you choose to start making money. My brother was only 13 when he got an idea to resell engine oil in small quantities to motorcycle owners, as we lived in a neighborhood that had a significant concentration of bikers. On Saturdays, he would go to the store to buy gallons

---

58   Tony Merevick, "This 11-Year-Old Just Made $11 Million Selling Her Lemonade to Whole Foods," Thrillist, March 31, 2016, https://www.thrillist.com/news/nation/mikaila-ulmer-beesweet-lemonade-lands-11-million-whole-foods-deal.

59   "Our Sweet Story," Me & the Bees Lemonade, accessed June 20, 2021, https://www.meandthebees.com/pages/about-us.

60   Alexandra Sternlicht, "These Teen Sisters Cooked Bath Bombs In Their Kitchen. Now It's a $20 Million-Plus Per Year Business," Forbes, February 21, 2020, https://www.forbes.com/sites/alexandrasternlicht/2020/02/21/these-teen-sisters-cooked-bath-bombs-in-their-kitchen-now-its-a-20-million-plus-per-year-business/?sh=42c611f47684.

of engine oil and set up his stall by our gate. When he saw one of them, he'd wave them down and tell them they didn't need to buy a full gallon of engine oil when they were low. This is how it all started for him, and later he turned this opportunity into a motorcycle business.

Perhaps the most basic way to build capacity is to get a job. If you're in a position to do so, try and get a job that will help you build skills and connections that you can use in future positions. There are a lot of entry-level jobs that can help you get a ton of experience, with most of them either in the business or restaurant worlds. Work your connections to find an opportunity that will help you not just today, but also with your future goals. Whatever your job is, give it everything you have and acquire as many skills as you can.

The mechanisms for building capacity are deeply entrenched in society. Some people get that first job and stop there. They rely on whatever meager raises their employer decides to dole out to them to get by as the cost-of-living increases. Oftentimes, they do this because that's what they saw members of their family do, and failed to acquire the codes to go to the next step.

You'll need to decide how much money is enough, though this will change over time. What's enough to you as a teenager isn't going to be enough when you're an adult with different responsibilities and expenses. This number changes for the time and stage of life you're in. It's different for a single person versus a family with young kids, for example. That's why you need to continually increase your capacity. As needs increase, means must increase commensurately.

As needs change and evolve, and there will also be more demands. The realization of your purpose will continue to unfold, and you'll always need money to keep up. Therefore, you must continue to increase your capacity. You can do this in a few ways.

One such way is to increase the depth of your knowledge and skills. This is when you dig down deep in your current field and work to become better at it. The more of an expert you are, the more money you can command for working in your career field. You can do this by taking courses, attending seminars, getting a certification, writing a manual, book, or white paper on the topic, or going to graduate school. Whatever you can do to learn more will help you earn more.

If you don't necessarily want to dig deeper in your current career you can go for breadth instead of depth by adding new skills. No matter what career you're in, there are complementary skills that you can develop, which give you more options and more flexibility when it comes to your career path. If you're in sales, you can also study marketing. If you practice one area of law, you can look at adding a second specialty—particularly if you find that it would be helpful to your potential client base. Pay attention to what your employer, coworkers and clients need, and by adding this new skill you'll help the company and increase your chances of getting that desired raise.

Even if you can't get a raise, one of the best ways to make more money is to add an extra income stream. According to the IRS, the average millionaire has seven streams of income.[61] The easiest way to do this is to profit from your passion. While you have a profession, you can profit from your passion on the side. Master the business of that passion and it can provide you with more money than you can make working at your profession.

---

61   Jenny Bourne and Lisa Rosenmerkel, "Over The Top: How Tax Returns Show that the Very Rich Are Different from You and Me," IRS, accessed June 20, 2021, https://www.irs.gov/pub/irs-soi/14rpoverthetopbournerosenmerkel.pdf.

Think big when it comes to creating new income streams. If you like renovating houses, try building a business that buys, fixes up, and flips good real estate deals. If you love to make crafts or find garage sale treasures, make a business that sells them. You don't even have to have a physical storefront. You can create a virtual one or sell through established sites like eBay, Etsy, or Amazon. If you have other services, you can offer people, advertise on social media and make videos to post online.

Once you've learned how to make money, this is when you can really start asking yourself if you're satisfied with how much you make and how you're managing your wealth. Odds are, when you think about it, you'll realize that just making money is a short-term solution to a long-term problem. You'll also need to look at whether there's room for continuous growth and realize that there's a limit to that growth unless you learn to manage and multiply your money.

Matthew's dad was at the same company doing the same job for 35 years before he retired. He instilled in Matthew the values of hard work and loyalty. However, Matthew didn't have the codes to help him succeed in a world where working at the same job for your entire career is no longer the norm. Matthew hadn't spent time learning more skills or becoming an expert in his own particular field. When he was laid off from his job, he was taken by surprise. He hadn't added appreciably to his skill set since college, and this made it harder for him to find something that would provide him with more money and responsibility. It also left him thinking that maybe he'd made a mistake not trying to more actively advance himself in either his field or his company.

Chapter 3

Managing Money

As you progress through the afternoon phase of your life, you need to transition from making money to managing it. When you start earning money from a job or your business, it's time to start thinking of the future. Roughly two-thirds of Americans live paycheck-to-paycheck.[62] That's not just workers living on modest paychecks either. Many in the middle- and upper-middle class are also living hand-to-mouth. The problem with this is that life is unpredictable. An accident can put someone out of work for weeks or months, or a medical emergency can turn into unexpected debt. If there's a natural disaster, you can lose your property if it's not covered by insurance. Even if it is, sometimes it can take months or years to recoup what you've lost, and you'll have to live in the meantime.

---

62   Susan Milligan, "Stretched Thin," U.S. News & World Report, January 11, 2019, https://www.usnews.com/news/the-report/articles/2019-01-11/stretched-thin-majority-of-americans-live-paycheck-to-paycheck.

It's not just the big, unexpected problems that can wreak havoc on your finances. Simple things like the air conditioner giving out in the middle of July can add up to large, unexpected expense that you suddenly must cover. Keep in mind that we're not even talking about trying to save for a child's college, or for your own future retirement. As we've seen recently with COVID-19, a pandemic can wipe out entire families and communities financially in a matter of weeks.

That's why it's crucial to learn how to manage money. Managing money means making sure that you're covering all your monthly expenses and not falling into the trap of getting farther and farther behind with credit card and other types of bad debt. More than that, though, managing money means planning for the future and the unexpected expenses of the present. I was once in a relationship with a lady who had a very lucrative career. She made more money than 90% of her friends and was doing very well for herself. However, as our relationship progressed, I noticed she ran out of money before the next pay day frequently. I was bothered by her poor money management skills, and although she had a great personality, excellent career, sound mental, physical and spiritual health, her finances were a wreck. She spent a lot of money on items she didn't need. For her, retail therapy was the solution to a bad day. For me to continue in that relationship, I knew I needed to do something about her relationship with money.

Have you ever gotten to tax season and wondered how you make so much and yet save so little? Worse yet, have you ever gotten to the last three or four days of the month and realized you were out of money? In order to keep yourself from having to eat junk food like a starving college student, or to keep yourself from working into your seventies or eighties, you need to start taking hold of your finances.

Some people think they make enough money that they don't have to pay much attention to it. This is usually the wrong way to look at things. In fact, the more money you make, the more you should be paying attention. It's shocking how many big lottery winners end up in poverty a few years after their big win. No matter how much money you have, if you don't manage it, that money will grow wings and fly away. This explains why people who once had money often die as paupers.

When it comes to managing money, it's crucial to have a budget. Here you can see the codes that you have really playing out. You need codes for self-control, good decision making, decisiveness, and prioritization. Without these codes, you can make a mess of your finances. It's important to note that indecisiveness in your finances can potentially result in loss of money. If you can't get your desires under control, then you become a slave to money.

After many years of building this money management code, I can account for every dollar I make. I do a realistic self-assessment for myself, and I coach others to do the same. I had a real conversation with my girlfriend at the time and we agreed to work on her money management skills together. We started by setting a budget for a week, month, quarter, and for the year. We set a spending limit for each of those, including a miscellaneous section for unforeseen emergency expenses. This was difficult in the beginning. I saw and felt her struggle but I was committed to helping her in that area.

Budgeting is something that can be helpful to get your spending under control. On a macro level, it's important to consider having a family budget too. Be sure to enlist members of your nuclear family in the money management journey. This way when something crops up that would make you go outside the budget, it becomes easier to make a rational choice together as a family. Learn to say no as much as possible.

This is where you can also start to have a serious conversation with yourself about giving back. Are you making enough and managing it well enough that you're able to give back to your community in some way? When you do reach this point, it's important to do so when you are able.

To develop good money management codes, there are some habits that will help with your budgeting and managing of money. These should be developed in order to make this process easier.

1. Track Your Spending

My then girlfriend and I evaluated her credit card statement and found that 35% of her spending was on clothing and jewelry. She had several subscriptions that she didn't use, and 17% of her income went to travel and restaurants purchases. This shows how important it is to know where every nickel goes. It can be eye-opening when you see how much money you're spending on that morning cup of coffee or snacks at the movies. You might also find that you gave your teenager some extra money for a night out with their friends, but that your spouse did, too!

Make sure to go through monthly subscriptions frequently and ask yourself if you're using them and if they're giving you value for what you're paying for them. Do you really need three streaming services and two online news subscriptions? Don't just look at the monthly cost— figure out what those subscriptions are going to cost you over the course of a year.

Similarly, interest is possibly the single biggest money waster there is. Every loan you have and every credit card you use costs you money in the form of interest. Figure out how much you're spending annually on interest and then break it down to see what it's costing you every week. Figure out how you can pay things off early and how much that will save you in interest.

2. Be Intentional

When you spend money, do so intentionally. Poor planning, impulse buys, and failing to choose well can cost you a lot of money over the course of the week and can be quite a staggering sum over a year. It's important to spend carefully, with full thought about what you are doing.

Fortunately, these days it's simple to pay most bills online, but watch out for hidden fees. Some charge extra if you pay using a credit card versus using an electronic check. Look for fees and service charges that crop up when you're paying for something. Pay cash whenever you can to avoid transaction fees or credit card interest. Even some gas stations offer discounts for cash payments instead of using debit cards. When picking out a credit card, find one that offers you cashback and has a low interest rate. When choosing a checking or savings account, look for ones that offer you the best rates.

Lots of things that you spend money on monthly (computer programs, business mailboxes, etc.) will give you a discount if you buy six, 12, or 24 months at once instead of just paying month-to-month. You can lose a lot of money by paying things every month instead of once a year if you can afford a single payment up front.

Today, there are websites and apps that will help you shop for coupons, which can offer you fantastic savings on things you need. Discount coupons can be incredibly helpful to save you money at the grocery store, pharmacy, restaurants, and entertainment venues. But they also provide a trap. Sometimes a deal seems too good to pass up, and you end up spending money on something you don't need.

A coupon for your favorite restaurant is tempting, and usually will come with an expiration date, which forces you to go out to dinner to get the savings. Unless you were already planning on going out to dinner that night, the coupon ends up enticing you into spending a lot of money you would not otherwise be spending. Ten dollars off a 40-dollar meal is still 30 dollars spent. That's not even including the tax and the tip. Realistically you could have eaten at home for less than the cost of the tax and tip and put the other 40 dollars into savings or investments.

Fees add up too. These include late fees, overage fees, usage fees, transaction fees, and fees for using an ATM from a different bank. A lot of people go wildly in debt paying for a wedding, their children's college, or a new car. It's important to start saving for big ticket items, particularly college funds, early. Set aside special savings accounts with high returns and put in a little every month.

Credit cards can also be a trap and are a big problem for many. If you've ever spent five minutes to read a credit card contract or figure out what's going on with your bill, you'll see that you can end up spending three, four, and five times as much for that one item than if you had paid cash for it. That Black Friday TV you bought for 200 dollars is a great deal, unless you put it on a credit card and didn't immediately pay it off. How does that TV look when you realize you've actually paid 800 dollars for it?

Once you have learned to manage your money properly, it's time to move on to learning how to multiply your money.

3. Set Budgets and Stick to Them

It's crucial to set budgets and follow them. A good budget covers all the weekly and monthly expenditures that are commonplace, and then has room for emergencies. Of course, you can spend hours putting together the perfect budget, but it's wasted time if you and your family members don't stick with it. If you set the weekly food budget at 200 dollars, that doesn't mean $215 or even $201.

It takes discipline and practice to stick to your budget. Once you have mastered this, you'll start to control your money instead of letting your money control you. Setting a budget was initially hard for Matthew and Kari because of her fears of scarcity, which arose from her childhood. She panicked when put on a strict budget, and the idea of not being able to buy something when she wanted terrified her. After several weeks, she began to see that a budget was a good thing, and that it was helping to ensure they didn't end up in the same position her family was when she was little. As she began to realize that the budget would help protect her, ensure that they could pay their monthly bills, and have plenty of money for food and other necessities, she calmed down and began to accept it.

Chapter 4

Multiplying Money

The key to financial freedom and getting your money to work for you is to learn how to multiply it. So many people spend their lives working hard, saving what little they can, and hope and pray that it's enough to get them through the nighttime of life. There's just one problem with that. You have no idea what your night is going to look like.

Say you've planned and saved so that you can comfortably live for 20 years after retirement. Well, what happens if you live longer than that? What happens if your spouse lives longer than that? What happens if something terrible happens to one of your children, and they need some financial help? What happens if unforeseen medical expenses or other difficulties chip away at your savings? In this instance, you'll be in serious trouble.

You don't want to spend the last part of your life worrying about money. No one wants to have to count pennies, tell your grandchild you can't buy them a bike, or think about having to sell your house just to pay bills. If you want to live comfortably and enjoy the nighttime, you need to have more than just a fixed amount of money in the bank. You need your money to renew itself. This is about investing, whether it's in mutual funds, real estate, or other businesses.

A lot of people unfortunately avoid investing in this way. They might have a mistrust or fear of the process, or they might think it's all too complicated and not worth the time. Whatever your reservations are, it's time to look again at the codes you've been given and see what you were raised to believe about money. Many people look at investments as a gamble and rely on savings accounts that provide only very weak returns. If your parents were this way, then you're going to have to adjust your thinking if you want to maximize your life and go farther with money than they did.

You need to make good investment choices and not just leave your hard work to savings or a government decision. You must proactively look for investments and ways to put your money to work. This can be a bit overwhelming at first since there are so many investment opportunities out there. Do your research, take time to learn, and find one that works for your situation.

This is when it can also be beneficial to figure out how to invest in yourself, your own businesses, and come up with ideas to grow them. Financial independence and security comes when passive income surpasses monthly needs. When you're multiplying your money, you still need to ask yourself how satisfied you are with how it's going. Now is the time to really focus on two questions: Is there opportunity to give back, and is there room for continuous growth? If the answer to either question is no, then it's time to take a hard look at what you're doing to multiply money and figure out how you can do so more effectively.

As always, it's important to pass on what you learn in each of these areas. You need to talk to your kids and your grandkids about money, demystifying it for future generations in order to give them a head start. The codes you program them with will either help them or hinder them as they try to make, manage, and multiply their own money. After working with my then girlfriend on the key areas of her money management deficits, she was able to cut down on her spending, increase her savings, and finally purchased her first investment property. With time and effort, you can learn to begin multiplying your money too.

Here are some money affirmations you can use to help along the way:

Affirmation #1: I am grateful for money.

- I am 100% grateful for money.
- Money is neutral, and what matters most is what I do with my money.
- I achieve great good with the wealth I accumulate. I am generous, big-hearted, and ready to help anyone in need. Wealth naturally flows to me, and as a result, I am grateful. I am grateful to my Creator for His abundant grace and generosity.
- I know that there's abundance in the world, and I choose to receive that abundance.
- I refuse to let past beliefs keep me from getting the wealth that I deserve. I reject any myths that I have believed that are unsupportive of my goals. I embrace my natural greatness and attract good things.

- I make more than enough money. When I make any money, I am filled with gratitude. I say thank you, for even the smallest amounts of money, because gratitude fills me with joy and attracts more good things into my life.
- Money is a good thing and I make *more* than enough. I am a wealth magnet.

Affirmation #2: I focus on abundance.

- My mind is incredibly powerful. What I focus on expands. What I give my attention to grows. My mind controls the outcomes that I experience in my life.
- I have a mindset of abundance. I attract positive things because I constantly think about positive things. My outer life is extremely positive because my inner life is also extremely positive.
- Because I focus on good things, I attract good things into my life. I attract wealth, goodness, and beauty. I gratefully receive the abundance that the Creator provides me.
- There's more than enough for every person in the world, including me, and I choose to receive what is rightfully mine. Because I believe in abundance, I manifest abundance wherever I go and in whatever I do.
- I know that my Creator has my back. I am constantly looking for ways to bring good into my life. I simply must open myself up to the endless possibilities the Creator offers me. I live life to the fullest, enjoying and exploring all the amazing opportunities that come my way.
- And because the Creator has my back, I am grateful. I receive wealth and blessings with open hands, thankful for all that I am receiving.

Turn to the workbook section at the back of the book, page 401, for your reflection exercises to help you commit to action.

PART 7:

CRACKING YOUR RELATIONSHIP CODE

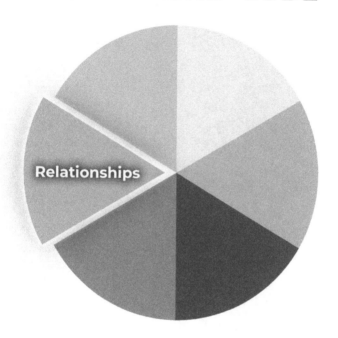

Chapter 1

Reforming Connections

Kari and Matthew spent the next three days fighting like they'd never fought in their lives. At different points, each of them stormed out the front door, leaving the other one to wonder if they'd ever come back. This time, it was Matthew's turn to walk the block, fuming.

They had very different ideas about what was and wasn't a necessary expense. He thought they should cancel all their streaming services, but Kari appeared ready to die on that hill. She told him that when she was exhausted at night and the kids were in bed, watching TV was what kept her sane. When she said she had nothing else to do, he suggested that she get a hobby, even though those cost money too.

He didn't get what the big deal was. After all, she hadn't even owned a TV in college. She hadn't needed it. Matthew stopped in his tracks as he thought about that. Why hadn't she needed a TV? A moment later he remembered. It was because she'd been busy going out with friends or spending time with him. When was the last time they'd hung out like they used to?

Slowly, he turned around and walked back to the house. Inside he found she was still sitting at the dining room table, fuming. The paperwork they'd been using to figure out their budget was still scattered all over the table.

"The boys went over to a friend's house," she said by way of greeting.

"Good," he said, heading for the hall closet.

He reached up onto the top shelf and finally pulled down a dusty deck of playing cards. He blew the dust off it as he returned to the table. With one dramatic sweep, he sent all the papers flying onto the floor.

"What are you doing?"

He slammed the cards down into the center of the table.

She stared at the cards, then up at him in confusion.

"I don't understand," she said.

"I'm sorry," he said.

That surprised her almost as much as it surprised him.

"Sorry for what?" she stammered.

"A lot of things. Specifically, at this moment, I'm sorry that we stopped having fun together."

Tears instantly sprang into her eyes.

"Me, too," she whispered.

He sat down.

"Would you like to play poker?"

The ghost of a smile touched her lips. "Is this like when you tried to get me to play strip poker in college?"

He smiled, too, at the memory.

"We can, but I was thinking of something more...stimulating."

"I'm listening."

"The loser of each hand has to tell the winner one thing they like about them."

"Okay," she said, sounding unconvinced.

"Wait," he said, popping up and going to raid the equally dusty Monopoly box.

He came back with two stacks of fake money, a total of 50 dollars each.

"Monopoly money isn't very exciting," she said.

"No, but 100 dollars of discretionary, unchallenged power in the monthly budget is."

"What?" she asked, eyes widening.

"The budget is important. We should have had one years ago. We're doing it for us. We need to stop letting it hurt our relationship the way we have the last few days. Instead of arguing over the cost of things like streaming services and other things that only one of us thinks is important, let's play for it. We'll set a timer, and in two hours whatever money each of us has, we get to spend on whatever we want for the monthly budget. Deal?"

"Deal!" she said, eyes gleaming.

Right then he mentally kicked himself. He'd forgotten just how much she loved to play games. Had he not forgotten and spent one night a week playing with her, they probably wouldn't have had to fight over the entertainment budget.

Relationships are another key element of life. In nearly everything you do you're connecting with other people. You have relationships with family, friends, neighbors, and people you work with, just to name a few. Even though relationships are strongly rooted in emotions, you still need to analyze your relationships logically, just like you analyze every other aspect of your life. You need to look at those family, friendship, and work relationships and ask the same questions you ask of everything else.

How satisfied are you with the relationship? What is the contribution you (and they) are making? Is there room for continuous growth? These questions will help you pinpoint which relationships could use more work and which ones have run their course.

This won't be easy, as relationships are difficult to be honest about. That's because honesty dictates when changes need to be made, which have the potential to have painful ramifications. If your job or romantic relationship isn't working for you, it can be scary to let go and move on. Unlike other areas of your life, relationships are not yours alone to manage and fix. They involve other people. Similar to your career, your relationships are about responsibility. Here, though, it's a shared responsibility. The codes that you have been programmed with are very significant and important in determining how far you go, how well you live, and how you maximize life in every area—including your relationships.

While examining your relationships, it's also important to take a good, hard look at your beliefs about those types of relationships and see the impact they're having. For example, let's say you're analyzing the relationship with your boyfriend or girlfriend. You might not see your current significant other as someone you'll ultimately marry and grow old with. Since there's no growth potential, it's logical that this relationship should either end or change. This is where you need to look at yourself before doing either of those things. Do you see yourself marrying or growing old with anyone? Did your parents raise you with the belief that marriage was positive and desirable, or negative and undesirable? Maybe the problem is that you don't believe that marriage is a viable option, or that it's something you want.

Identify the negative codes that you have about relationships, and attempt to fix those before you do anything drastic. The last thing you want to do is ditch a best friend because you have trust issues, or alienate a good boss because you have a problem taking orders. Many people have bad codes when it comes to relationships. Erroneous beliefs and destructive stereotypes about marital relationships, and employer-employee relationships, tend to run rampant and are often perpetuated in families and in society.

There are stereotypes out there about what women's work is versus what men's work is, often pegging the woman as being solely responsible for the household even if she also holds down a job. It's common to hear people complain that bosses are mean, demanding, unreasonable, don't care, or just don't understand. But by identifying your own bad codes and rewriting them with new, good codes, you can begin to work on objectively evaluating the relationships in your life.

Let's say that you have two children. One of the things you'll teach them growing up is that they have to share. You're programming them with the code of sharing. When they grow up, they're likely to apply it to their friendships and romantic relationships. Programmed into them will be a shared responsibility for the relationship.

Relationships are valuable, not only to your survival and happiness, but also for what they can help teach you. Oftentimes people find pieces of good code are missing when they engage in friendships or romantic relationships. When you make that connection with another person, you get exposed to certain values that you may never have been exposed to in your bubble growing up. Sometimes the difference can be so profound that it can be almost like learning a new programming language.

Chapter 2

Trust

Cracking the Code: A Case Study

Lori grew up in a house where abuse was rampant. As a result, she has a deep mistrust of men that makes it difficult for her to have meaningful conversations, let alone relationships.

In college, she ended up with a roommate named Jenny who had been brought up in a much different environment and enjoyed close, loving relationships with her father and grandfathers. When the two young women met, their differences became apparent immediately. While they both were raised in the same part of the country and had many interests and goals in common, their differing life experiences meant that they approached most things in vastly different ways.

At first Lori struggled with the fact that Jenny trusted men and found it difficult to believe her when she talked about the loving, supportive male family members and friends she had. Lori's initial thought was that Jenny might be naïve or even delusional when she insisted that there were plenty of good men in the world, and that Lori shouldn't judge them all based on the ones she'd grown up with.

Through exposure to Jenny and her family, Lori started to reassess what she knew to be true about men and families in general. She began to trust and rely on Jenny's family, especially Jenny's dad. It changed Lori's entire attitude, and she built new codes which allowed her to change her beliefs. Many years down the line, Lori's new codes of trust were helpful in her newly found loving relationship. Lori encountered a trusting man on a short flight to Seattle one summer. Two years later, Lori got married to this man and is happily raising a family with two kids. If it hadn't been for her exposure to good codes and her attempts to rewrite the bad ones, this loving relationship would never have happened.

When attempting to understands codes concerning relationships and figuring out what to do in order to improve existing relationships, there are several important things you should attempt to work on. This includes trust, communication, respect, honesty, support, balance, and accountability. For Lori and many others, the first step in changing occurred when she was able to trust.

Following my experiences with my ex-fiancé, my view of the role of trust in a relationship changed slightly. My investment in emotion and resources was thrown away overnight. The more difficult part for me was knowing that the woman I was about to be married to was pregnant with another man's baby. I gave her all my love and trust and expected the same in return. Unfortunately, this wasn't the case for me in our relationship. I believed we each had each other's back, and no matter what happened we were going to be together forever. Of all the emotions I felt, I believe the most difficult one was the breach of trust. Trust can play a crucial role in building and sustaining relationships over the long haul.

Trust is the hallmark of safety. When trust exists, you'll not have to check your partner's phone each time he or she leaves the room. Some relationship experts have argued that marital vows without trust is just an exchange of empty words. Trust is what gives meaning and power to words. Your words don't hold water if trust fails to exist. As an adult, this takes a significant amount of work to build. When you're a child, trust comes easily, and you tend to trust the people around you until experience tells you otherwise. As negative experiences with adults or other children begin to pile up, you become more and more untrusting.

By the time you're an adult, no matter how generally open you are toward people, trust is something that they usually must earn—particularly to make the transition from casual acquaintance to friend, and again from friend to close friend. It can take years to build, and yet be destroyed in the space of a few seconds, often permanently. It can be a tenuous, fragile thing, but is a necessary bedrock of any real relationship.

Trust is often characterized by vulnerability. In her book, *Daring Greatly*, Brené Brown describes vulnerability as "uncertainty, risk, and emotional exposure."[63] It's that unstable feeling we get when we step out of our comfort zone or do something that forces us to loosen control. When the wall of vulnerability goes up, it takes trust to bring them down. Distrust is your way of deciding that what's important to you is not safe with that other person.

Think about some of your closest, deepest friendships. They're most certainly with the people that you have shared more of your fears, dreams, and even embarrassing stories with. There's a need

---

63   Brené Brown, *Daring Greatly: How the Courage to Be Vulnerable Transforms the Way We Live, Love, Parent, and Lead* (New York, NY: Avery, 2015).

to be known by others that you admire, respect, and care for, and this expresses itself every time you share a part of you that's not public knowledge or surface information.

In my upcoming book *Naked*, I delved into vulnerability and trust as critical attribute of highly effective leaders. The best organizational culture is those built on trust between management and employees. There's an assumption that leaders must be tough, hard, and put up a front. This could not be farther from the truth. Leadership is all about influence. The most effective way to lead is to build trust. The way to build trust is to be willing to be vulnerable with the people you lead. The most effective leaders are the ones who can express vulnerability because then they get followers to connect with them as a person and not just connect with the position.[64]

The more you let others in and the more vulnerable you are with them, the more trust is established. This is a survival mechanism, because without trust you would live in a constant state of anxiety about how vulnerable you actually are. This can be seen in cases when you suddenly realize you have overshared, either because of stress, a desire to connect, impaired function, or some other reason. There's that sense of dread that follows those incidents when you realize you don't know if any secrets you shared with that person will be kept, or if any parts of yourself that you revealed to them will be respected or mocked.

There's a tendency by many people to never let anyone in. This is bad code at work, though. Letting people in does mean you run the risk of getting hurt, but not doing so keeps you from experiencing deeper connections with others and living a more fulfilled, satisfying life. At some point you must take the risk and open up.

---

64   Carley Sime, "Could a Little Vulnerability Be the Key to Better Leadership?" *Forbes*, March 27, 2019, https://www.forbes.com/sites/carleysime/2019/03/27/could-a-little-vulnerability-be-the-key-to-better-leadership/.

How much you do often correlates to how much trust you have and are willing to put in the other person.

You tell your best friend things you wouldn't tell your mother. You tell your mother things you wouldn't tell your coworker, and you tell your coworker things you wouldn't tell your nosy next-door neighbor. The amount of information you give out about yourself is proportional to the level of trust you have with that individual. There are, and should be, many levels of trust that you experience.

People progress to different layers of trust over time as they prove themselves trustworthy. Sometimes, though, it might be necessary to speed up the trust process. This is often especially important in work situations. When this needs to happen quickly, trust exercises can help.

Without a doubt, your spouse or significant other is the one who deserves the most trust from you, even if that isn't always the case. It can be that you were hurt by a former romantic partner, as I was with my ex-fiancé, or even that your current romantic partner did something to betray your trust. Whatever the cause, it is crucial to build or rebuild trust with the one you love.

One way to do this is through eye contact. Spending five minutes facing each other and staring into your significant other's eyes builds rapport and can also bring up intense emotions. This is a great opportunity to talk them out, whatever they are.

When you do mess up, which everyone does at some point, don't be afraid to apologize quickly and sincerely. When your partner messes up and apologizes to you, accept it graciously and unconditionally. As a personal principle, I don't like to apologize for the same thing repeatedly. For this reason, I make it my duty to ensure my apologies are backed with practical actions to prevent a repeat of the same action. Apologies are empty if you don't make conscious decision to avoid repeating the actions that hurt your loved ones.

Even when apologies have been made, sometimes guilt lingers over something that you've done. When this happens, sit down with your partner and apologize again, even if the event in question happened years earlier. Tell them how you feel and what that's doing to you. When Matthew apologized to Kari during their argument over the budget, it gave her peace. He wasn't even apologizing necessarily for anything that had happened during their fight over the budget. He was apologizing for something else that had contributed to distance between them. In that moment he defused the situation and allowed her to reassess the discussion. They then were able to move in a new, more positive direction instead of digging in deeper to their respective sides.

Spending some time taking turns telling each other what you love or are grateful for about the other person is another good way to establish trust. You can alternate back and forth or have one person speak about their initial list and then the other. Either way, it helps affirm the other person and build a stronger connection. It can also help to remind you of all the reasons you fell in love with them and promote positive feelings toward them and the relationship.

Even for those who have been together for a long time, there are often still secrets. People carry around with them a lot of pain from their childhoods, previous relationships, and life's disappointments. While a lot of this is shared with your significant other, there's often something, big or small, that you've never told them. A 1997 study by Arthur Aron and others found that sharing a secret with another person intensifies the intimacy between you.[65] Of course, the secret shared should be one that doesn't harm the other person.

Trust takes time to build, and once broken it will need to be rebuilt. Above all, show patience and understanding with each other. Be honest and forgiving with your partner and with yourself.

Ironically, many people find it difficult to completely trust themselves. They either doubt their own intelligence, abilities, judgement, or intentions. This mistrust makes it impossible to operate at peak efficiency. It's also a sign of bad code that has been instilled in you, likely since childhood.

The best thing you can do is to identify the negative codes you were programmed with. What did adults say about you when you were young that made you distrust yourself? What can you do in order to help you build good codes?

Kids by their very nature have lapses in judgement. In fact, studies have shown that the brain of an 18-year-old has more in common with a four-year-old than it does a 21-year-old when it comes to impulse control.[66] Kids are also busy learning coordination skills that they might not fully master until they're adults. Just because you had butterfingers when you were 14 doesn't mean you'll have them all your life. Of course, the mind is powerful. What it believes to be true often finds ways to make true or at least provide evidence to support the theory. That means if you have a bad code that says you're still a klutz, the mind might help the body prove that.

65   Arthur Aron, Edward Melinat, et al, "The Experimental Generation of Interpersonal Closeness: A Procedure and Some Preliminary Findings," *Personality And Social Psychology Bulletin* 23, no. 4 (1997): 363-377, https://doi.org/10.1177/0146167297234003.

66   Daniel Romer, "Adolescent risk taking, impulsivity, and brain development: Implications for prevention," *Developmental Psychobiology* 52, no. 3 (2010): 263-76, https://www.doi.org/10.1002/dev.20442.

This is why it's important to constantly affirm yourself, both your character and your abilities. You must always be honest with yourself about who you are. This means you might have to readjust a lot of your thinking to get rid of hyper critical code that says you always do the wrong thing, or change egocentric code that says you can do no wrong and everyone else is the problem.

When you let yourself down, as you will at some point, it's important to do your best to move forward. Just like a relationship with another person, you need to work on the relationship with yourself. When trust is broken, it's time to rebuild it.

Anytime trust is lost, it can be devastating. This is true no matter what type of relationship it is. Don't expect to give or receive a whole lot of trust after trust has been broken. There are some instances when someone might have done something so heinous that trust should never be rebuilt for your own protection. However, if you want to keep the relationship, it's important to start rebuilding trust. It can be a long, hard journey that's anything but easy. The five steps you should follow to rebuild trust are gaining some perspective, reminding yourself of other areas of trustworthiness, forgiving them, starting small, and rewarding good behavior.

Step 1: Gaining perspective

A breach of trust often seems like the end of the world, even when it's not. You can't force yourself to hurry up and get over the hurt. It's going to take however long it's going to take for you to feel better about the other person. What you can do, though, is try and gain some perspective about what's happened.

Take a good hard look at the area where the person broke trust with you. Ask yourself pertinent questions like was this a pattern of behavior, or did they have a moment of human weakness and slip up? Was the breach intentional or accidental? Did your actions or words contribute in any way to the breach of trust? Do you and the other person have a relationship where open communication is encouraged?

By examining the event rationally and objectively without the painful emotions attached, you can start to cope with what happened and see if there are any changes you need to make that may have contributed to the problem. Most things don't happen in a vacuum, particularly when relationships are concerned. While there are times when one person is clearly, logically 100% at fault, most of the time there's either extenuating circumstances or some blame that can be shared. Only when you're clear on what went wrong can you truly move forward and begin to work on rebuilding the relationship and reestablishing trust.

Step 2: Remind yourself of all the times the other person was trustworthy

If the relationship has lasted any length of time, you should have examples of the other person living up to the trust that you put in them. This might be in the area in which they broke trust. Think about all the times they have been trustworthy and haven't broken your trust. A relationship is not just one event, it is instead a culmination of every event on every day that includes all the things that have gone right.

By keeping the other person's good qualities and the times they've been there for you in mind, it will make it easier as you attempt to rebuild the relationship and heal faster. Too often people get hung up on the negative aspects of life and relationship. Instead, research has shown that when people focus on the positive, particularly on the things that they are grateful for, it can have a profound impact on their mood, health, and outlook on life.[67] Instead of focusing on the areas where someone has let you down, focus instead on the way where they have kept the faith and earned your trust.

Step 3: Forgive them

This might seem easier said than done, but if you hope to rebuild trust and salvage the relationship, you need to forgive the other person for what they've done. It's easier to do this once you've gotten some clarity about the situation and reminded yourself of all the other times the person has done right by you.

Even if you don't want to forgive for the other person's sake, you need to do so for yours. Studies have shown that the anger and bitterness people harbor toward those they haven't forgiven can cause mental and physical and relationship problems.[68] These negative emotions can act like a cancer in your body and mind, and it's best to get rid of them and free yourself up to focus on the future and continue moving onward and upward. Focusing on the past and constantly letting it drag you down keeps you from achieving everything you can and should in life.

Remember that forgiveness isn't a weakness and is instead a strength. Forgiveness isn't opening yourself up for more pain and failure. It's acknowledging that flawed people do flawed things, and that you don't need to carry on with toxic emotions that result from those actions. Forgiveness is a gift you give to yourself which frees you from the bondage of all that toxic negativity.

---

67   Sara B. Algoe and Baldwin M. Way, "Evidence for a role of the oxytocin system, indexed by genetic variation in CD38, in the social bonding effects of expressed gratitude," *Social Cognitive Affective Neuroscience* 9, no. 12 (2014): 1855-1861, https://www.doi.org/10.1093/scan/nst182.

68   "Forgiveness: Your Health Depends on It," Johns Hopkins Medicine, accessed June 20, 2021, https://www.hopkinsmedicine.org/health/wellness-and-prevention/forgiveness-your-health-depends-on-it.

Step 4: Start small

Give trust in relation to small things. This will be easier to do in areas of the relationship that are unrelated to those where trust was broken. Eventually, though, you will have to give trust in that area as well.

This doesn't have to be done all at once. Baby steps can help both of you feel more comfortable. There does have to be a steady progression in order to keep the feeling of momentum and hope that trust will be restored to the level it once was. You can't just give trust in one or two ways and then stall out indefinitely. If you find that you're unable to do this, then it's time to rethink the relationship and whether or not you're serious about keeping it.

As trust is earned back, it's appropriate to touch base with the other person every so often. Be sure to do so in a positive way and without making them feel bad all over again for the original transgression.

Step 5: Reward good behavior

If the other person is doing well, don't ignore it. Thank them either verbally, by showing increased levels of trust and intimacy, or ideally both. Let them know that you appreciate all their effort and tell them how it's impacting how you feel. When people feel unappreciated or like their work is going unnoticed, they get frustrated. It's important to positively reinforce their efforts so they keep going instead of giving up on the relationship altogether.

It's important to build trust to have an effective relationship. Whether it's a family relationship, a friendship, or a work relationship, trust is a crucial element to making the relationship work. Without it, effective communication about anything that truly matters will cease to exist.

Chapter 3

Communication

Communication is key to any successful relationship. This should come as no surprise. Communication builds upon the codes that people receive as kids. For this reason, it's especially important to help your kids with communication skills. A great way to do this is to have play dates with other children when they're young. This allows them to gain experience with peers instead of only communicating with older family members. Communication will vary slightly with different people depending on personalities and the type of relationship. As kids, all you must do is take one look at a parent's face to know if you're going to be in trouble later. Kids have different codes for their interactions with each other. These codes help protect the relationship. But no matter what kind of relationship it is, for truly effective communication to occur there should be respect, compassion, and gratitude.

To have a good relationship, respectful communication is important. Your words sink in and impact people in ways that aren't always instantly obvious. Sometimes what you consider teasing ends up being incredibly hurtful or damaging to someone else, particularly if they don't have the same codes hardwired into them that you do. Verbal and non-verbal communication both need to be handled with respect.

Earlier you read about Lori and Jenny. Lori grew up in an abusive household. For her, many forms of touch, including tickling, were used as a literal form of torture. For Jenny, who grew up in a loving home, tickling was a way of playfully sharing affection. This created an incredible conflict when these two young women first became friends. It ultimately led to a very painful conversation.

Because Lori had the courage to tell Jenny what the action meant to her, Jenny was able to modify her behavior. The funny part was, it was short-lived, as Lori forced herself to break the bad code given to her by her family and embrace the good code she saw modeled by Jenny's family. The first time Lori tickled Jenny, it was awkward for both of them, but it led to a new level of understanding, friendship, and respect. It also helped Lori learn how to communicate verbally without rancor about something traumatic, and to open up to non-verbal displays of communication and affection.

Non-verbal communication can be just as important as verbal communication. Expressions can be a way to signal approval or disapproval, and touching can be a way to demonstrate closeness and affection. These cues that people give out help maintain structure in a relationship.

Compassion is another crucial element of good communication. It gives you a different opportunity within your relationships. If you want others to be happy, you need to practice showing compassion. You need to understand your friend, partner, child, parent, or coworker and realize that the experiences they've had in the past might be explaining how they act today. You can see the codes programmed in them. When you have compassion and care, it helps you to stop judging and accept your loved ones more easily.

When you demonstrate this compassion, it gives you an opportunity to diffuse arguments, avoid finger-pointing and blame throwing, and release resentment and anger. Even when you need to express tough love, you can do so with care and concern for the other person. Digging in and obsessing on being right about everything ultimately does you little good. When you win fights at the expense of compassion, you lose sales, friends, and can find yourself alone.

While you're at it, show some compassion to yourself as well. Understand that the experiences you've had in the past, both good and bad, have shaped your codes. These in turn have control over your behavior. If that behavior is negative, then you need to fix it. Don't spend time beating yourself up, though. Instead, get on with the business of replacing the bad code with good and vow to do better whenever you can.

A good rule of thumb is to speak to others in a way that you'd like to be spoken to. If you want understanding, sympathy, and compassion from others, you need to express it. Another thing you should always do for those close to you is express your gratitude for them.

Gratitude is an especially important thing to communicate to others. You need to constantly express it to those you care about, as it's virtually guaranteed that your partner will never get tired of hearing you say things like I love you. Take some time to write a note to a friend and let them know you're thinking of them. Do the same for family members. Sometimes communication can be solely about gratitude and nothing else—not business or chores or life updates. This is a strong way to empower the relationship.

Remember, the other person doesn't have to be your friend, business partner, or spouse. Nobody has to do things for you that improve your life. They do so out of their own free will, and that should be recognized by you and appreciated for the gift it is.

Like everything, expressing gratitude should be a shared responsibility of the relationship. If this doesn't come easy to you, it's time to take a look at those codes that you have and see why and adjust them as needed. Then try one of these tricks to get your message across to the other person.

1. *Express gratitude frequently.* Make sure to express your gratitude to those in your life on a consistent basis. For most relationships, weekly is fine, although for some business relationships biweekly or monthly might work well, too. For closer relationships such as significant others or children, expressing gratitude daily is better.

2. *Be sincere.* Don't just repeat yourself every time you express gratitude to someone. Worse yet, don't write one note and then send it to a dozen different people. Expressions of gratitude should be authentic, timely, personal, and specific. Let them know what you appreciate about them, why what they just did meant something to you.

3. *Mix things up.* Express your gratitude in more than one way. If you usually give a verbal expression, mix it up and write a note, love letter, or poem. Say it with a card on a gift of flowers, or event tickets to an event. It's good to do this for a couple of reasons. First, it keeps the expression from getting stale or seeming to be routine instead of a heartfelt thank you. Second, not everyone experiences love or attention in

the same way. Some people need to hear words, others want to read them, and some appreciate gifts. This way, no matter how someone is most receptive to what you have to say, they will fully hear and understand what you're trying to tell them.

4. *Set aside gratitude time.* You can set aside time with those closest to you to praise and thank each other for the contributions you make to each other's lives and well-being. This need only take five minutes. But by setting aside time, it makes the expression of gratitude intentional and mutual. Expressing gratitude is one of the ways that you can boost your own sense of well-being and optimism. Doing this regularly with someone you're close with will strengthen your bond and connect them in your mind with feelings of happiness and positivity. Taking the time to do this intentionally also shows respect for the other person and everything they do for you, which is also an important element of communication.

Chapter 4

Respect

Everyone wants respect—not just in the way they're communicated with, but as an individual. Respect in a relationship also shows acceptance and lets the other person know you value them. This is important in every relationship. Being in a relationship is a choice and you need to respect the other person's choices and decisions. This is all about accepting them for who they are rather than trying to change the core of their being.

The two types of relationships that are especially susceptible to the problem of one person trying to change another are romantic and parent-child relationships. So many people get into romantic relationships and even marry someone thinking they can change the other person. First, true change is rare and has to stem from the individual's recognition that change is desirable and necessary. No amount of pushing, prodding, cajoling, threatening, or behavior modeling from another person, even a romantic partner, will do anything except breed resentment. Second, this shows a fundamental lack of respect. You need to be happy with the other person as they are and recognize that their faults and foibles are their own, and instead of changing them, you must be willing to accept them if you want the relationship to progress.

Remember reading earlier about those people you know who can never sustain a relationship and blame everyone but themselves? This is often the root of the problem. If they respected the other person for who they were and worked only on changing themselves, then things might go differently. If you can't accept the other person and can't change your attitude, then it's a relationship you shouldn't be in.

The other type of relationship that frequently suffers from a lack of respect and one person's desire to change the other one is the parent-child relationship. Parents often don't realize that they need to respect their kids, but they do. Respect is one of the pillars of a good relationship.

How to do this requires a lot of maturity and careful self-analysis on the part of the parent. There's a difference between instilling good code and values in a child and trying to change or mold them into someone they're not. If your child has the soul of an artist, expecting them to be happy with rigid, boring routines and trying to prepare them for a career that embraces those is going to cause a lot of friction between the two of you.

A lot of parents expect a child to follow in their footsteps. This pressure can be especially intense if there's a family business involved that the parents are hoping or expecting their children to take over. You have to remember, that's *your* business. Whether or not your child wants to run it when they grow up is entirely up to them. Even if your parents forced you to take over the business, you shouldn't repeat the error and force your own child to do the same. Instead, do what your parents couldn't do. Accept your child for who they are. If they want to follow in your footsteps, if their dream is running the family business, great. If they want to do something entirely different, communicate that the decision to do so is fine, too.

If you want to have a strong relationship with your children and still be able to communicate with them once they're grown, you need to practice mutual respect when they're young. You can help to inspire and guide them, but you can't change them. Understand this and accept who they are. Better yet, help them as they develop in line with their own desires and life path.

Before you can have a successful relationship with anyone else, you need to have a successful relationship with yourself. Self-respect is something a lot of people talk about, but dangerously few have. It means that you thoroughly understand yourself and your values and choose to live up to them without compromising your principles. It means also giving value to yourself as worthy of love and good things. Too many people look to parents, romantic partners, or even bosses to give them value. You must first look inside yourself for that value.

To love and respect yourself can take a lot of work. This is especially true if you grew up in an abusive environment or are coming out of an abusive relationship. No one deserves to be treated poorly. Refuse to accept that for yourself. Make a list of all your good qualities and remind yourself of them daily. Outline what you're looking for in a partner, a friend, or a boss, and until you learn to really respect yourself compare each potential person to that list. If it's an up-and-coming company that would be exciting to work for, but you know the boss disrespects and verbally abuses his employees, have the self-respect to not get into that relationship. If a really fun person is willing to be your friend only when they get to dictate everything the two of you do, have the self-respect to realize you deserve friends who value your opinion.

Where a lack of self-respect can cause very serious, long-reaching problems is when you get into romantic relationships. It can be easy to become trapped, relying on your partner for validation or approval and letting them dictate the rules of the relationship. This is how people end up in unhappy marriages. One person is subservient to the other instead of living together as two equals with mutual admiration and love. Sadly, many women still in the modern age look to men to define them. It is, however, not an exclusively female problem. Many men also find themselves trapped in a certain position because of the expectations of family or society.

It's important to respect yourself and all those you plan on having any kind of meaningful relationship with. Any relationship built on a foundation of anything other than mutual respect is flawed and doomed for failure. This is true no matter what type of relationship it is. Have the courage to be honest with yourself when getting into any new relationship. Ask yourself, do you respect the other person? If the answer is no, then you need to seriously think about the repercussions of going forward.

Chapter 5

Honesty

Honesty is another key aspect to a successful relationship. This may seem like a foregone conclusion, but it can actually be something very hard to stick to. It requires you to be honest first and foremost with yourself, which can often be overwhelming. It also means that you forego the social niceties that you have learned to use in place of actual, real, frank conversation.

This is another area where getting honest with yourself can be a difficult proposition but is utterly crucial. If you can't be honest with yourself about your needs, wants, and expectations, then it's impossible to honestly and clearly communicate those to friends, coworkers, and family members. This includes having the courage to dig deeper and understand where your wants and expectations might be unrealistic or unfair to other people. Just as you don't want to be in a relationship where the other person dictates everything, so, too, you cannot expect to be in a relationship where you do that to the other person.

Maybe your wants and desires seem fair and reasonable. However, you need to check them against reality.

Cracking the Code: A Case Study

Claire had the belief that if both spouses were working, then both spouses should split the housework. This seemed to her like a reasonable expectation. In her household growing up, there was a division of labor between her parents that had been modeled for her. She also had codes that told her that the more physically demanding and disgusting tasks, such as hauling trash, should be the responsibility of the man.

During college, she had her relationship codes further refined by her roommates. They had a house rule that whoever cooked didn't have to clean the dishes. That responsibility would fall on the other two who'd shared in the meal. Claire believed this same division of labor would naturally flow into a marriage.

Claire did get married out of college, but the choice of spouse ended up bringing challenges she hadn't anticipated when she was first forming and later refining her relationship codes. Her husband was disabled, and as a result couldn't do the household chores that she had anticipated he would.

Several months into the marriage, Claire found herself beginning to resent her husband because she felt that she put in more work than he did. On paper, yes, she did. Because of his physical limitations, cooking, cleaning, laundry, even taking out the trash fell on her.

Before long, she found herself beginning to snap at her husband and make snide remarks. She realized something was wrong, but it took her getting honest with herself to figure out what the problem was. When she realized that she resented him for not fulfilling her expectations of what a spouse would do, she felt terrible. She married him knowing he had physical limitations, but because she had never consciously updated her code, she was making life difficult on both of them, bringing unrest into what had been a happy relationship.

She had to come to the realization that her original expectations were unfair considering her actual circumstances. Because of this she had to rewrite her own code instead of picking concrete things that her spouse had to do. She set up expectations of the amount of time and effort he would spend working on the relationship and the shared responsibilities overall.

Once she was honest with herself, Claire was able to talk with her husband and figure out a way so that they both felt like they were contributing to the household. Her husband was more than sympathetic to the problem once she made him aware of it, and they were able to work out an acceptable solution.

He took over-paying the bills so she didn't have to spend time on that. They also hired a twice-a-month maid service to handle the cleaning, scrubbing, and vacuuming, removing that completely from their hands. Claire still cooked, did laundry, and took out the trash, but she no longer felt like the entire household burden was falling on her shoulders.

What Claire and her husband discovered was that when couples are honest with each other, it takes away a lot of hassle and keeps resentment from building up. Of course, that wouldn't have happened if Claire hadn't had the courage to be honest with herself first. It's impossible to have a good relationship without inspecting yourself first and discovering if your demands, expectations, dreams, wishes, and desires are reasonable. Do your best not to violate the other person's rights or put an impossible burden on their shoulders.

Chapter 6

Support and Balance

Each person in a relationship is a pillar holding that relationship up. If one person crumbles in an area of support, the relationship is liable to fall apart. Each person has to play a role of support, being able to differentiate their needs from the other person's and letting them grow professionally and personally into who they're supposed to be. If you're not supporting, you're not allowing the other person to maximize their life. Relationships are a tool that help you fulfill a greater goal.

If you have a friend who's not supporting you, they're really not a friend. This can be an incredibly hard lesson to learn and is oftentimes painful. Again, honesty and respect are things you can look at to help you be clear on this. Does your friend respect you, and are they honest with you about things? Do you do the same for them?

Every relationship is give and take. When one side gives all the time and another side takes all the time, the relationship will fall apart. It's like trying to balance while standing on the center of a teeter-totter. You're going to fall if both sides aren't working to keep things level.

When you're talking about your friends and family, it's not enough to meet halfway. Relationships aren't 50-50. They're 100-100. Each person needs to give 100% to make the relationship work. When you give all that you have, you're all in. When the other person does as well, then you have a bond that's unbreakable.

While it's true that some relationships are more transitory by their very nature, whenever possible you need to carefully choose your relationships, especially any that could end up lasting a while. When you think of a relationship being a marathon, it becomes more important to decide who you want to hang with.

It's not enough to give love, you must be willing and able to receive love. It really isn't easy even though people think that it is. So many relationship problems occur because someone doesn't know how to receive love, and that frustrates the other person. There's a great series of books by Gary Chapman covering this entire topic. He discusses the five love languages and how different people need to feel love in different ways.[69] This can be an incredibly eye-opening read, especially for couples who don't express and receive love in the same way (i.e., one person responds to touch, and another responds to shared time together, etc.).

Even the ability to accept love from another human being is a code programmed into you when you're young. It might be that you came from a family where love was scarcely, if ever, displayed, or was used as some kind of bargaining chip. In that case, you're going to need to work to create new code and understand that

69   Gary Chapman, *The 5 Love Languages: The Secret to Love That Lasts* (Chicago, IL: Northfield Publishing, 2015).

love should be a free expression of positive emotion given without condition, expectation, or coercion.

Some strong, independent women were given codes when they were young that make it hard for them to receive those little signals of love, and it becomes difficult for a man to pierce that tough curtain with a tiny show of love. Some men are given codes that say men have to be tough, and real men don't cry. They can become so hard that they don't know how to receive love or might even have difficulties giving it. That external stoicism can make an impossible wall for a woman who needs to verbally communicate in order to feel loved and appreciated.

Some people with bad backgrounds can't forgive themselves for the things they've done and think no one else can either. Those with low or no self-respect might not think they're worthy of love. Both types have a problem accepting that someone else could love them and need to be willing to accept grace from another person. Some people give and give but never get back. It doesn't matter what the other person says at that point. All talk and no give makes love a dull affair.

Love is an action word. You have to give, and you have to receive. This is one of those areas where people who are dating need to take special notice of the way their partner responds to them. When the blush of newfound attraction is over, does the other person receive and express love in a way that can sustain the relationship for a lifetime?

Balance in a relationship is crucial. The effort, time spent, and the intimacy of the language used are three things that are crucial to evaluate between friends or partners when attempting to understand how well balanced your relationships actually are.

No one wants to feel like they're doing all the work. Most people have experienced a relationship that felt one-sided in this way.

Whether it was working for a lazy boss, struggling to please an un-giving significant other, or being the friend that has to make the ef-fort—it's no fun and doesn't lead to solid long-term relationships.

Both parties in any relationship need to expend effort to keep the relationship alive and healthy. There are times in most rela-tionships where circumstances or necessity dictates that one per-son will spend more effort than another. This inequity should only last for a short amount of time in order to keep from dramatically changing the nature of the relationship.

When one spouse becomes seriously ill, all the household duties plus care of the ill spouse and children will fall upon the healthy spouse. For a short time, things are out of balance in rela-tion to effort spent. Once the ill spouse recovers, though, balance should be restored and both partners should return to putting ef-fort into taking care of the house, the children, and each other. If it doesn't, then serious conversations need to ensue to figure out why it hasn't, and what needs to be done in order to get things back on track.

In cases where one spouse becomes permanently ill or disabled, the amount of effort might seem to be permanently thrown out of balance. This does not have to be true. Remember the case of Claire who married a disabled man? They worked together to find ways that he could put effort into the marriage. The same should be true for a couple who finds themselves suddenly in this new position of having one spouse permanently ill or injured. All that's required is communication and creative thinking about how to re-adjust things. It's possible that hiring a maid, nurse, tutors for the children, or working with a grocery delivery service can lift some of the burden off the healthy spouse. Additionally, in all except extreme cases, the injured spouse should be able to find ways that they can contribute while working with their new limitations.

They can possibly take over more of the paperwork, find ways to help the children with their homework, or be the one to plan the meals and do the food ordering. The important thing is to do what you can to keep the effort spent on the relationship from becoming all one-sided or far enough out of balance. Inequity of effort spent on the relationship can breed resentment just as inequity of time spent on the relationship can. There are situations where it's totally impossible for a sick partner to make any type of contribution at all. This is understandable.

Everyone has the same 24 hours in their day. While it's true that different people have more demands on their time than others, it's crucial for relationships of any kind that both people try to commit to spending the same amount of time with each other or doing things for each other. This might require a very frank conversation, and the person with more time in their schedule sacrificing to match the time that the busier person can spend. This might get frustrating for the person who wants to and can do more, but it's a better solution than letting the busier person be consumed by guilt and feelings of failure because they can't spend as much time as the other person can.

In the movie *Ghost,* there was a lot made from the fact that the Demi Moore character would say "I love you" and the Patrick Swayze character would respond "Ditto."[70] It took him dying and embarking on his journey to heaven to actually tell her he loved her. While this might be cute in a movie, it is not cute in real life.

For things to work, both people need to be on the same page about word choice. Word choices won't go unnoticed by your heart and your subconscious. This is true regardless of the type of relationship. Kids know this instinctively, making a big deal over who their best friend is, and making sure that the term is recipro-

---

70   Jerry Zucker, dir., *Ghost,* Paramount Pictures, 1990, 128 mins.

cated. It's no fun to have your best friend think of you as just one of their many friends. You want to be as special to them as they are to you.

Your language needs to be balanced. However, you cannot do this at the expense of honesty. If one person says, "I love you" and the other person isn't at that place yet, saying it back isn't really the right decision. Instead, it's better to have an honest conversation about how you feel and where you're at mentally and emotionally. In order to keep from building that sense of inequity and resentment, you can ask the other person to match what you're willing to say and step up the intimacy of the language when you're both comfortable. It's an awkward conversation to have, but you both need to be on the same page and not force each other to say things you don't mean or express different levels of intimacy with each other either.

Maintaining balance is an important aspect of communication and relationships. One area you should be sure to have balance is working jointly to keep each other accountable.

Chapter 7

Accountability

You need to hold yourself and your friends accountable. A person who doesn't want to be accountable is self-destructive. When that happens, sometimes you need to take a break from those friends or family to protect yourself. Ultimately, a relationship without accountability is a waste of time.

It's important to be accountable for your actions, emotions, and words. So many times, people say that actions speak louder than words. While that can be true, words are still vital to a relationship. They can destroy or heal in the space of a few seconds.

When you go through life, you'll find yourself collecting a lot of friends and acquaintances. Not all these relationships will give value to you. Look for friends who make you a better person, not ones who enable your bad habits. True friends want what's best for the other person, not just what's enjoyable or convenient for themselves. In this regard, you need to carefully monitor both yourself and your friends to ensure that all of you are living up to the highest standards and bringing out the best in one another.

In order to have successful friendships, there are several things you need to do. This includes setting clear expectations, empowering each other, having honest conversations, setting aside time and sticking to it, evaluating who you are when you're together, and adjusting as necessary.

There's an old joke that friends help you move but real friends help you move bodies. It's funny but it speaks to the heart of the commitment level in the relationship. If you're going to have more than a surface friendship with someone, then you need to empower them, and vice versa. Everyone wants friends to cheer them on and tell them they're doing a great job. But the truth is, you can hire people to do that for you. While everyone wants to be encouraged and praised, that's not the true value that a friend brings to the table. A friend is the one who can offer you honest feedback, criticism, and advice from a place of love and compassion. A true friend wants you to succeed, so they're not just going to tell you whatever you want to hear. They'll take the time, effort, and hardship that comes along with it in order to tell you the truth.

At times, this can be stressful for both parties. No one wants to hear bad news or difficult feedback, and most people don't enjoy giving it either. Just think of the dreaded "Does this make me look fat?" question that no one ever wants to be asked by a significant other. If the truth is that yes, the outfit makes the person look fat, a true friend should never lie and say no. No isn't a helpful answer and means that you were too much of a coward to tell the truth. You cared more about a few seconds of awkwardness than you did about the fact that your friend might be embarrassed if they wear that out in public. In this light, you should be concerned with your friend's image and how they want to appear, answering honestly and being genuinely helpful instead of just placating. Of course, there are a lot of nice ways to say yes. Tell them that the color works but the cut is wrong. Help them figure out why the outfit doesn't work so that they can choose something more flattering next time.

Both people in the friendship should be empowered to speak the truth with kindness and compassion. If your friend is dating someone that's all wrong for them, speak up. You don't have to be mean but do be honest. On the opposite side, the friend receiving the information should hear it out even if they don't agree. You need to empower the other person to give their honest opinion based on everything they know about you. The alternative is that everyone might just keep their mouths shut and let you make the mistake of your life by staying with someone who is completely wrong for you, and ultimately will cause you grief. You don't have to agree with your friend's advice or opinion, but you do need to give them the respect of listening to it. After all, they're giving you respect by trying to help you.

This might require you to rewrite some of the communication codes you've been given. Many people were raised to believe that white lies are acceptable, and that you don't tell people the truth if it will hurt them. Helping each other be better is more important than sparing each other's feelings.

You might also have been raised with codes that tell you that it's okay to cut down others because it's funny, or because it will make you look better. This is also something you need to rectify immediately. Cutting, sarcastic comments destroy relationships. They're never funny, no matter how hard people laugh, because they cut into the psyche of the person they're aimed at, undermining their self-esteem and slowly poisoning the relationship the two of you have. This can be particularly destructive when dealing with your significant other. Saying something is just a joke might seem like a valid excuse to you, but their subconscious isn't laughing. In the same vein, be honest with your friend or significant other if they do this to you. Let them know that it does hurt you and that you want them to stop. If they respect and value the relationship, they should listen and modify their speech accordingly.

This two-way street of empowered communication isn't limited to these areas. You need to be honest with each other about what you think you're doing right and wrong in every area of your life. Your artist friend might not know anything about the world of high finance like you do, but they know you. They know who you are, your core values, what you like and dislike. He or she can speak to that and offer advice as to how you're interacting with your current job and what might suit you better.

The goal here is to constantly build each other up and push each other to be the best version of yourself. If you don't want someone trying to do this for you, then it begs the question of why you want them in your life in the first place. That, like everything else, is something you need to have the courage to have an honest conversation about.

It's impossible to hold others accountable to a friendship or a standard of behavior without honest conversations. This ties in with empowering people to help you, like in the example of telling someone whether or not they look fat in a particular outfit. Honest conversations need to happen at every stage of a friendship. The more honest you can be in the beginning and the middle, the less likely you'll need to have honest conversations because the relationship is ending.

Sometimes it can be helpful to schedule time to discuss whatever's on your mind. If you don't want to do something formal, make sure that from time to time you ask the other person how they're doing and how they'd rate the relationship. It might seem like a strange idea but ask them on a scale of 1 to 10 how you're doing as a friend and how the friendship is working for them. Then, you should answer those questions as well. This can help the two of you grow the friendship and better understand each other's needs, particularly as they may change over time.

Don't let these opportunities slip. It might even be helpful to set reminders for yourself to take the time to check in with your friends and find out how they're doing and how the friendship is doing. That way you can honestly evaluate the friendship and make sure you're aware of what's happening in each other's lives. In order to do this most effectively, you need to make sure that you're spending quality time together.

We all have friends who constantly flake on plans. It's annoying, and it teaches you that they can't be counted on. It can also undermine the relationship in other important ways, making the other person feel unimportant. Some people's lives have challenges that can make sticking to a schedule or keeping social plans difficult. Ailing family members, unpredictable work hours, and other elements can lead to a lot of missed dinners or skipped parties. It's important when these factors are in play that there's understanding and effort put forth on both sides. If your friend is in this situation, you might find that you need to be more flexible to accommodate their crazy schedule. Instead of planning a lunch meeting two weeks in advance, you might need to make it more spontaneous and be adaptable on the day of. Flexibility can be an important tool in this area.

That said, be intentional about time spent with your friends. If you're not, six months can slip by, and you won't have spent any quality time together. This is how friends drift apart. Everyone is busy, so just accept that. Even your friend who stays at home to take care of the household is busy. Your retired friend has hobbies and other activities taking up his time. Go into relationships expecting that your friends' time is just as valuable and scarce as yours. That way you'll respect the time they're giving you and be less inclined to cancel at the last minute because you're tired or need to work late, or frankly, have something more interesting to do.

It's important to be consistent, whether it's daily, weekly, or monthly. This sense of repetitive togetherness builds trust in the friendship and allows your relationship to get into a rhythm with that person. Whether the time you spend is in deep philosophical conversation, brainstorming about how to make areas of your life better, or just hanging out and playing games, the activity is something your mind and body will start to rely on to fulfill different needs. Too many missed appointments are not only detrimental to the friendship, but also to your mental and emotional well-being.

Here, too, it's important that you establish expectations early. How much time and of what type is important? If one person needs to touch base every other day and the other really would prefer to interact every other week, then you have a problem. Either one person is sacrificing time, or the other person is sacrificing space. This is one of those things that should be worked out in advance. If expectations aren't being met or needs have changed, then it's time for one of those honest conversations.

Time spent with each other should be a benefit to both of you. It should help to relax, educate, or in some way enhance your life. If it's not, then that's something you need to address as well.

Not everyone will be a good match for you. There are some friends who don't help you grow or enhance your life, and who are actually detrimental. Some people engage in bad or even dangerous behaviors and love to get other people to join them. When you're with a true friend, most of the time you should be at your best. They should inspire you and push you, not drag you down.

Do you have a friend who might encourage you to have fun but engages in destructive behaviors? Maybe it's a friend from college who loves to go out drinking, but you often find yourself waking up the next morning with a pounding head and fuzzy memories. The binge drinking isn't good for your body or your mind, and ultimately isn't beneficial in any way, no matter how much fun you tell yourself you're having. Friends like that can be funny, dynamic, and very persuasive, which can make it hard to say no to them.

Of course, the truth is, they're not true friends, they're just acquaintances who are encouraging and enabling bad behavior. Oftentimes with people like that you'll find that if you try to say no to them, they'll bully, beg, mock, and do everything they can to try to get you to cave and do what they want. This person is not your friend. They're actually your enemy, because they're attacking your self-esteem, your will, and your values. Treat them as such and cut them out of your life. There are plenty of other people out there you can have fun with who will make you feel better afterward and not worse.

Take a good, hard look at each of your friendships. Who are you with each person? Do they bring out your best? Or do they bring out your worst? Are you cheerful and optimistic with them, or are you grumbling and pessimistic? Friends help shape you as a person. One of the fastest ways to change yourself, your outlook, and many other areas of your life is to change your friends. True friends push you to a higher level of joy, self-actualization, and success. False friends pull you down, often to their level, and will try to stomp you down even lower if they can. You're deeply influenced and impacted by the beliefs and actions of the five closest people in your circle. Choose only winners in that circle who will in turn work to make you a winner.

You need to decide who helps you on your journey and spend more time cultivating those friendships. You'll probably also find that you're in several destructive or non-beneficial friendships that you need to end. When you find companions that truly have your best interests at heart and who strive to push you to be your best, then no matter how life changes, those friendships are usually the ones that stay rock solid.

Keep in mind that even if you have created a friendship with certain expectations and boundaries, you find that eventually the relationship changes and other factors come into play that one or both of you are no longer satisfied with. When this occurs it's time to have another honest conversation and see how the other person is feeling.

Nothing ever stays the same in life. Some of your friends might be closer at different stages. For example, if you're diagnosed with cancer, you might suddenly find that one of your friends who's a cancer survivor is your new primary support structure even though you rarely connected previously. True friends are able to withstand the ebbs and flows of life and be closer or a little more distant through the different times of your life. Your closest friend when you were in your 20s might take a back seat to the friend who has kids when your first child is born. This dance is a natural part of life, and if you have clear, honest communication with your friends and are still intentional with the time you do schedule together, most friendships can weather the highs and lows of life.

It's important, though, to give each other respect and communicate when expectations and realities change. You can't have a shift in your own mind and expect the other person to just automatically shift theirs. Friends aren't psychic, and there's only so much they can intuit about what's going on with you and your changing needs. To prevent misunderstandings and hurt feelings, be honest when your expectations of the friendship need to be adjusted.

It's important in any relationship, whether with it's with friends, business partners, or family members, to offer respect and accountability in the relationship. Your significant other, children, or parents deserve the same communication of expectations, empowerment, honesty, and intentional time as your friends and business partners do.

Basically, it all comes down to providing a safety net for your relationships. That's why you need trust, communication, respect, honesty, support, balance, and accountability. A lack of any of those can destroy the safety net of the relationship. The primary responsibility should always be to provide safety for everyone in the relationship, and each person is responsible for that.

Again, with each relationship you need to go through and evaluate it. Is it working for you? Is there room to continue to grow? Remember, you need a thriving, healthy relationship in order to help you on your journey to maximizing your potential as a person. Relationships are an important aspect of the wheel of life and help to keep us all balanced and constantly pushing forward.

Here are a few relationship affirmations and self-reflection questions that can help you along the way:

- **I am a relationship builder.** It's important to have solid, honest relationships, and I embrace the support I get from these good relationships. My friends, family, co-workers and others whose trust I rely on are part of my backbone.

- **I know that positive relationships take time to build**. I am committed to staying the course because I know the benefits of having good people on my side. I spend much of my time doing things with and for others that help to solidify our bond.

- **I show support to those around me by listening keenly when they speak.** Whether they share lamentations or expressions of joy, I take the time to listen actively and show that I'm interested in the progressions of their daily life. My active participation is a sign that I care and can be counted on in times of need.

- **I strive to share my emotions with others so they can know where I am coming from.** When people in my circle of influence receive honest feedback from me, the bond of trust is strengthened.

- **Today, I commit to being a relationship builder**. I vow to have honest, effective, and meaningful interactions with others so I can live in harmony with them. My relationships partly define my successes in life and serve to make the world a better place.

- **I affirm that I have and attract positive people.** I receive and cherish genuine love without hesitation.

Self-Reflection Questions:

1. What steps do I take daily to strengthen my bond with friends?
2. Do I actively work on my family relationships, so I don't take them for granted?
3. How do I respond when my actions have hurt someone?
4. How effectively do I communicate my needs?

Turn to the workbook section at the back of the book, page 417, for your reflection exercises to help you commit to action.

PART 8:

CRACKING YOUR SPIRITUAL CODE

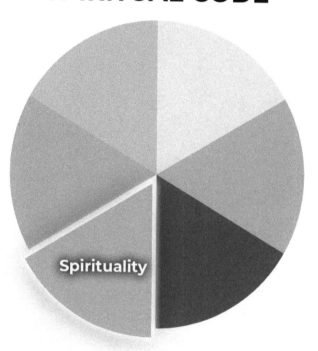

Chapter 1

An Often Overlooked Necessity

There was a time in my life when I thought I had everything going for me—a successful career, a beautiful relationship, a properly managed investment portfolio, and a healthy, fit body. Yet, sometimes, I still woke up feeling dry and empty. At this point in my life, I had broken many bad codes and replaced them with the right set of codes for a more flourishing life. But there was something missing. I was satisfied but I didn't quite have a sense of fulfillment. As I sought to troubleshoot the reason for my occasional feelings of emptiness, I soon realized I had fallen behind in the spirituality aspect of my life.

It was only then that I decided to give spirituality the attention it deserved, and as I did, that feeling of dryness began to slowly disappear. Man is, by design, a spiritual creature. Some people might try to deny it, but the soul is what sets man apart from other creatures. There's a thirst, a longing ingrained in your DNA to be part of something bigger than yourself, and to find a quest for meaning. There's a part of you that always yearns for some connection to something else, even if you don't know exactly what to call it. When in crisis and trauma, it's natural to reach out for help from something or someone. When life is great and people are blessed, they feel the need to express gratitude and often give to charities as an offering, with the hope that their fortune will continue.

However it came to be and whatever it is you think you're trying to connect to, the truth is that your life is out of balance if you ignore the spiritual aspect of your nature. You can have all the education in the world, a perfect job, great relationships, plenty of money, and be in great physical health. But without addressing the spiritual part of life you'll still have a huge, gaping, hole in your life, and your wheel won't be balanced.

Kari felt bad about having to stand Linda up for the yoga and lunch date. When she called her, she'd been kind enough to reschedule for the following week. Kari really enjoyed the yoga session, which just made it even harder to tell Linda at lunch that she couldn't afford to take her class.

"You know, I believe that God is trying to tell you something," Linda said with a mysterious smile.

"What's that? Kari asked.

"My receptionist is moving, which means I have a job opening. The pay is okay, but free classes are one of the perks."

Kari stared at her in shock.

"That's—wow. It's just, I can't, though. I have the boys."

Linda laughed. "I have kids, too. That's why the studio is only open weekdays during school hours. I cater to busy moms who still need to take care of themselves in what little time they have."

Kari again felt something stirring inside her. Was the universe, or God, trying to tell her something? Her bumping into Linda immediately after the conversation with her doctor somehow didn't feel like a coincidence.

But what would God want with her? She hadn't been to church since she was a kid, and once she'd gone away to college, she hadn't given much thought to anything like that.

"God doesn't believe in coincidences," Linda said softly, almost as though reading her mind.

Kari nodded slowly as a warm glow filled her eyes. She took a deep breath as she thought about that some more.

Life is chaos. Things fall out of place, plans fall through, and people can let you down. There are many things that happen that are outside your control. Instead of throwing your hands up in despair and giving up, you need to put your faith in something else. There's a saying, "Let go and let God." It depicts that moment when things are out of your control but does so in a positive spin. You're not abandoning everything, you're instead giving over the worry to someone else who sees farther than you do, and who cares about your problems as well.

For some people, it's God. For others, it's nature. Some believe that the universe is sentient and that things run in an orderly manner. Whatever you believe, it's vital to your mental health and your overall life balance that you get in touch with that part of you.

Otherwise, it's like you're taking care of every other part of an expensive car, the tires, the transmission, and the safety features, but are never bothering to make the whole car come to life by putting the key in the engine and turning it on. It's that moment, that spark, that turns a lifeless hunk of metal into a roaring, beautiful creation that can take you on incredible journeys. Just so, man is only truly alive when he stops focusing on the things he can see and begins to focus on those he can't. That's when he turns the key, igniting his soul and embarking on the most fantastic adventure life can offer.

In order to truly fulfill this part of your life you need to assess where you've been and where you're going. Start by taking a look at the codes that have been programmed into you and decide if they're good or are bad and if they need replacing.

In many ways, your spiritual code will end up being the most highly personalized part of your code regardless of how much it changes over time. Your spiritual life is, by design, intensely personal. No one else can share your exact journey. That's why you need to take responsibility for it. You can't just leave this up to tradition or someone else to dictate to you what to believe and how to live that belief.

Faith, no matter what or who it's placed in, can move mountains. There are thousands of examples of people surviving horrific experiences or coming back from the brink of death because of the power of their faith—their belief in a strong spiritual force, which for some is God and for others is a higher power. Even those who claim to have no religious beliefs often display an unwavering faith in something else such as science, or luck, or the law of attraction. That's because that need to connect to something else is universal, even if the expression of the connection is highly personal.

Chapter 2

Connection

It's important to be able to connect with your spirit and then connect your spirit to something beyond yourself. Some people spend a lifetime and never really meet themselves. Self-reflection doesn't come easily for everyone. Again, this is where your codes come into play. If the adults in your life when you were younger gave value to self-discovery, understanding motivations, and building the foundations for beliefs, then you will, too. If they went through life avoiding holding up a mirror to their own soul, then the very thought of doing so might make you intensely uncomfortable.

The first step to spiritual enlightenment is to understand who you are and what you think your place in the universe is. You must recognize that your thoughts, emotions, and everything that makes you unique is important. Whether you call it a soul or your inner self, you need to understand who you are and what you want. Once you have some sense of that, it's time to look beyond yourself and see how you fit into the larger pattern of the universe.

To a Hindu, their souls try to perfect themselves by living life after life, striving to achieve harmony and become one with the universe.[71] A Christian believes they are children of God who have accepted the sacrifice of a savior.[72] Whatever the belief, there's a connection to something beyond the self that helps fulfill that need that's been inside you, since your life began.

Everyone is raised with some sort of belief on this topic, even if there's nothing to believe in. Many people never dig deeper than this, upholding the spiritual practices and traditions (or lack thereof) that their parents held. It's fine to believe what your parents did, but until you look deeper, past the traditions and activities that you were raised with, you could struggle to progress on your spiritual journey.

Right here, today, what do you perceive to be your truth? Do you believe man is alone in the universe? Do you believe in a higher power that you can't honestly name? Do you believe in something or someone specific? What do you think your relationship is to the universe, or that higher power? How sure are you?

Once you understand what you believe, then you can start to investigate it. Sometimes you might discover things that deepen your belief, or that will cause you to change it. Either way you need a clear picture of where you are or have been in order to begin to figure out where you're heading.

Everyone has a reason for their beliefs, whatever they are. Some reasons are compelling, while others are less so. Ask yourself where

71   "Moksha," BBC Religions, updated July 19, 2006, https://www.bbc.co.uk/religion/religions/hinduism/beliefs/moksha.shtml.

72   William P. Loewe, "Jesus the Savior," BYU Religious Studies Center, accessed June 20, 2020, https://rsc.byu.edu/salvation-christ-comparative-christian-views/jesus-savior.

your beliefs come from. Did a relative or teacher instill them in you? Were you raised a certain way, and if so, did you ever question it? Did you do research and decide what made sense to you? Have you ever had what might be called a religious experience? On the other side of things, did you *not* have a religious experience when you hoped or expected to have one?

This exercise is not about questioning or trying to destroy your faith. Instead, it's an opportunity for you to discover where your faith or lack of faith comes from. Remember, your spiritual journey is a highly personal one. If your answer is something akin to the fact that it's just what everyone in your family believes, that's not a great foundation to launch your spiritual journey from. This is about why *you* believe, not why your parents or spouse or siblings believe.

Once you have an idea about what it is that you believe and why, it's time to dig deeper. How much do you actually know about the religion or other path that you're following? Knowledge is important for several reasons, as it can help you to understand the path you're on during those dark days when you find yourself lacking in faith. It can also help you succinctly explain it to others when they ask. Knowledge helps you deepen your own faith and gives context to your experiences.

When trying to figure out what you believe and what you don't, it's helpful to look at your own life. Everyone has experiences that could be categorized as divine. Timely and beneficial coincidences can easily be perceived as miracles. Experiences can become more intense and more personalized from there. What you've experienced can often point the way to something outside yourself. Once you understand these events they can help to inform and deepen your belief.

It's always a good idea to understand more about a religion that you're following. What are the tenets? Why are they important? Some people go through classes like this in their churches or synagogues when they're young. If you didn't, it's never too late to do some research about your beliefs.

If you're unsure of what you believe or even if you have no beliefs, try taking a comparative religion class at a local college or online. It will help to explain what the various religions believe and why. That could help you understand which one more closely resembles your own world view.

In his book, *You Are the Universe*, Deepak Chopra explains that one of the first steps to finding and deepening your spirituality is to connect with yourself.[73] To do this, you're going to want to set aside a day or two of intense soul searching. If you can manage to do this as a getaway where you can be alone, this is ideal. If not, you can just block out uninterrupted time to get it done.

Make sure that however you choose to get in touch with yourself that you have plenty of privacy. You'll need somewhere quiet where you won't be interrupted while you do some soul searching. If you've got your mobile device with you, make sure to put it in *do not disturb* mode.

To ensure you have everything you need, have a notebook, a pen, a comfortable place to sit, and whatever else you may need already on hand. If there's certain music that moves you in a spiritual sense, have something to play it on. If you think and relax best while listening to sounds of rain or the ocean, then there are tons of apps for your phone that can provide you with the needed sounds. Some people like to use white noise to block everything out. Whatever makes you feel comfortable, make sure to bring it

73   Deepak Chopra, *You Are the Universe: Discovering You Cosmic Self and Why It Matters* (New York, NY: Harmony, 2017).

into your safe space. You might also want to bring some water or snacks.

Sometimes it can be hard to sit quietly by yourself for an extended period. The real world might try to intrude on your thoughts. It's possible that you could even feel guilty, awkward, or embarrassed about having this deep discussion with yourself. Don't let that stop you. Acknowledge the feelings and then let them go. Remind yourself that this is a crucial part of your life journey, and that if you don't take care of your spirituality, it will throw your entire wheel out of balance.

It's time to ask yourself some deep questions. Who are you? What is your moral center? What are your values? What would you never compromise on? Why? Do you believe that you have a soul, something that is not just your body or your mind? Why or why not? What codes were you given as a child that relate to religion and spirituality? Have those codes been beneficial to you or not? Spend as much time as you need asking and answering these questions and all the others that will pop up. You're not talking to God or a higher power at this point. You're just talking to yourself and trying to get to know yourself on a deeper level.

Don't be afraid to talk out loud and even record yourself if you want to. If you're more comfortable expressing yourself writing, have your notebook handy and write it all down. You don't have to worry about keeping things organized. If you maintain a record of what you're thinking and feeling, you can clean it up later if you so choose. Given that you have a lot to talk about with yourself, this can be a great way to keep track of your thoughts.

This is not the time to pass moral judgements on yourself. You're not trying to decide if you're a good person, a good Christian, a good Hindu, or anything at this point. You're just trying to be as real and honest as you can be.

Ask yourself whether your current religious practices and beliefs (or lack thereof) are working for you. Do you feel fulfilled? What do you feel is lacking? Once you've spent time getting real with yourself and who you are as a person, it's time to start defining what it is you believe in.

Once you have explored yourself and your beliefs thoroughly, it's time to try and make a closer connection to your higher power, whoever or whatever that is. This is usually done through prayer or meditation of some sort.

The whole point in connecting to God or whatever you believe in is to have a source of help and comfort that comes from outside yourself. There's part of your being that's designed to make that connection, and you won't be truly happy or fulfilled until you do. When you pray or meditate, don't just do all the talking. You need to spend some of that time listening for the answer. Sometimes it might be a quiet voice in your head or a feeling deep inside. The idea is to keep reaching out until you feel that you have established communication and connection.

Just like with any relationship, you need to work on your communication with God. You need to be open, honest, and consistent. If you're reaching out only on major holidays or once a week at church, then you're not going to be seeing a whole lot of deepening of that relationship, which will end up severely stunting your spiritual growth.

Once you have done some self-exploration to discover who you are, and spent some time trying to connect to God, you might wish to reach out to other people. Connecting with a community that shares your beliefs can be an important aspect of spiritual growth.

It's important to find spiritual teachers that you can trust who speak to you—and remember that you can have more than one at a time. Try doing some research online and see whose articles, sermons, blogs, videocasts, or books appeal to you. Ask yourself whether they believe what you do. Also ask whether they challenge you to grow. When researching someone, check out three or four of their articles or videos. Not everything they say must really impress you or make you think. However, if after half a dozen sermons or blogs they haven't spoken to you, they're probably not the teacher you're looking for.

What's fantastic is the sheer number of teachers you have access to thanks to modern technology. You don't have to learn from someone who lives in the same area. You can learn at the virtual feet of people who live on other continents. The important thing is to find people whose message makes sense and who demonstrate a real interest in helping others learn and grow.

If there are congregations or group meetings in your area, try several of them. It's important to connect both with those who will be teaching you and those who will be learning beside you. Looking around for the best fit is crucial, as you need to find a place where you can learn, grow, flourish, and be supported throughout the process. If you like the teaching but can't really connect with the people, keep looking. The same is true for the reverse. You need to find a community where you connect on both levels.

There's long been a push for the in-person meetings, but in this day and age, you have a variety of tools at your disposal that will allow you to reach out beyond your town or city to find a group that you can really connect with. Vet them just as you would any in-person group. It's ok to shop around until you find exactly what you need. A good community will support you while also pushing you to be a better person than you are today.

Don't overlook opportunities just because they're not what you're used to. Here you might have to do some more work breaking your codes. In recent years, there have been big innovations in how people gather and worship. You can attend a home church which gathers in someone's house, sign up for an online Bible study, or find groups that keep Jewish tradition and culture alive and relevant to their beliefs. Just as Deepak Chopra created a mobile app so you are never alone, there are several religious apps that make spiritual connection more easily accessible. The point is there are countless possibilities available, and you can find something that will fit your schedule and still allow you to interact with others who believe as you do.

Once you have made that connection to something beyond yourself, you then need to practice deepening it. This is done through meditation, documentation, and practice.

Chapter 3

Meditation, Documentation, and Practice

M editation, which was discussed earlier in relation to mindfulness, is an important aspect of spiritual experience as well.
Meditation can take many forms, which can include guided visual-
ization, focused breathing, quiet reflection, and times of prayer. Regardless of what you call it or how you spend the time, you should
be engaging in meditation daily. This practice can help you to focus
and provide you with a calm place to listen to yourself or to God.

Beyond the mental benefits, meditation and prayer have doc-
umented physical benefits as well, helping to lower blood pressure and calm your nervous system.[74] When you're having a tough

---

74   Manoj K. Bhasin et al, "Specific Transcriptome Changes Associated with
Blood Pressure Reduction in Hypertensive Patients After Relaxation Response Training,"
Journal of Alternative Complementary Medicine 24, no. 5 (2018): 486-504, https://www.
doi.org/10.1089/acm.2017.0053.

time concentrating or struggling with a challenging day, you can stop and engage in this quiet time for as few as five minutes and emerge with a more settled mind and a better attitude with which to tackle the challenges ahead.

As with anything else, the codes you've learned will impact how you engage in this type of activity. Some people were raised with the belief that this type of practice must take one specific form, such as memorized prayers or chants. For them it can be hard to break that code, but it can be deeply beneficial. Prayers, mantras, and even guided meditation are often the most powerful and effective when they come from a person's own heart and mind and aren't just something they're reciting by rote.

For others, prayer might have been relegated to a particular time or activity, such as before a meal or bedtime, or on Sunday morning at church. Again, freeing yourself from these codes and opening yourself up to expressing yourself in these ways whenever and wherever you want can be incredibly rewarding while pushing you farther along your spiritual journey.

Many religions provide opportunities to pray, meditate, or worship in a group. This can provide a sense of empowerment and deepen your feeling of connection to the spiritual realm. It can also deepen your relationship with the people you are participating with. Some groups don't even require you to share the same beliefs in order to participate.

For example, Ruth is a devout Jewish woman who takes great pride in her heritage and loves to sing. Over the years she discovered that she had a deep passion for Christmas carols. The beauty of the carols touched something deep in her soul, and singing them became a very spiritual act for her. A few years ago, Ruth found a local Christian church that put on a big Christmas concert every year. She approached the music director and told him that she wanted to sing in the choir at the church's concert. She explained that she was Jewish, not Christian. While it was a bit unusual, he agreed to let her rehearse with the choir and sing at the Christmas concert. She has since made it an annual tradition that gives her deep joy and a sense of connectedness.

For many, an important part of your spiritual growth might be the need to participate in a retreat at least once a year. The retreat can last a day, a weekend, or even longer if you desire. There are many organized retreats put on by different organizations and retreat centers. You can opt to attend as part of a small or large group. These kinds of retreats usually offer study, worship, and often games or group team-building exercises or challenges. There are retreats geared just for men, women, couples, or for entire families. You might even try different retreats based on what it is you're looking for and who might go with you. These retreats almost without exception allow you some free time by yourself to reflect and connect with your higher power. As a practice, I make time for retreats every year around my birthday. During this time, I prefer to quiet my spirit and invest in spiritual development. This is the time when I review the old year and set intentions for the new year. I've found this to be a powerful way to launch into the new biological year.

Another type of retreat that you can go on is a silent retreat. These are often held at monasteries and allow you the opportunity to spend a weekend in complete silence, freeing up your mind to focus solely on your spiritual pursuits. Meditation and prayer are the sole focus of this type of retreat and can leave you with a profound sense of peace and provide a life-changing experience.

Another alternative is to design your own retreat. You might choose to go camping or fishing, or even go to a health spa. There are many options, and a spiritual retreat of your own design is only limited by your imagination. The goal is to take time out from everyday life in order to focus on your spiritual health and growth. Time spent doing this can be refreshing and lead to deeper insight and connectedness to yourself and your higher power. When doing a retreat of this type, it's always a good idea to bring along a notebook to document what you learn during the experience.

Just as it's important to practice various forms of meditation, it's important to chronicle your spiritual progress. For many people a journal is an easy way to do this. You can write your thoughts freely, set goals for yourself, or even participate in structured studies. Do whatever makes you feel comfortable and helps you track the lessons you've learned and the progress you've made.

Have you ever had that experience of waking up in the middle of the night from a dream and had a profound thought that then disappeared in the morning? Journaling helps you hold onto those thoughts, ideas, spiritual breakthroughs, and revelations that you find meaningful. It can help keep you on your spiritual track, allow you to easily identify things that are worrying you, areas that you'd like to improve on, and show you just how far you've actually come in life.

It also can prove to be something of a life journey as well as a spiritual one. You can look back and see how some of your perspectives have changed as your life progresses. Gathering your thoughts together in a concrete way also helps to identify whether you're satisfied with your current spiritual growth, what you can do to improve it, and how you can help others learn from your lessons and mistakes. This last part is crucial when it comes to passing down good codes to the next generation.

The last part of this process is documentation. Faith is like a muscle, and you'll need to work it out in order to improve and get stronger. When you go to the gym and work out, it hurts, but you still go back because that pain means you're making progress. You tear the muscle apart and then rebuild it stronger. The same is true with your faith. It's not enough to say that you're spiritual. You must continue to practice every tenet of what you believe so you're in tune with your spirit.

Sometimes this isn't easy and will feel like you're pushing past opposition. This is when real growth happens. As with every other area of life, if you're not growing, you're stagnating. Faith isn't meant to be static, as it should be living and breathing, changing, and evolving with you as you progress on your journey.

Time spent in spiritual reflection is something that's likely to slip through the cracks of a busy week if it isn't scheduled. If you're part of any kind of organized group or study, it will provide a concrete timeslot that you can put on your weekly schedule. However, it's not enough to just show up for an hour once a week and assume you're all good. Real spiritual growth takes time and effort.

You need to set aside time each week for spiritual study and reflection. Many people find it beneficial to schedule a little time every day, often in the morning. This way they start the day feeling grounded, and what they learned or contemplated stays in the back of their mind all day. Others find it helpful to set aside one or two blocks of time each week where they can really dig in and feel like they're spending some focused, quality time. Whichever works better for you, be intentional. Schedule it on the calendar like you would anything else. Then, when it's time for your appointment with yourself or God, keep that appointment.

Some people have discovered that fasting helps give them more spiritual clarity and a greater feeling of closeness with God. There are many resources online that can help if you decide to go down this path. Fasting can be as short as skipping one meal or be as drastic as a liquid-only fast for 40 days. For those with specific dietary constraints, other types of fasting, such as fasting from social media, can be beneficial as well. When you fast, you should take the opportunity to be focused on prayer and greater spiritual connection with God. Fasting, while having benefitted a great number of people on their spiritual journey, is not for everyone, and if going on a food-related fast you should first consult your doctor.

Complacency with practice can often be a problem, and you should strike out the words *good enough* from your vocabulary. The goal should always be to strive for excellence in every area of your life, and that includes your spiritual life. Try to live every aspect of your life to the fullest, and when you do so you'll find that doing less is completely unacceptable.

So, work at your spiritual life like your work at your business, your relationships, and your health. In a very real way, it's all of those things and more. Then, when you've learned how to truly grow spiritually and are practicing it successfully, you can help change your family and perhaps the world. Through practice, you can easily share your spiritual truths with your kids and your grandkids. Engaging in activities that can be shared will help to build familial bonds, good memories, and good codes. After all, expanding your spiritual life is one of the most important aspects of your own development.

When you need help, use some of these spiritual affirmations:

- **I am spiritually grounded.**
- **I am grateful for the wonderful creation I am, even when I feel like a mess.** My spirit is alert, alive, and deeply rooted. I am grateful for the guidance I get from my spirit.
- **My spiritual roots are growing deeper.** I am content knowing I am who and where God wants me to be. Today, I am centered in the universe, and I draw goodness from it.

- **My life is a living miracle.** I manifest tranquility, stability, and higher purpose. Spiritual enlightenment comes naturally to me. My life is full of gratitude, my spirit is unwavering. Life and love flow through me. I allow God to guide everything I do.

Turn to the workbook section at the back of the book, page 431, for your reflection exercises to help you commit to action.

PART 9:

CRACKING YOUR PERSONAL GROWTH AND DEVELOPMENT CODES

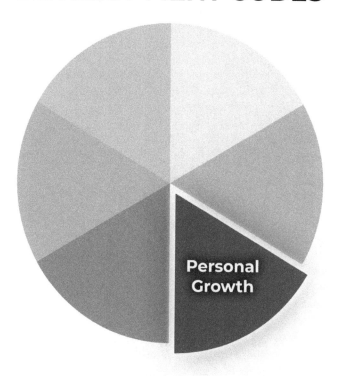

Chapter 1

Life Codes Case Study: Matthew and Kari Revisited

M atthew knew things were changing when he realized that he and Kari spent an evening at home without the kids reading. She studied something called *the wheel of life*, while he was busy reading a book about finding one's purpose. Occasionally, one of them stopped to read a passage out loud to the other. He couldn't remember having such an enjoyable evening in a long time. As he thought about it, he realized that they'd both been doing more reading and game playing the last two weeks. The streaming services, which Kari had won in their game of poker, weren't being used. This made him smile. Maybe they could soon remove those from the budget altogether.

"Did you realize that if any area of your life is out of balance, your entire life is?" Kari said.

"No, but given the wheel analogy you explained to me, that makes sense."

"Have you figured out what your purpose is yet?" she asked.

"To make you happy?" he teased.

She looked up from her e-reader with a smile and then playfully threw a pillow at him.

"I have read about this mentor named Babs. I think I want to check out some of his videos. He says that we're programmed from childhood with codes, and that not all of them are good. He says that we need to work to replace the bad ones with good ones."

"That sounds interesting," she said. "Maybe we can watch his videos and read his books together."

He grinned. He was finding he had a voracious appetite for learning. It was appropriate that he and Kari were learning together, since they had first met in a classroom.

Only this time, he vowed to pay attention and take notes.

We spend our lives in pursuit of doing better, being better, and finding perfect happiness and success. We ride the wave of excitement at the thought of becoming more successful. Then, we ride the wave back down with disappointment because we've tried and failed. Everything starts in the mind. This includes both success and failure. When you succeed at something, that success first came from your thoughts and the codes you operate from.

By the same token, when you fail, that failure also stems from your mind, from those same thoughts and codes. That means that starting off with the proper mindset is indeed critical to your success. The mind is what processes information, and information flows through your mind, giving energy to your thoughts and internal and external actions. We're all entirely unique with unique experiences and ways of dealing with those experiences. The way we feel, what we believe about ourselves, and how we perceive the world is completely distinctive from anyone else. The patterns of our minds are shaped by our experiences, life events, surroundings, and the way we process information.

If you want a hint as to the kind of beliefs and codes that are hardwired into your brain, listen to the words you use. Are your words negative, and filled with doubt? If you often say things like "I'm not sure I can," this is a defeatist language that should be avoided. Even innocuous seeming things like "I'll try," show that your intent is coming from a place of doubt.

Your mind is to dreams what soil is to plants. Many great and powerful dreams never blossom or come to fruition because the mind that conceived them was not fertile. If you place a plant in soil that isn't fertile, the plant is stunted, choked, and doesn't grow. Many people conceive dreams, but because of weakness in the mind they can't water them or give them nutrition, and therefore are never able to birth that great business or invention they may have envisioned.

That's why it's critical to invest in your mind and personal development. Without that you can't maximize the other areas of your life. It doesn't matter if you're doing well in other areas because you can't achieve your full potential without developing yourself in this way.

For example, if you have money, you still need the right mind to know what to invest in. The mind channels your passion and guides your purpose. It's important to build yourself personally and constantly grow. You must establish good codes, as it impacts your beliefs, behavior, balance, boundaries, and bliss.

Chapter 2

What You Believe

In her book *Mindset*, Carol Dweck discussed the groundbreaking theories behind the power of mindset.[75] She revealed that success in any life endeavor begins with the mindset. Your beliefs are those things that you hold to be true about the world, life, and even yourself. With these beliefs you create your own reality. If you didn't have someone to pat you on the back and tell you that you were doing a great job as a kid, you might not believe it now. If you had someone who praised you no matter what happened, you might not understand why you're having a difficult time succeeding when no one is there to coddle you. These beliefs become hardcoded into you as you grow up. And like anything else, many people end up with faulty codes that are a disservice to them.

---

75   Carol Dweck, *Mindset: The New Psychology of Success* (New York, NY: Ballantine Books, 2007).

When it comes to beliefs, there are two types of mindsets: fixed and growth. Fixed mindset explains that not everything is achievable, and that there's not a lot you can do about it. Growth mindset, on the other hand, believes that things can be done, and that there's always a way to accomplish and overcome even the most challenging of obstacles.

Fixed mindset says, "This is who I am, this is who I've always been. It's a natural talent." Growth mindset says, "I can be better, learn, and make progress. I can shape the outcome of my life, bounce back from a fall, no matter how hard it is. I can handle whatever life throws at me. Each day of my life is an adventure. I'm driven by purpose."

The fixed mindset is dangerous because it keeps you stuck in old patterns of behavior. You have limiting beliefs about who you are and what you can achieve. Instead, your beliefs should be what sustain you, not what betrays you. Subconscious limiting beliefs are why some people fail to grow in different areas of their lives. The sad truth is that you're not born this way. You're born with all the potential in the world. When you're little you believe you can do anything. But as you grow to adulthood, gradually, little by little, society reins in your mind so that you become self-conscious and hyperaware of perceived limitations.

Subconscious limiting beliefs are why many people fail to grow in different areas. Therefore, it's important to break limiting beliefs, build positive beliefs, and beautify the world with those positive beliefs.

In order to break limiting beliefs, you must first identify them. However, it can be tricky to differentiate between good, protective beliefs and bad, limiting beliefs. A child who was once scared by a dog when they were younger grows up with fear and limitations. These can impact not only their ability to enjoy animals in the future but also their ability to connect with friends who do. Here are some steps you can take to identify your own limiting beliefs.

Limiting beliefs are strongholds that hold you down, stifle your creativity, and keep you from achieving your goals. In order to truly crack the life code and live a dynamic life of freedom and fulfillment, you need to get rid of those limiting beliefs. The first step is to identify what's holding you back.

You may or may not have an instinctive understanding of the answer to this question. Whether you do or not, it's important to go through the exercise, as you might be surprised at some of the things you discover about yourself, your family, or even the world. To complete this exercise successfully, you must ask yourself several questions in order to identify each of your limiting beliefs.

Many people aren't where they want to be in life. In order to break free of the things that keep you fettered, you need to first identify your limiting beliefs. One of the best ways to do this is to closely examine your life and your past experiences by taking a moment to analyze your life. Look at the last 10, 20, 30 years of your life and look for patterns. Do you not leap when you should because you're afraid to take the risk? Or do you leap too late because you're afraid of changing, or trying something new? What were the things that kept you chained to the ground and kept you or your business from soaring? What triggers made you get cold feet and back out of business deals or relationships when you should have been pushing forward?

When a relationship reaches a certain point, do you find yourself always ending it instead of taking the next step? Why? Are you afraid of getting hurt? Do you believe that marriage doesn't last? Do you have low self-esteem, which causes you to believe that for someone to care about you there must be something wrong with them? Do you think you're too young for a serious relationship, or too old?

When a business opportunity that seems promising comes along, do you back away? Why is this? Are you afraid of falling flat on your face? Do you believe that what you have is good enough or that if you reach for more, you'll risk what you already have? Do you believe that good things don't happen to you, or that if other people had a good idea, they wouldn't be reaching out to you for help? Think of every time you turned down an opportunity to expand your business or grow in your career. What stopped you? Odds are there's some limiting belief that you carry that made the decision for you. Spend some time examining those situations and see if you can find your own pattern of negative beliefs that hold you back and keep you from reaching your full potential.

Family plays an important role here too. You've seen in previous chapters how your family plays a critical role in creating the codes you live by. Family beliefs, including biases, defeatist attitudes, and even traditions and legends can leave you with personal limiting beliefs that hurt and hold you back from achieving all you were set on this earth to achieve.

Now is the time to look for family patterns and trends, not only in your immediate family but also in the stories and histories passed down to you. Think about your family. Is there a belief that all women get divorced, or that a bachelor's degree is the best one can ever hope for? Has no one ever made more than a certain amount of money, and it's seen as a ceiling for what someone like you can achieve? Is there a history of everyone in your family doing the same kind of job, whether it's working in the same industry or for the same employer?

Some of these patterns may be obvious. Alcoholism, other types of addiction, and abuse often run-in families and afflict many generations. When these things occur, it can be easy to just assume that's the way it is and that you shouldn't expect anything different for your own family.

Maybe there's an expectation that you'll always live in the same town you were born in. These beliefs might keep you from exploring the world, being your own person, or from taking a fantastic job opportunity because it's in another town, state, or country.

It could be that the men in your family die young, even when they seem healthy. This could lead you to not taking care of yourself like you should because there's an underlying belief that it won't ultimately matter. It could also keep you from planning for retirement or doing several other things you might want or need to do if you didn't feel like you had an axe over your head.

The limiting beliefs can be even more subtle. They can relate to where you come from, whether it's the wrong side of the tracks or a third world country. Perhaps you come from a small town or farm country. For all these, there can be an expectation that you won't ever have, or truly appreciate, the finer things in life. Your family might even have a history of despising the wealthy or the arts out of ignorance or jealousy. If you try to break free of that, you might be met with hostility, and be told that you don't know your place and that you're forgetting where you came from.

Some beliefs don't even have to be spoken. If you grew up in a family where few or none of the women worked, then you might end up with a limiting belief about the role of women in the workplace. If your father didn't lift a hand to help raise you or your siblings, then you might not think it's your place or responsibility to help raise your own children.

Look at the members of your family and their actions and inactions. Look at the patterns that you see in their lives, both on an individual level and on the family unit level. After a while, you'll begin to see the beliefs, both spoken and unspoken, that your family holds. Then you can start to see how some of these beliefs are limiting, and if you don't discard them, they'll only hold you back.

Examining family trends really ended up helping Matthew. He discovered that it wasn't just his father who had stayed at the same job, without really advancing, for his entire career. The same had been true for his grandfather, three uncles, and even several cousins. He realized that he had received codes that made him believe that a stable job was the most he should hope for. As his eyes began to open, he realized that fear of losing that stability and his fear of failure had been the driving force in the lives of several of his family members.

He began to see the layoff as a blessing. Without it, he probably would have let those same fears keep him in the same dead-end job until he retired. He began to realize that not only could he make more money for his family elsewhere, but that he could also do more meaningful work that would pay him more, make him happy, and allow him to help others. With the use of a mentor, he managed to break free of the negative codes that had been instilled in him since he was a child.

In order to understand your beliefs, examine your choice of words, especially when you're under intense pressure. When life squeezes you, the juice that comes out is the real content of your character and a display of who you are. When the pressure is on, what do you say? Do you demean yourself? Do you constantly say that you're a failure, or grumble that good things don't happen to you, or that you just always have bad luck? These are all verbal cues as to what you're thinking and what your true beliefs are.

Sure, when things are going well, you're probably able to put on a brave face and say all the right things with a positive attitude. But how do you speak to yourself? What names do you call yourself? Do you call yourself a loser who will never win, or do you call yourself a winner who is just facing your next challenge? Do you hold pity parties or pep rallies for yourself? Are you wallowing in perceived defeat, or cheering yourself on to victory?

In the realm of the mind, words hold a lot of power. You tend to believe whatever you say whether it's true or not. So, if you constantly complain that you have bad luck, your mind will accept that as truth and will seek evidence to support that theory. No cloud will have a silver lining, and every bump in the road will turn into an impossible mountain.

On the other hand, if you constantly remind yourself that you have good luck, your mind will also accept that as truth and try to prove it. Suddenly you see the silver lining for the cloud. That bump in the road might prove to be a speedbump that slows you down so that you can see something you might have missed and that will ultimately benefit you. Every negative thing you believe about yourself and the world around you will sooner or later come out in front of a group of sympathetic listeners or alone to yourself when you think no one else can hear you.

I knew a businesswoman named Rachel who was smart, funny, and talented. She was a real up-and-comer and could command a room. However, she couldn't accept compliments. If you tried to tell her anything positive, regardless of what it was about, she would instantly reject the statement. If you told her she'd led a great presentation, she'd instantly point out everywhere it went wrong and if there were good aspects, she'd credit them to others, even if she was the one who did the work. If you told her she looked nice, she'd instantly reject the compliment, saying that she needed to lose weight, or that there was something wrong with her hair and how it had been cut, colored, or styled.

From her perspective, she was being humble or gracious, but I could see the truth in her word choices. This powerful woman had incredibly poor self-esteem. She didn't believe herself worthy no matter how many promotions she received, how many people admired or complimented her. She always thought she wasn't good enough. It was tragic, and constantly held her back. She wouldn't step out and go after the things she really wanted because of that same low self-esteem. She also sowed seeds of doubt about herself with those who were trying to help and promote her. During my coaching call with Rachel, we identified how she had shaped her self-esteem with her own words. I encouraged her to join my 30-day *Word-Up* challenge where participants were required to practice using only positive, empowering, and uplifting words in their everyday interactions.

During this period, I shared my affirmation e-book with Rachel and encouraged her to physically confess the affirmations daily. After the challenge, Rachel continued the practice for 60 days. In the process, she began to build herself up with her own words. Her esteem improved tremendously, and it became noticeable to everyone around her. When I met Rachel for in-person coaching 45 days in, I gave her a compliment. This time, Rachel responded and said, "Thank you. I am really feeling more confident in myself these days."

Once she stopped contradicting all the people who complimented her, she started to listen more and take to heart the things people said about her. She used this feedback to build new, positive beliefs about herself and her work. This helped to bolster her self-esteem, and she started to value her own time and contributions more. She also began to look at what made her happy and was able to admit that the field she was in actually had nothing to do with her passion or her life's purpose. With the newfound self-esteem she adopted, she was able to quit her job and enroll in graduate school. Now she works in a field that she finds deeply fulfilling and can impact others' lives, teaching them to break their limiting beliefs and build new, empowering ones.

Beliefs can often be traced back to your education. I'm in a doctoral program and I still have concerns about formal education. Formal education is fantastic, but sometimes it can actually create limiting beliefs. Some truths you need to query and investigate. It can be as simple as having a bias against alumni of a rival school or can be more complex, such as favoring one way of doing something because a trusted teacher preferred it. Even the way things are done in school can create limiting beliefs about the way the world works.

Life's trials, challenges, and tribulations are not pre-announced. If you go to school and your professor says that he'll give a test in two weeks, you prepare. You get used to the idea that you know what's going to be thrown at you, and oftentimes even when. Life's tests are never pre-announced. They don't tell you that tomorrow you're going to lose your home or that next year there'll be a global pandemic. Life will always test your beliefs, that's why you need to be on top of your beliefs.

To move forward, you'll need to begin to examine your inherent biases. This is because you're most prone to accept information that you find agreeable. Things that make sense to you or place you in a flattering light can be easy to believe, even if they aren't true. You also can find that you sometimes have inherent bias regarding the topic based on the source. You're more likely to accept wisdom from a person with a fancy house and expensive cars than you are from a homeless man, regardless of the helpfulness or truth of that wisdom.

If a person is similar to you, the information you receive is more likely to be accepted—especially when they are the same race, gender, religious belief, profession, and culture as you. Since childhood, you're programmed to listen to and believe adults, particularly those in authority over you. When you start to search yourself to understand where your beliefs come from, you'll often find that you've picked up things and ideas from people of authority, professionals, doctors, teachers, and spiritual and political leaders. It's easy to just take whatever they say as truth. Sometimes these conclusions become limiting beliefs, and you realize that those authority figures are speaking out of their own biases and limiting beliefs.

Kari struggled in her new job for the first few days until she realized that she'd received an inherent bias from her family, particularly her mother. She believed that women didn't belong in the workplace and was embarrassed to admit it because she liked to think of herself as a modern woman, and the belief went against her perception of herself. She ended up sharing her struggle with her boss, Linda, who confided in her that she'd been told by several family members that a woman's job was in the home and not running a business. Kari was able to learn from Linda's experiences and to adopt new codes that helped her thrive at her new job.

In order to break a limiting belief, you must first identify it, then reject it. Sometimes you can do this all at once. Other times, it takes time to thoroughly reject and break the codes that you've been operating by. It's not enough just to destroy limiting beliefs, you need to also replace them with positive beliefs. For every lie you've believed you must now believe a truth. While you're building positive beliefs about yourself, it's important to take charge of your environment and physical space. It's yours and you can create what you want. Surround yourself with positivity, create an empowering environment, and let everything around you speak to you in a powerful, way.

Always attempt to focus on the positive side of things. Focus on your goals and everything that helps you expand your abilities or knowledge. Reach out to positive people. If you can't reach positive people you admire, read their books. Get materials that reinforce your new beliefs, or find a coach or a mentor to help.

It's easy to slip back into old beliefs. Constantly reinforce the new beliefs to minimize this risk. Practice positive verbal confessions and affirmations. I believe very strongly that what you confess with your mouth is more ingrained in your spirit. Embrace minimalization, decluttering, and detachment from material things. Focus instead on what's truly important and seek clarity and honesty. Finally, don't forget to pass on the positive beliefs you've embraced.

Also don't forget to pass on your positive beliefs. It's not okay for you to just be successful. Pass on your knowledge to future generations and help others get rid of their limiting beliefs. Lift up those around you and pass new, good codes on to your kids and grandkids so that those beliefs will exist long after you're gone. Share them around the dinner table. Talk about your belief system with your grandchildren. Turn them into family traditions and find ways to make them a part of your family life. Be the first counselor family members want to talk to when they need advice or have a problem.

Your beliefs are vitally important to you and those you teach them to. Beliefs aren't just intangible things—they're living and vital. Your beliefs are what drive and inform your actions. Beliefs are the foundation for behavior.

Chapter 3

Behavior

Behavior is your beliefs in action. Since beliefs inform behavior, if you hold a certain belief, you're most likely to behave in congruence with that belief. For example, if you believe that conflict is a bad thing and should be avoided, a corresponding behavior is that you don't like saying what's on your mind when someone offends you. This can cause several problems and lead to building feelings of anger and resentment that can ultimately destroy business and personal relationships. There are several behaviors successful people develop to stay at the top of their game. These include continuous learning, goal setting, time management, maintaining a positive attitude, and building a trustworthy network.

When you stop learning, regression is the most likely result. This is true for every aspect of your life, including your career, relationships, and aspects of your health and spirituality. Trends are always changing, and with the advancement in technology the whole world has become a small village, with the same resources available to you that are available to the entire world. The implication of this is that competition is higher. There are more people, fewer resources, and a lot more people scrambling for the same assets. This is the direct result of globalization. Competition has increased, and to keep up with changes, especially in technology, skills, expertise, and knowledge, you've got to keep learning. Successful people never say, "That's how we've always done it." Rather, they're constantly adapting and seeking to acquire new knowledge and skills, and to sharpen them.

If you don't know where you're going, how do you know how to get there? According to Dr. Gail Mathews' goals research, people who set goals tend to achieve more than those who don't. Goal setting helps you focus on your goal and not your road.[76] The road to success is full of potholes, and if you focus on the road, you get weary, discouraged, and often give up. That's why you must keep your head up and focus on the goal instead. The goal serves as your motivating factor and will keep you going. The end justifies the means in this regard.

Time is life. That means that time wasted equals life wasted. Take a moment to really think about that. It's a simple mathematical equation, but so powerful when you realize its impact on your life. This really puts the phrase *killing time* into stark perspective, as it's not just time that you're killing.

Successful people are adept at managing their time effectively. Time is a universal resource. Everyone gets the same amount of time in a day. It doesn't matter your age, gender, race, or anything else. Time is the great equalizer. Everyone has an equal amount of

76   Gail Matthews, "Goals Research Summary," Sonitrol, accessed June 20, 2021, https://braveheartsales.com/wp-content/uploads/Goals-Research-Summary.pdf?x60870.

it every day. Successful people understand the power of prioritization. They have also learned to delegate non-essential activities.

Keep in mind that every day will not be filled with sunshine. This is true no matter who you are. Successful people are not magically blessed with good things and easy lives. They suffer through trials, tribulations, setbacks, and tragedies just like everyone else. The difference is the attitude with which they approach difficult times. Successful people believe there's always a way to work through their problems. Even when they fail, having this attitude makes it so that failure doesn't feel like a loss. Instead, having a positive attitude helps them see the lessons in failure.

I have failed at a lot of things in my life. Just name it, and I've failed at it. From businesses to relationships and everything in between. However, today I earn a lot of money teaching people the lessons I learned from my mistakes and failures. And now I can boldly say that failing can be a source of income. Honestly, if I had known that I could make money from all my failures, I would have wished that I failed even more. Today, I teach people and guide them to a path that I only discovered because of my failures and the lessons I've learned.

Embrace failure instead of shrinking from it as if it's some terrible thing. I choose mentors based on this. A person has no value to add to my growth unless they've failed. People who've been successful all their lives have nothing to teach me. Those who have repeatedly fallen and then stood up again have a wealth of knowledge that they can share.

Having a bad attitude is like trying to drive a car with four flat tires—you won't be able to get anywhere. With a positive attitude, on the other hand, you'll know that even though life might have you on your back, you're going to stand up and hit back. If your attitude is right, you'll be back on your feet in no time. The right attitude says, "I may not be where I want to be, but I'm not where I used to be either. I will win. Maybe not today, but eventually."

I cannot overstress the value of building a network of trusted friends, partners, and contemporaries. These people can provide significant support for you on your journey. The road to success can be a very lonely one. A strong network can make the journey a little less lonely. A mentor can help you achieve your goals faster. If you're in the corporate world, you always need to find a corporate sponsor who speaks for you when you're not in the room. With your contemporaries, you can compare notes to see if their understanding of the current situation matches up with yours.

Every professional should make it a goal to create a board of trusted advisors who they can always go to. They can be people who've been on your path and succeeded, or people who have knowledge, experience, or influence that can be useful to you. That board should be filled with people from different fields who can each speak to something important in life. You want a variety of experts that can help you find balance. Negative behaviors stem from erroneous, negative beliefs. This bad code needs to be changed so that you may modify your behavior.

Bad behaviors keep you from maximizing your life. Some are limiting, some are self-sabotaging, and some are self-destructive. There are a lot of obvious ones that everyone can point to, such as substance abuse. Others, however, can be more subtle but no less insidious. In my book *Naked*, I mentioned that for a long time I didn't think men should cry. The culture that raised me was one that encouraged men to mask emotions. When I fell and bruised my leg as a child, I was told to *man up*, implying that strong boys don't cry. On the other hand, when my female cousins fell and bruised their legs, all the adults pampered them. So, I grew up believing that as a man, I needed to bottle my emotions, and I struggled to allow anyone see me in a vulnerable state. This lack of vulnerability and twisted perception of masculinity had a negative impact on my early relationships.

I was also taught to maintain peace and calm in the house. As the first child, it was my responsibility to ensure there was no fighting or ill-mannered behavior in a family of boys. That was definitely a tough task for a child 12 years of age. As I grew older, I became averse to conflict. I was the one who wanted everything to go smoothly, and made sure no one was upset with me, that everyone liked me, and that my relationships had a peaceful and calm environment. The combination of the belief that men don't cry and the perception that conflict is always a bad thing was a recipe for disaster in my young adult life. I would not take help from anyone, and I thought I was self-sufficient. I would avoid confrontation and conflict like a plague. Oftentimes, you can look to your erroneous beliefs and link those to behaviors that are based on bad beliefs.

It's important to get rid of the habits that are stunting your growth in every area of your life. Maybe your lack of preparation or constant tardiness have lost you business opportunities or even friendships. As I progressed in my career, it became imperative for me to manage cases of conflict in my role as a manager. I also had to give constructive criticism of the work presented to me as part of my work and had to deal with this limiting belief. In the beginning, I had to take baby steps, saying no more when I didn't have the bandwidth for certain requests.

Always take a look at your bad habits and know that everyone has them. As you look at yours, write them down on a piece of paper. Once you've identified them, ask yourself where they come from. What beliefs do you have that fuel these behaviors?

Ask yourself if these beliefs are true or if they're part of bad code you've received. For example, are you constantly hitting the snooze button in the morning instead of getting up with your alarm? You might discover that you believe that five, 10, or 15 minutes of sleep is helpful when you're tired. This is simply not true. Science has shown that hitting the snooze button throws off your entire wake/sleep cycle and that it can leave you groggy and rundown for hours.[77] So, once you know what the underlying faulty belief is, you can change it. Now you can say to yourself that it's better for you to wake up with the alarm instead of trying to get a few minutes of extra sleep.

Remember that it's not just enough to break bad habits, you must also build good ones. If it takes 30 days to break a habit, it takes 30 days to build a new habit to take its place. For instance, say you stopped the bad habit of hitting the snooze button. That's great, but you need to examine the state of things. When I realized how beautiful it felt when I first said no to someone, I wondered why I lived most of my younger life saying yes to everyone. Eventually, I began to feel more comfortable with saying no and embracing healthy conflict.

In the situation with the alarm clock, did you hit the snooze button because you're always tired and not getting enough sleep? This is an indication that you need to build a healthy habit of getting six to eight hours of sleep a night. Set a hard deadline for when you'll need to go to bed each night and stick to it. After making a conscious effort to break the belief that I need to bottle up my emotions, it was clear to me that I needed to embrace vulnerability and allow myself to feel and express certain emotions publicly. I remember the first day I cried publicly too. They were

---

77   Sarah Young, "Why hitting the snooze button can actually make you more tired," the *Independent*, November 3, 2016, https://www.independent.co.uk/life-style/health-and-families/sleep-tips-snooze-button-makes-you-more-tired-a7395476.html .

tears of joy, and the experience of letting tears roll down my cheeks was liberating.

It's helpful when trying to build habits to keep firmly in mind the belief behind it. Why is it an important or necessary habit? In the case of sleep, we understand that while everyone has their own biorhythm, an adult needs a reasonable amount of sleep a night.[78] It's also shown that no matter how much some people might enjoy being night owls, that it's better to get up early to find extra hours to work than it is to stay up late.[79]

New behavior should be consistently reinforced. Sometimes change can be easier and more effective if you change your environment or the people around you. However you plan on changing, you need to create a plan that helps you track your progress. Write down what your new code or belief is. Then tie the new habit to it as directly as possible. Set alarms for yourself, or put-up reminders on bathroom mirrors, refrigerators, or wherever you need to in order to be reminded of the new habit you're trying to integrate into your life.

Whether you surround yourself with a new environment, new people, or have to tough it out in your normal day-to-day life, it's important to give yourself time and support while changing habits. Make sure those around you are aware of and support the change you're trying to make. It does no good to swear off desserts if your spouse is constantly nagging you to split one with them. By letting others know what you're doing and why you're doing it, you give them the opportunity to help you, which can be invaluable.

---

78   "World's largest sleep study shows too much shut-eye can be bad for your brain," ScienceDaily, October 9, 2018, www.sciencedaily.com/releases/2018/10/181009135845.htm.

79   Peter Economy, "11 Reasons Why Early Birds Are Exceptionally Successful," Inc., April 23, 2015, https://www.inc.com/peter-economy/11-scientifically-proven-reasons-why-early-birds-are-exceptionally-successful.html.

With the right set of behaviors, success appears to be natural. When someone says, "You're a natural," what they're saying is that you have the right set of positive behaviors. Once you've succeeded in breaking bad habits and establishing good ones, don't forget to pass them on.

Chapter 4

Finding Balance

When your car's tires aren't properly balanced, the ride is much bumpier and can cause extra wear and tear on your vehicle, including premature wear. The same is true with life. When your life is out of balance, it makes everything more of a struggle, and can cause damage in every other area of your life.

People often speak of the work-life balance. When you're young, there's an especially strong temptation to ignore this, thinking that if you work hard, grueling hours now that somehow you can make up for it later. All you're really doing is establishing negative behaviors that will be difficult to change. This is also how you can quickly ruin your health, opening yourself up for injury and an early grave.

Of course, it's a bit more complex than that since you need to balance more than just work and life. There's this idea that family and leisure time is what the life part is. If you devote half your time to work and half your time to life, you're still going to be in trouble because you're trying to cram too much of the life thing into that small space. Instead, you need to have balance between work, health, relationships, spirituality, finances, and personal growth.

Everyone must find their own balance in this regard. If even one of these areas is out of balance or not getting the attention it deserves, it will throw off everything else. The longer you allow things to remain out of balance, the more damage it will do. For Kari, when her doctor told her that her life was out of balance, it was a wake-up call. It led to her re-engaging with her faith, getting a job that allowed her to still be there for her family, get in shape, and spread her wings in a way she never had before. At her next annual exam, the doctor noticed the improvements she had made. Her muscles were toned, she had lost a few pounds, and her blood pressure was lower. She thanked him for the tough conversation that set her on the path to improving her life and finding greater balance.

One of the things that can throw you off balance is your emotions. In order to lead a rich, fulfilling life, you need to be the master of your emotions. Start by using a fine-tooth comb to run through your emotions to help separate and distinguish them. Once you understand exactly what emotions you're having, you can regulate them more easily. If you have them all lumped up, it's too difficult to tell the difference. When you separate and identify them it helps to access more information that can help to better assess your behavior and manage the situation. Studies show that people who can separate their emotions are less likely to be under stress.[80]

---

80   Sonja Weilenmann et al, "Emotion Transfer, Emotion Regulation, and Empathy-Related Processes in Physician-Patient Interactions and Their Association with Physician Well-Being: A Theoretical Model," *Frontiers in Psychiatry* 9, no. 389 (2018), https://doi.org/10.3389/fpsyt.2018.00389.

Sometimes you have emotional responses that are out of proportion or inappropriate for the circumstances. This is often due to bad code that you've received. Some people get angry, embarrassed, or scared if a peer or superior offers a critique of their work. No one likes being criticized, but a genuine critique, offered with an eye to help improve you or your work shouldn't cause you to fly off the handle. It's offered in good faith for your benefit.

The problem is many people were raised with codes that tell them that failure of any kind is bad. They believe that if there's room for improvement that they let themselves or their team down. When parents are overly critical of their children, this can instill in them a sense of dread and cause intense negative emotions, which can keep them from being able to take the lesson and learn from it.

Do you believe failure is bad? Do you believe criticism comes from a place of anger or disappointment? Do you believe that if you have room to improve, then you should be embarrassed and feel like you are terrible at what you do? All of these are bad codes that need to be rewritten.

Once you've identified the bad code, you need to replace it with a good code. Learn that failure is a powerful tool. Those who want you to succeed will offer you honest critique and criticism. Having room to improve doesn't mean that you're inadequate or should be embarrassed by your efforts. Everyone has a different learning curve, and that's nothing to be ashamed of.

Personal growth is about balance. You need to be the master of your emotions, and there are several things that can help do this. The first step is to gain self-awareness. It's important to understand your emotions and how they may affect your decisions and other people around you. Know your strengths and weaknesses, as they are triggers. Knowing these triggers can help you better manage expectations and experience less disappointment. If you know your limits, your expectations will be clearer, and that reduces disappointment. Track your experiences and how they relate to your emotions. Journaling is always a good tool for this. When you're experiencing a strong emotion, examine the way you feel, take a break, and choose wisely.

People who do this effectively rarely engage in verbal attacks, stereotype other people, or compromise their values. It's all about control and self-regulation. While you can't always control what's happening around you, you can control your response. Learn to stay calm when facing challenging situations and know that your actions and reactions are 100% your responsibility.

Stay calm and practice deep breathing. Define your values and your personal code of ethics. When you do this, you can determine what values are important to you and what values you won't compromise on. This will serve as your guide when you're faced with difficult life situations. By doing this, you can also hold yourself accountable for your actions and responses.

Successful people don't feel entitled, and are, instead, self-motivated. They don't expect others to do for them. In order to understand your own motivation, you need to look within and find an internal source. Don't blame the world—focus on you. Why do you do what you do? What spurs you to achieve? When you have figured this out, use it to stay optimistic in the face of challenges.

Empathy is your ability to sympathize with others and to feel for them. This is the code that helps you feel sorrow for someone else's misfortune and drives you to help others who are experiencing trouble. One of the codes programmed into you as a child was social skills. Social skills are the currency you spend in society. You can get more out of society if you harness your social skills. Charismatic leaders are exceptional with social skills. With the advent of social media, social currency is becoming almost as valuable as financial currency.

Personal social skills are equally valuable to your career and relationships. Learn how to give compliments, improve your communication, and gain better conflict resolution skills. Your family, co-workers, employers, and friends will thank you for it.

As always, once you've achieved balance, learned the positive code, and disrupted the negative code, you need to pass it on to future generations. One of the most important things you can do for kids is to teach them to embrace failure instead of running from it. No one wants to fail, and kids are no exception. But treating it as natural, or even as a positive part of life, you will help them find lessons in their failures and provide a solid foundation. They need to build codes that accepts criticism and discovers what they can use from it.

Being in balance is a key to personal growth. It's also helpful when figuring out how to establish good boundaries. Boundaries are crucial in every area of life and are crucial for every relationship. Anything that tells you that boundaries are bad, needs to be rethought.

Avoid boundary traps by keeping an eye out for traps of emotion, time, energy, and values. These types of thoughts all fall into that category:

- I'm too heavy for anyone else to love.
- This is a little better than the last relationship.
- If I just give it a little more time, energy, and money it will get better.
- He or she depends on me for everything.

All these statements are meant to create feelings of inadequacy, guilt, futility, or false hope. If any of these statements resonate, then you need to take a serious look at your beliefs and why you feel this way. Once you've figured out the bad code, replace it with the good code. You are worthy, deserve good relationships, and don't have to settle for broken relationships that aren't working. You aren't responsible for someone else's life, only your own. This starts by giving yourself permission to set boundaries. More than that, you must understand that it's crucial to your mental, physical, and financial well-being that you do.

When you set standards and define your boundaries, you can hold other people accountable for their actions. This is just so other people's lack of preparation doesn't become your emergency. Access is one of the greatest assets you have. What's most powerful about access is that as an individual you can choose who you give access to. If you give someone access to yourself, you're giving them a gift. People need to recognize that access is a gift. Boundaries protect the core of your being. Lack of boundaries are an indication of disrespect.

Suicide rates lower in December,[81] but homicide rates are higher during major holidays, usually between Thanksgiving and New Year's. This relates to more frequent complaints about family and household disturbances being higher during major holidays, and is a clear indication that the challenges of family dynamics can often be overwhelming. It's important to set healthy boundaries during intense family time to maintain your family relationships.

Setting healthy boundaries is crucial to building healthy relationships. It's also crucial to improving self-esteem and reduce stress and anxiety. When you don't have boundaries, you let everyone else determine your needs, emotions, and desires, allowing others to control you. Boundaries ensure that you're in charge, and

---

81   Marc Shapiro, "Suicide Rates Spike in Spring, Not Winter," John Hopkins Medicine, May 8, 2019, https://www.hopkinsmedicine.org/news/articles/suicide-rates-spike-in-spring-not-winter.

can be emotional, physical (your body or your personal space), privacy related, or time protectors.

Some people are toxic, while others are manipulative and can drain you emotionally. Emotional boundaries include separating your feelings from other people's. It means holding them at arm's length and refusing to engage in their negative talk, pity parties, gossip, or cave to their guilt trips. Sometimes this means that you won't feel as close to someone as you have in the past. Think about it. Anyone who is exhibiting these negative emotions and inflicting them on you is not necessarily someone you want to be close to. You can limit the time you spend with these people and be firm about what you will and will not talk about with them. Reinforce these boundaries gently but firmly by disengaging when they break the rules.

Don't forget that you're allowed to have your own personal space and keep people from invading it. You're also allowed to decide how much touching and of what type you will accept from people. It doesn't matter if everyone thinks creepy cousin Joe is harmless—you don't have to let him hug you if you don't want to. In fact, you don't even have to have him in your house. If other people think they can't have Thanksgiving without him, then they can host at their house.

It's also your right to decide what you will and will not discuss with other people. This includes information about your kids, finances, marriage, even where you live. Anyone who can't respect or doesn't respect you, doesn't need to be in your life.

When it comes to your time, overstepping these boundaries can perhaps be the most insidious. Everyone wants a little piece of your time, and it feels good to help when you can. There's an old joke that if you have a truck, everyone you know will eventually ask you to help them move. And because they're a good friend, neighbor, relative, coworker, or cousin of someone's roommate twice removed, you're expected to drop everything and do it even if that means that you've lost every weekend in the year to doing stuff for other people.

Children start life with no boundaries, which can be very sweet. However, it's incumbent on you to teach them the value of good boundaries and provide them the code that lets them know they don't have to agree to do what their friends want them to do. This can be a bit tricky because you also need to let them know that setting boundaries doesn't give them the right to disobey authority figures such as parents and teachers just because they feel like it. You can teach them, though, how to stand by their principles and withstand peer pressure, which is an early form of manipulation and boundary erosion practiced by kids on each other.

Chapter 5

Enjoying Bliss

The last thing you need is bliss. Bliss is about basking in the abundance of happiness, joy, and grace. This is when you are living life to the fullest and living in the moment. This is also about capturing moments and making memories, which is an important aspect of life.

In this busy, fragmented world, so many things can get in the way of you living life in the moment. There are a thousand demands on your time, all of which seem important. Perhaps the number one thing you can do for yourself is to break free of your addiction to all things digital. Digital minimalizing and giving yourself a break from digital life is crucial. Bliss is about being in the moment and capturing it, but you can't do that if you're attached to digital devices and things like social media all the time. Once in a while, learn to totally declutter your digital life.

So many people are overdependent that they deny opportunities of being in the moment, enjoying the moment, and capturing important memories. An example of this is trying to take photos when you should be enjoying the experience of where you're at. To enhance bliss, you need to reduce dependency on digital devices and digital life. This will allow you to enjoy vacations and your time with family better and be more fulfilled by the moment.

Primarily, what you need to do is practice self-love and self-care. Self-care is not vanity—it's an expression of sanity. You have to be sane to know that you need to love other people, and yourself. Throwing yourself some love helps you maintain your sanity. It's the blanket you need to survive the cold world we live in.

Practice gratitude as well. Gratitude is what turns a plate of food into a feast. It's what turns a neighbor into family, and a bed into a good night's sleep. It's all about perspective. When you have the perspective of gratitude what's little becomes plentiful. Focus on what you have and enjoy and not what you don't have. Ultimately, it's not about the bigger, better houses, cars, and vacations. It's all about the little things that really matter.

I hear so many people complain that their kids are constantly on their phones and not connecting with people, especially with family. While smart phones have changed the way you experience technology, this problem isn't new. Previous generations were glued to their computer monitors and their TV screens.

Remember, kids learn what you model for them. How often are you 100% attentive to your children, particularly when they're younger and most impressionable? It seems like there's always other things vying for your time, such as work, friends, or your own desire to veg out in whatever form that takes. Demonstrate to your kids gratitude for family and the time you have together by setting the example. You do this by putting away your phone, turning off the television, and ignoring your computer. Spend time together talking, sharing a hobby, or playing a game. This is how you teach kids that actual life has something to offer that virtual life doesn't.

Turn to the workbook section at the back of the book, page 435, for your reflection exercises to help you commit to action.

PART 10:

DO THE WORK: WORKBOOK QUESTIONS

Part 1

Summary and Questions

1. What do you consider to be the most important lessons (right, wrong, good, or bad) that your parents (or other caregivers) taught you?

_____

_____

_____

2. When was the first time you experienced something that made you wonder if something your parents, guardians, or a teacher had taught you was wrong?

_____

_____

_____

3. What was your reaction?

_____

_____

_____

4. What did you ultimately do about it?

_____

_____

_____

5. Do you have beliefs or habits that you already know are holding you back from achieving something you want to achieve? If so, what are they?

_____

_____

_____

6. Are you ready to do something about those?

_____

_____

_____

7. Do you feel that what you were taught as a child has helped or hindered you on your journey?

_____

_____

8. What have you done, if anything, to overcome the bad codes you might have been programmed with?

_____

_____

_____

9. If you're in the *afternoon stage*, are you prepared for the *night stage* or are you hoping that it will take care of itself when the time comes?

_____

_____

_____

10. If you haven't prepared, is there something you can do to change that? What would it take?

_____

_____

_____

11. If you are in the *night stage*, what are you doing to teach subsequent generations? Do you feel you're making an impact? What more should you be doing?

_____

_____

_____

Part 2

Summary and Questions

1. Do you already have an idea what your purpose might be? It's ok to say no, but if you have an idea, write it down.

_____

_____

_____

2. Can you describe this purpose in a few words?

_____

_____

_____

3. What kind of activities or causes drew your attention as a child?

_____

_____

4. Is there a common pattern for things you voluntarily did as a child, particularly if they involved other people?

_____

_____

_____

5. Have others pointed out that you're gifted at something or come to you consistently for help in specific areas? What areas are these?

_____

_____

_____

6. At the end of your life, what is it you would like to have accomplished or be remembered for?

_____

_____

_____

The Role of Passion

1. What are some things that you're passionate about?

_____

_____

_____

2. If you think about it, do you see a common thread?

_____

_____

_____

3. Can you take your passion and channel it to serve a higher purpose?

_____

_____

_____

The Need for a Platform

1. Do you already have a platform?

_____

_____

_____

2. Is there an existing platform that you can use?

_____

_____

_____

_____

_____

3. If not, what would it take for you to create one?

_____

_____

_____

The Importance of People

1. Who are the people who have gotten you to where you are now?

_____

_____

_____

2. What did they do for you?

_____

_____

_____

3. What more can they help you to accomplish?

_____

_____

_____

4. Do you have at least one mentor?

_____

_____

If so, are you using them to the fullest?

_____

_____

If not, how can you get more out of the relationship?

_____

_____

Name three areas of your life where you could use a mentor and don't have one. Now, name a few people who would be good mentors in this area. The sky is the limit. They don't even have to be people you know.

1. How could you reach out to the above people?

_____

_____

2. What are the potential benefits of contacting these people?

_____

_____

3. What are the potential risks?

_____

_____

4. What are you waiting for?

_____

_____

_____

Your Codes and Your Purpose

Like every area of your life, bad codes can hold you back when you're trying to fulfill your purpose. For example, you might think your purpose is to revolutionize a certain industry, but you could have codes that tell you that it's never good to be too ambitious or that trying to do something grandiose always ends in failure. You might even have codes that make you think that someone of your age, gender, background, status, or even race doesn't belong in the industry you want to revolutionize. Those codes need to be replaced with good codes that tell you that you can do and be anything you want.

1. Do you feel like elements of your upbringing or the beliefs that were programmed into you by family or teachers are holding you back from your purpose?

_____

_____

_____

If so, what are these codes, erroneous beliefs, or bad habits?

_____

_____

_____

2. What step can you take today to start to change those?

_____

_____

_____

3. Are you ready to look at your life and figure out what needs to be fixed?

_____

_____

_____

4. Do you have a clear idea in your ahead of your purpose and the goals you want to achieve on your journey?

_____

_____

_____

5. What are you currently doing to fulfill your purpose?

_____

_____

_____

6. What small step can you make today or this week to bring yourself more fully into alignment with your purpose?

_____

_____

7. Is there any area of your life that you can think of just off the top of your head that's not in alignment with your purpose?

_____

_____

_____

8. Why do you think this is?

_____

_____

_____

9. Are there negative codes holding you back?

_____

_____

_____

10. What can you do about it?

_____

_____

_____

_____

_____

Part 3

Summary and Questions

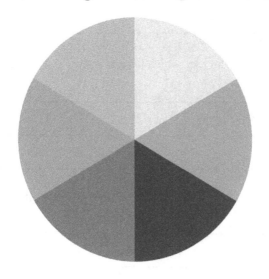

- Career & Business
- Personal Growth & Development
- Finances
- Spirituality
- Relationships
- Health & Wellness

1. After glancing at the wheel, do you already have an idea which areas you pay more attention to?

_____

_____

_____

2. Are you satisfied with where most of your time, energy, and attention is going?

_____

_____

_____

3. Do you have an idea which is your biggest problem area?

_____

_____

_____

4. Why do you think that area is causing you difficulty?

_____

_____

_____

_____

_____

5. Briefly can you think of at least one way you're contributing to your family, community, or society in each of those areas?

_____

_____

_____

6. How out of balance do you think your wheel is right now?

_____

_____

_____

7. Where do you think your biggest growth opportunities are?

_____

_____

_____

8. Do you already have a clear vision of where you want to be in each of those areas of your life?

_____

_____

_____

_____

_____

CRACKING THE LIFE CODE

9. Do you already know that you have some bad codes that are causing bad habits, beliefs, or actions involving one or more areas of your life?

_____

_____

_____

Your Codes and the Wheel

Of course, each of these areas of your life are affected by your life codes, both the ones you were programmed with and the ones you acquired along the line. Oftentimes, it's these bad codes that get in the way. Bad codes tell you things like, "I'll rest when I'm dead," and "There'll be time to think about family, retirement, or health later," or "I don't need to learn anything new to accomplish what I want."

In order to live life to its fullest and be your best, you need to pay attention to all these areas. It doesn't work to say you'll focus on a couple now and get around to the others. Whether it's one year or one day, being out of balance hurts your life and gets in the way of you fulfilling your purpose.

1. What are your beliefs or behaviors (both good and bad) in relation to career and business?

_____

_____

_____

_____

_____

2. Where do these come from?

_____

_____

_____

3. Do you feel like any of these are holding you back?

_____

_____

_____

If so, what might be a better code to replace it with?

_____

_____

_____

4. What are your beliefs/behaviors (both good and bad) in relation to health and wellness?

_____

_____

_____

5. Where do these come from?

_____

_____

_____

6. Do you feel like any of these are holding you back?

_____

_____

_____

If so, what might be a better code to replace it with?

_____

_____

7. What are your beliefs and behaviors (both good and bad) in relation to your finances?

_____

_____

_____

8. Where do these come from?

_____

_____

_____

9. Do you feel like any of these are holding you back?

_____

_____

If so, what might be a better code to replace it with?

_____

_____

_____

10. What are your beliefs and behaviors (both good and bad) in relation to relationships?

_____

_____

_____

11. Where do these come from?

_____

_____

_____

12. Do you feel like any of these are holding you back?

_____

_____

_____

13. If so, what might be a better code to replace it with?

_____

_____

_____

14. What are your beliefs and behaviors (both good and bad) in relation to spirituality?

_____

_____

_____

15. Where do these come from?

_____

_____

_____

16. Do you feel like any of these are holding you back?

_____

_____

If so, what might be a better code to replace it with?

_____

_____

_____

17. What are your beliefs/behaviors (both good and bad) in relation to personal growth and development?

_____

_____

_____

18. Where do these come from?

_____

_____

_____

19. Do you feel like any of these are holding you back?

_____

_____

_____

20. If so, what might be a better code to replace it with?

_____

_____

The Importance of Self-Assessment

For every area on the wheel, you need to routinely sit down and take stock. What are you happy with? What are you unhappy with? What steps do you need to take to change that?

While these are six separate areas of your life that you need to examine, don't think that they're completely unrelated to each other. All the spokes on the wheel are interconnected. You change one and it will impact the others in some way.

As you begin to improve one area of your life it can lead to discoveries about other areas. You might have thought that your romantic relationship was a problem because you don't see eye-to-eye with your partner. You might find as you more closely examine your relationship that the only thing you really don't see eye-to-eye on is money because your finances are a disaster. Fix the finances and it might help fix problems with the relationship.

If you find that you're having problems keeping up with your work, look at your health habits. It could be that you're not getting enough sleep and that's making it hard for you to stay focused and sharp at work. Or perhaps you need to get more exercise, which helps build endurance and in general makes you more energetic overall. It could be that constant fights with your spouse could also be keeping you up and affecting your sleep, therefore negatively impacting the quality or quantity of your work.

While it's important to do an assessment on each part of the wheel, realize that you might not truly understand what the root problems are until you start pushing that wheel and making changes, even tiny ones. Then you'll see how everything in your wheel is working together (or not)!

When doing an assessment on your life, it's important to evaluate each area in terms of Satisfaction, Contribution, and Growth Potential. Have the courage to be honest with yourself here. There is no reason to feel guilty about your answers. You can't begin to fix what's out of balance in your life until you're ready to face the truth of what is and isn't working for you.

1. In terms of Career and Business, how would you rate your:

- Satisfaction: _____

- Contribution: _____

- Growth Potential: _____

2. What would you say is the single best part of your life in this area?

_____

_____

_____

3. What is the part of your life that you would change first in this area if you could?

_____

_____

_____

4. In terms of health and wellness, how would you rate your:

   • Satisfaction: _____

   • Contribution: _____

   • Growth Potential: _____

5. What would you say is the single best part of your life in this area?

_____

_____

_____

6. What is the part of your life that you would change first in this area if you could?

_____

_____

7. In terms of finances, how would you rate your:

- Satisfaction: _____

- Contribution: _____

- Growth Potential: _____

8. What would you say is the single best part of your life in this area?

_____

_____

_____

9. What's the part of your life that you would change first in this area if you could?

_____

_____

_____

10. In terms of relationships, how would you rate your:

- Satisfaction: _____

- Contribution: _____

- Growth Potential: _____

11. What would you say is the single best part of your life in this area?

_____

_____

12. What is the part of your life that you would change first in this area if you could?

_____

_____

_____

13. In terms of spirituality, how would you rate your:

- Satisfaction: _____

- Contribution: _____

- Growth Potential: _____

14. What would you say is the single best part of your life in this area?

_____

_____

_____

15. What is the part of your life that you would change first in this area if you could?

_____

_____

_____

_____

_____

16. In terms of personal growth and development, how would you rate your:

- Satisfaction: _____

- Contribution: _____

- Growth Potential: _____

17. What would you say is the single best part of your life in this area?

_____

_____

18. What's the part of your life that you would change first in this area if you could?

_____

_____

19. What one small change could you make today or this week in each area of your life to increase your satisfaction, contribution, or growth potential?

- Career & Business:

- Health & Wellness:

- Finances:

- Relationships:

- Spirituality:

- Personal Growth & Development:

Part 4

Summary and Questions

There's a difference between a career and a business. Your career is a job you work at. In your career you are part of a bigger picture. You're building a career that has hundreds of thousands of other people working toward a shared goal. You're contributing to a pool in a professional space. You usually make money at your career, but it's possible to have a career you don't generate income from.

Your business, on the other hand, is the platform you build for other people to contribute to. You lead with the vision and are responsible for building the groundwork of the platform and directing the affairs of the vision. Business is about income, product, services, and flow of cash within the supply and demand space.

Satisfaction

1. On a scale of 1 to 10, with 10 being blissfully happy, how satisfied are you with your job?

_____

_____

_____

2. *Code Question*: What did you learn when you were a child about work? Should it make you happy or miserable? Did you learn that you stay no matter how much you don't like it or that it's okay to change jobs or even entire careers?

_____

_____

_____

3. How satisfied are you with your relationship with your boss?

_____

_____

_____

4. *Code Question*: What did you learn from your parents about bosses? Are they to be trusted or mistrusted? Are they friends or foes?

_____

_____

5. How well do you get along with your coworkers? Are there any you have trouble working with or personally dislike?

_____

_____

_____

6. *Code Question*: Do you believe you are a people person? Did your parents enjoy working with others or prefer working alone?

_____

_____

_____

   If you weren't being paid, would you still do this job?

_____

_____

_____

7. How would that affect your satisfaction level?

_____

_____

_____

_____

_____

_____

8. *Code Question*: Is money the only reason to work or do anything?

_____

_____

_____

9. What aspects of your job make you give it the satisfaction rating that you did?

_____

_____

_____

10. What are the top three problems with your job as you see it?

_____

_____

11. Code Question: When looking at these problems, what beliefs/codes do you have regarding these types of issues?

_____

_____

_____

_____

_____

12. Would fixing or improving these issues increase your level of satisfaction?

_____

_____

_____

13. Is it within your power to resolve these three problems?

_____

_____

_____

14. *Code Question*: Did your parents instill in you a sense of empowerment or make you feel that nothing ever changes and trying to change things will just get you grief?

_____

_____

If not, who does have the power to resolve these three problems?

_____

_____

15. Do you foresee a way in which you could discuss these problems with that individual and get a satisfactory resolution?

_____

_____

16. *Code Question*: What are your codes/beliefs about conflict?

_____

_____

_____

17. One year from now do you think you will be more or less satisfied with the job than you are right now? Why or why not?

_____

_____

_____

18. How does this job compliment or detract from your own self-image?

_____

_____

_____

19. *Code Question*: Are there elements of your self-image that are based on bad codes/information told you by others?

_____

_____

_____

20. Is this job in any way aligned with your purpose?

_____

_____

21. Does this job give you any skills or tools you need to fulfill your greater purpose?

_____

_____

_____

22. Are there any additional skills that you could learn at this job?

_____

_____

_____

Contribution

Some people are looking to change the world, some want to just make a valuable contribution even if it's on a small scale. Which are you?

1. *Code Question*: Were you taught that you could change the world or were you taught that change is hard and that you can't really impact more than just your own family?

_____

_____

_____

2. Do you feel that the job you do contributes to the well-being of your family in a significant way?

_____

_____

_____

CRACKING THE LIFE CODE

3. Does it contribute to the well-being of the company?

_____

_____

_____

4. Does it contribute to the well-being of society?

_____

_____

_____

5. *Code Question*: Were you taught to care about society or to just look out for yourself or your immediate family?

_____

_____

_____

6. Is there a way you could make a greater contribution while still working at this same job?

_____

_____

_____

7. *Code Question*: Were you taught to give 110% or to just do enough to get by?

_____

8. If you don't feel that you are making a significant contribution with your work, is there something you can change with what you're doing in the job to impact that?

_____

_____

_____

Growth Opportunity

1. How long have you been working at this job?

_____

_____

_____

2. *Code Question*: How long do you think people should work at the same job?

_____

_____

_____

3. How much growth have you experienced in that time?

_____

_____

_____

_____

_____

4. *Code Question.* Do you believe you should learn and grow from your job or just put in your time?

_____

_____

_____

5. Is it more or less than you anticipated?

_____

_____

_____

6. If it's less, is there a reason for this?

_____

_____

_____

7. Are there opportunities for growth in the job within the next one to three years?

_____

_____

_____

8. *Code Question*: How ambitious were those adults you were around as a child? How has that impacted you?

_____

_____

_____

9. Are those opportunities automatic or will you have to work for them?

_____

_____

_____

10. *Code Question*: Did your parents work hard for things, or did they expect them to be handed to them?

_____

_____

_____

11. Are there new skills you need to acquire in order to advance farther in your career?

_____

_____

_____

12. *Code Question*: What codes do you have about learning new things?

_____

_____

_____

13. Where is it you would like to be in five years? Ten? Fifteen?

_____

_____

_____

14. Can you get there from where you are now?

_____

_____

15. What would you have to change in order to get there more easily or faster?

_____

_____

_____

Which Way from Here?

Look at the answers specifically to the *Code Questions*. Are there any bad codes you can detect that might be negatively affecting your career or business?

1. What would happen if you changed those codes? How do you think your other self-assessment answers would change (or not)?

_____

_____

_____

2. Looking at the path you're on now, what's the next career opportunity available to you? (This could be a promotion, an opportunity to transfer to a different department, or anything that will represent a change.)

_____

_____

_____

3. Do you take that opportunity?

_____

_____

_____

If yes, where will that lead you five years from now? Ten?

_____

_____

_____

_____

_____

If no, what's the alternative path you might choose?

_____

_____

_____

4. Where will that lead you in five years? Ten?

_____

_____

_____

5. Look at where you want to be in 10 years. Is the path from where you are now to where you want to go clear? Can you travel that path while staying at the same job?

_____

_____

_____

If yes, are there any additional skills you need to learn?

_____

_____

_____

If no, what would be a step you would need to make now in order to put yourself on the path to where you want to go?

_____

_____

What will happen next if you take this step?

_____

_____

_____

What will happen next if you don't?

_____

_____

_____

_____

_____

_____

Part 5

Summary and Questions

1. What shape is your body in?

_____

_____

_____

2. How satisfied are you with that?

_____

_____

_____

3. What shape is your mind in?

_____

_____

4. How satisfied are you with that?

_____

_____

_____

5. Is there a way you can get your mind or body into better shape?

_____

_____

_____

6. What are the growth opportunities for your physical health? Your mental health?

_____

_____

_____

Mindfulness

If you've ever played around with one of those fitness trackers, you've likely heard about mindfulness. Mindfulness is being in the present moment and aware of your body, your thoughts, and emotions—all without casting judgment on them. These days that can be hard to do. Learn the importance of unplugging and be intentional about taking a break. Sometimes you need to turn off your phone and make time for hobbies, interests, and even just to sit and focus on nothing, letting your body and mind relax and get in tune. It sounds easy, but it can be a challenge, especially in the modern business world. Your mind is constantly running to the next meeting, the next call, what you'll do tomorrow or next week or next year. It's easy to spend so much time focusing on the future that you miss out on the present.

When you're not mindful, there are several unpleasant consequences. First, you might miss out on signals your body is giving you that something is wrong and needs attending to. Second, you can be so fixated on other things that you miss being in the moment and enjoying time with family and friends. Third, you can miss out on creative breakthroughs because you're not focused and paying attention.

1. How much time would you say you spend in the moment as opposed to thinking about the future or the past?

---

2. Do you spend some time each day being mindful?

Why or why not?

---

3. Do you ever find yourself zoning out and missing conversations?

_____

_____

_____

4. Have you ever tried meditation or journaling to focus, relax, or be more mindful?

_____

_____

_____

How did it go?

_____

_____

_____

5. *Code Question*: What are the beliefs that were instilled in you about meditation and journaling? Do you see them as helpful? A load of hooey? Girly? Or do you see them as vital tools for everyone?

_____

_____

_____

_____

6. Could you set aside 20 minutes a day to mediate or journal?

_____

_____

_____

7. What benefits would there be if you were able to focus more, stay more in the moment, and organize your thoughts?

_____

_____

_____

8. Try this experiment. Either meditate (there are several apps that can help with this) or write in a journal for 20 minutes every day for two weeks. When you're done, take note of what you noticed about the experience and any differences between the first day and the last.

_____

_____

_____

Rest and Relaxation

Every living creature needs time to let the body and mind rest in order to recharge. When the human body gets the rest it requires, it improves your mood, eases stress, lowers your risk for serious health problems, allows you to get along better with others, and enhances your ability to think clearly and make good decisions.

While few people could argue against the mountain of evidence about how much sleep is required, many people still ignore the fact that the mind needs just as much opportunity to rest as the body does. While the mind does rest some at night, it is also still busy processing data from the day before and preparing you for the day ahead. So, while the body might be at rest for seven hours, the mind is not. The mind requires something more, relaxation.

1. How much uninterrupted sleep do you get at night?

_____

_____

_____

2. Do you feel that's enough? Do you awake refreshed?

_____

_____

_____

3. Do you make time every day for relaxation? Every week? Every year?

_____

_____

_____

_____

_____

4. When was the last time you took a vacation and really unplugged?

_____

_____

_____

How did you feel during and after?

_____

_____

_____

5. What is your dream vacation?

_____

_____

_____

How can you make that happen within the next year?

_____

_____

_____

What do you think the benefits of this would be?

_____

_____

_____

6. Do you routinely do new and stimulating things? Why or why not?

_____

_____

_____

7. Do you feel like you're going through the motions a lot? Does your brain check out when doing routine tasks, such as driving to home or the office?

_____

_____

_____

8. What can you do differently to keep your brain stimulated?

_____

_____

_____

Exercise

It's important to get your heart pumping and your muscles moving. This continues to keep your body strong, limber, and healthy. You know that old saying, use it or lose it? The same is true with your muscles and your mind. Doing so brings fresh supplies of oxygen to your blood which carries it to all your muscles, including your mind. Human bodies weren't designed to sit in a chair all day. They were designed to be up, moving. If you don't get a certain amount of exercise, it becomes harder for you to move your joints and to keep all your organs in top shape. Stretching, strength training, and cardio exercises all play a part in keeping you strong and healthy.

1. Do you exercise each day?

_____

_____

_____

2. How much and what types of exercise do you get in a week?

_____

_____

_____

Do you feel this is sufficient?

_____

_____

_____

How could you benefit from new or more exercise in your routine?

_____

_____

_____

_____

_____

Eating Right

You need to take control of what you eat. Nutrition is an important element in keeping your body going. It's important to be mindful of what you're eating, how much you're eating, and when you're eating. You should take care to know what's in your food, choose based on nutrition not convenience, learn how your body interacts with foods, particularly if you have any allergies, and drink plenty of water. Doing this can have a huge impact on your health.

1. Do you eat healthy meals?

_____

_____

_____

2. If you had to, could you name every ingredient that went into what you ate for your last three meals?

_____

_____

_____

3. Do you eat processed food?

_____

_____

_____

4. Do you eat at regular intervals at predictable times?

_____

_____

_____

5. Do you actively choose what you're going to eat, or do you eat whatever presents itself at the moment?

_____

_____

_____

6. Are there healthier choices you can make when eating during work hours? Are there better restaurants, smarter menu items, or do you can bring your own lunch?

_____

_____

_____

7. *Code Question*: How were you raised to feel about food? Did the source of your meals matter? Was fast food a staple of your diet? Were meals ever homecooked or always acquired from a restaurant? Were there any unhealthy eating choices you learned when you were young?

_____

_____

8. How would breaking any bad codes you received improve your health, well-being, or finances?

_____

_____

_____

What beliefs about food are holding you captive?

_____

_____

_____

9. Do you have any health issues that could be addressed or helped by changing your diet?

_____

_____

_____

10. Do you drink 64 ounces of water a day?

_____

_____

_____

11. How many times a day are you dehydrating your body with caffeinated drinks?

_____

_____

12. Do you know what food allergies or food intolerances you might have?

_____

_____

_____

13. Do you have access to healthy snacking choices? If not, how can you change this?

_____

_____

_____

14. Do you eat at regular intervals at predictable times of day to help your body keep blood sugar under control?

_____

_____

_____

If not, what can you do to change this?

_____

_____

_____

15. Are you mindful about what you eat, trying to engage all your senses in the experience?

_____

_____

16. Run an experiment. Spend two weeks reading labels, making healthy choices, preparing your own food when you can, limiting your caffeine, increasing your water intake, and eating at regular intervals. Note any differences in how you look or feel, physically or mentally, during those two weeks and after.

_____

_____

_____

Which Way Element: If This, Then That

1. Imagine that you've read the labels to all the food products that you eat in a week. The list includes a dozen chemicals you can't even pronounce, preservatives, and food coloring. Do you eat it anyway?

_____

_____

If yes, what do you think will eventually happen?

_____

_____

If no, what might you eat instead that would be healthier?

_____

_____

_____

2. If you exercised every day, what do you think would happen to your body?

_____

_____

_____

Would this be a desirable result?

_____

_____

_____

Which do you choose, to exercise or to not exercise?

_____

_____

_____

Part 6

Summary and Questions

1. Are you satisfied with your current capacity to make money?

_____

_____

_____

2. How can you increase this capacity? Can you increase your skills, add a new skill, or create a new income stream?

_____

_____

_____

_____

_____

3. Spend a few minutes thinking about how you can repurpose your skills and create a new income stream.

_____

_____

_____

Can you start a consulting or freelancing business?

_____

_____

Can you write a book or give seminars on your area of expertise?

_____

_____

Is there a way to use those skills to make money some other way?

_____

_____

What platform would you need? Does it exist or could you create it?

_____

_____

_____

What new skill could you add that would be a benefit to you or your current employer?

_____

_____

_____

What would it take to acquire that skill?

_____

_____

_____

Can you get your employer to pay for additional education or training?

_____

_____

_____

What small step could you take today to start to increase your capacity?

_____

_____

_____

4. *Code Question*: How did your parents treat money and their capacity to make it? Were they always learning, always trying to advance themselves or did they stay in the same job not advancing much for most of their career? Did they instill in you a desire to constantly strive to be better or to just put in your

40 hours and not complain too loudly? Did they value education and risk taking or not? What beliefs/behaviors do you have when it comes to making money and for striving to increase how much you can make?

_____

_____

How have those beliefs helped or hindered you in your capacity to make money?

_____

_____

_____

5. Does the amount of money you make allow you to give back?

_____

_____

If not, how much would you need to make in order to do so?

_____

_____

Can you contribute time, knowledge, or skill to your community instead?

_____

_____

Is there a way to give back to your community while at the same time increasing your capacity (getting more depth or breadth of experience or starting a new venture)?

_____

_____

6. *Code Question*: Did your parents, guardians, or teachers believe in giving back to the community through charitable giving, tithing, or community service? What beliefs did they instill in you about this?

_____

_____

_____

How have those beliefs helped or hindered you?

_____

_____

_____

7. Is there room for growth in how you're currently making money? Can you get a promotion in your current organization?

_____

_____

_____

If not, is there a rival company who might pay more for your skills?

_____

_____

If not, is there a particular skill you can learn to make you more valuable to your current employer or to future ones?

_____

_____

8. *Code Question*: Did the adults in your life know when you were growing up to instill codes that told you to stick with one company and be loyal to them no matter what? Or did they instill in your codes to follow opportunities?

_____

_____

_____

9. How has what you learned as a kid helped or hindered you?

_____

_____

_____

Managing Money

As you progress through the afternoon phase of your life, you need to move from making to managing money. Managing money means making sure that you're covering all your monthly expenses so that you're not falling into the trap of getting farther and farther behind with credit card and other types of bad debt. More than that, though, managing money means planning for the future and the unexpected expenses of the present. It's crucial to have a budget and be intentional about what you're spending.

10. Are you satisfied with the way you are managing money?

\
\
\

11. Do you have a weekly, monthly, and yearly budget?

\
\
\

If so, how closely do you stick to it?

\
\
\

Do you consider money to be held for emergencies?

\
\
\

12. Do you know where every dollar goes?

_____

_____

_____

13. Have you ever run out of money before the end of the month?

_____

_____

_____

If so, how would it feel to never have to worry about that again?

_____

_____

_____

14. Have you ever bought something on impulse that you didn't really need?

_____

_____

_____

15. How much money are you losing in interest every year to credit cards, personal loans, student loans, car loans, etc.? Take the time to add it all up.

_____

_____

What could you do with that money if you weren't wasting it on interest fees?

_____

_____

_____

16. How much money are you losing a year in transactional fees, late fees, overdraft charges, foreign ATM fees, etc.? Take the time to add it all up.

_____

_____

_____

What could you do with that money if it weren't being wasted?

_____

_____

_____

17. Do you actively look for coupons and discounts, particularly when buying larger ticket items?

_____

_____

_____

_____

_____

18. Can you name right now every subscription service that you have that automatically bills you every month whether or not you're actively using it?

_____

_____

_____

19. *Code Question*: How will did your parents, grandparents, or other caregivers manage money? What did you learn from them about that?

_____

_____

_____

Have those codes helped you or hindered you? What do you need to change?

_____

_____

_____

20. What step can you take today to start eliminating waste from your budget?

_____

_____

_____

21. What step can you take today to become more intentional about your spending?

_____

_____

_____

Multiplying Money

The key to financial freedom, to really getting your money to work for you, is multiplying it. So many people spend their lives working hard, saving what little they can, and hope and pray that it's enough to get them through the nighttime of life. There's just one problem with that. You have no idea what your night is going to look like.

You don't want to spend the last part of your life worrying about money. You don't want to have to count your pennies, tell your grandchild you can't buy them a bike, or think about having to sell your house just to pay bills. If you want to live comfortably and enjoy the nighttime, you need to have more than just a fixed amount of money in the bank. You need your money to be renewing itself. This is about investing, whether it's in mutual funds, real estate, or other businesses.

1. Are you satisfied with your multiplication plan?

_____

_____

_____

_____

_____

CRACKING THE LIFE CODE

2. What does your ideal retirement life look like?

_____

_____

_____

How much will that cost?

_____

_____

Can your current multiplication plan ensure that you get to have this life?

_____

_____

_____

3. *Code Question*: How did your parents treat investing?

_____

_____

_____

4. *Code Question*: Were your parents or grandparents able to live comfortably after retiring?

_____

_____

_____

5. *Code Question*: What were your takeaways from watching the adults in your life when it comes to saving and investing for the future?

_____

_____

_____

6. How has this helped or hindered you?

_____

_____

_____

7. What codes do you need to change?

_____

_____

_____

8. How much time have you spent actively researching investments or talking to an expert in the field?

_____

_____

_____

_____

_____

9. Do you have enough money invested so that you could survive 20 years on it? Thirty? More?

_____

_____

_____

10. What one step could you take today to start or enhance your multiplication plan?

_____

_____

_____

11. Over the past 10 years has your need for money increased?

_____

_____

_____

If yes, has your capacity increased?

_____

_____

_____

If no, then what can you do today to start fixing that?

_____

_____

_____

12. If you're dating someone, do you know where they stand financially?

_____

_____

If yes, are your goals and money management styles compatible?

_____

_____

If no, when can you sit down to have a serious financial discussion with them?

_____

_____

_____

Part 7

Summary and Questions

1. How do you view yourself?

_____

_____

2. Are you worthy of friendship?

_____

_____

3. Are you worthy of love?

_____

_____

4. *Code Question*: What did the adults in your life tell you about you? Did they call you unlovable? Did they think you were flighty or untrustworthy? Or did they build you up and tell you that you were a good friend and a great catch?

_____

_____

_____

How has what you were told as a kid about yourself impacted all your relationships to date? (Friends, Romantic Partners, Bosses, etc.)

_____

_____

_____

What truths do you need to believe to supplant any lies you were fed as a kid?

_____

_____

_____

How will it change your life and your relationships going forward if you do?

_____

_____

_____

Friendships

Friendships nourish and sustain you. They also range in intimacy and casualness from the very casual to the closer-than-brothers type. What's important is to find people who will accept you while still holding you accountable, will encourage you and not hold you back, will lend you an ear as well as a hand, and will make you a better person just by knowing them. Anyone else is not a true friend and is more a glorified acquaintance. While those have their place, you need to spend most of your time with those who lift you up.

Friendships can change over time. Sometimes you and a friend can drift apart. Other times someone you thought of as just a casual friend turns out to be your hero when your life turns upside down. It's okay when things change if everyone is honest with feelings and expectations.

1. Do you have a few great friends?

_____

_____

_____

2. Does each of those relationships nourish and sustain you?

_____

_____

_____

3. Are you a good friend and do you make yourself available?

_____

_____

4. Do you love and make the most of the time you spend with your friends?

_____

_____

_____

5. Who are the three friends that you spend the most time with?

_____

_____

6. What does each of them bring to the friendship? How do they contribute to your happiness or well-being?

_____

_____

_____

7. Are you satisfied with the relationship the way it is, or is there room for improvement?

_____

_____

_____

_____

_____

8. What would it take to improve the relationship?

_____

_____

_____

Can you discuss that with your friend?

_____

_____

_____

What would be the benefit of doing so?

_____

_____

9. Are you giving as much as you're receiving? Is there balance?

_____

_____

_____

10. Does this friendship have the potential to sustain you and be beneficial for years to come?

_____

_____

_____

11. Think of one or two friends who aren't necessarily the ones you spend the most time with but who might enrich your life more than the others. Who are they?

_____

_____

_____

How does knowing them make you a better person?

_____

_____

_____

Why don't you spend more time with them?

_____

_____

What would happen if you did spend more time with them?

_____

_____

_____

_____

_____

12. *Code Question*: How did the adults in your life treat their friends? Did they have close friends they could rely on? Did they make time for them? What beliefs do you have about friendship that you learned when you were a child watching your parents or guardians interacting with their friends?

_____

_____

_____

13. Are there any erroneous beliefs you need to change so that you can be a better friend or enjoy healthier relationships?

_____

_____

_____

14. *Code Question*: Kids can be cruel and stupid. They haven't figured out life yet and are just muddling along as best they can, dealing with the codes they've received. Did you have any bad experiences with friends when you were little that made you distrust or kept you from being able to freely express yourself?

_____

_____

How can you put those childhood problems squarely in the past?

_____

_____

_____

Familial Relationships

1. Are you satisfied with the level of contact you have with your family members?

_____

_____

_____

Why or why not?

_____

_____

_____

Is there room for improvement?

_____

_____

_____

2. Is spending time with your family members a positive experience or a negative one?

_____

_____

_____

_____

_____

3. Are there family members that you should avoid being around because they drag you down, disrespect you, etc.?

_____

_____

_____

4. While you can't choose your blood family, you can choose how much to let them impact your life. Are there blood family members who cause you problems?

_____

_____

_____

   What can you do to put an end to this?

_____

_____

_____

5. If you don't have family members who are close either physically or emotionally, have you created a family for yourself out of close friends?

_____

_____

_____

6. Do you have an older person or couple who can act as surrogate parents or grandparents who can advise and encourage you?

_____

_____

_____

7. Do you have someone who can act as a sibling, who can love you unconditionally, listen when no one else will, and push you to be your best self?

_____

_____

_____

If you don't have these people in your life, can you find them?

_____

_____

_____

8. *Code Question*: What did you learn growing up about the way families are supposed to be with each other. Did you learn that blood means everything, even if the family members are hurtful? Did you learn the value of a created family?

_____

_____

_____

9. What are the beliefs/behaviors that you have that might be holding you back from stronger, healthier "family" relationships?

_____

_____

_____

Romantic Relationships

Romantic relationships are the most exciting and can be the most problematic because they require a higher degree of intimacy, trust, and honesty than all others. If you or your significant other have problems with this, it can make it nearly impossible to make the relationship work. It's important to identify early on any negative codes you've received that might keep you from able to fully engage in this type of relationship.

1. Are you open to creating an intimate loving relationship?

_____

_____

_____

2. Are you willing to risk yourself for the sake of intimacy?

_____

_____

_____

_____

3. Are you free from past resentments?

_____

_____

_____

4. *Code Question*: Did your parents have a good relationship? Did they struggle to model positive romantic relationships? What beliefs did you get from them?

_____

_____

_____

Are there beliefs or behaviors in a relationship that are holding you back?

_____

_____

_____

5. *Code Question*: Have you noticed a pattern in your romantic relationships? Do your partners always complain about the same thing about you?

_____

_____

_____

Is there something you're doing to sabotage the relationships?

_____

_____

_____

Are there negative beliefs you're holding that are making it hard to have loving, trusting relationships?

_____

_____

_____

Which Way Element: If This, Then That

1. Are there any bad codes you can detect that might be negatively affecting your relationships?

_____

_____

_____

2. What would happen if you changed those codes? How do you think your other self-assessment answers would change (or not)?

_____

_____

_____

Part 8

Summary and Questions

1. Do you have a spiritual life? If so, how satisfied are you with your current spiritual life?

_____

_____

_____

2. *Code Question*: Did your parents practice any kind of religion openly? What expectations did they place upon you?

_____

_____

_____

_____

_____

Have these codes been helpful or limiting?

_____

_____

_____

Have you explored religion beyond what you may have been exposed to as a child?

_____

_____

_____

3. Is there room for growth in your spiritual life?

_____

_____

_____

4. What do you believe? Why?

_____

_____

_____

5. Does this belief (or lack of) resonate with you? Why or why not?

_____

_____

6. If you have an existing belief, how often are you engaging with it?

_____

_____

_____

How do you do so?

_____

_____

_____

Do you think you would benefit from more engagement?

_____

_____

_____

7. Have you had experience chronicling your spiritual journey?

_____

_____

_____

If so, what benefit did you find in it?

_____

_____

_____

If not, consider keeping a journal for two weeks as an experiment. You can write your thoughts freely, set goals for yourself, or even participate in structured studies when doing this.

8. Do whatever makes you feel comfortable and helps you track the lessons you've learned and the progress you've made.

_____

_____

_____

Which Way Element: If This, Then That

1. If you've never explored your spirituality, would you be open to trying?

_____

_____

_____

If yes, what can you do to take a first step?

_____

_____

_____

If no, why do you think you can ignore this aspect of your life?

_____

_____

_____

Part 9

Summary and Questions

1. What negative beliefs do you have that are keeping you from living your best life?

_____

_____

_____

2. *Code Question*: Where do these beliefs originate? How did you come to learn them?

_____

_____

_____

_____

_____

3. What positive beliefs can you replace the negative beliefs with?

_____

_____

_____

4. How do you think this will impact your life?

_____

_____

_____

Behavior

There are several behaviors successful people develop to stay at the top of their game. These include continuous learning, goal setting, time management, maintaining a positive attitude, and building a trustworthy network.

1. What negative behaviors do you have that are keeping you from living your best life?

_____

_____

_____

2. *Code Question*: Where do these behaviors originate? How did you come to learn them? (Examine past behaviors and family trends while thinking about this.)

_____

_____

3. What positive behaviors can you replace them with?

_____

_____

_____

4. How will you keep yourself accountable?

_____

_____

_____

5. How do you think this will impact your life?

_____

_____

_____

Balance

1. What areas of your life feel like they are out of balance?

_____

_____

_____

2. What can you do to bring your life into balance?

_____

_____

_____

3. How do you think this will impact your life?

_____

_____

_____

4. What is one small step you can take today to start creating balance?

_____

_____

_____

Boundaries

1. Look at the boundaries you have in your relationships (professional, family, friends, romantic). Are they all healthy?

_____

_____

_____

2. If you have nonexistent or unhealthy boundaries, where do you think that comes from?

_____

_____

_____

What can you do to change them?

_____

_____

_____

How do you think this will impact those relationships?

_____

_____

_____

Bliss

Bliss is about basking in the abundance of happiness, joy, and grace. This is when you are living life to the fullest. It's about living in the moment. Capturing moments and making memories is an important aspect of life.

1. Are you practicing gratitude?

_____

_____

_____

2. Are you living in the moment?

_____

_____

_____

3. How can you provide yourself more self-care?

_____

_____

_____

Which Way Element: If This, Then That

Pick one area to focus on (belief, behavior, balance, boundaries, bliss).

1. If you improve this area, what do you think will happen?

_____

_____

_____

2. Will it improve your life?

_____

_____

_____

If yes, why?

_____

_____

_____

_____

_____

If no, why not?

_____

_____

_____

3. If it does improve your life, are you willing to work on a second area? Which one will you choose?

_____

_____

_____

4. How do you think that will change your life?

_____

_____

_____

5. If it didn't improve your life, why do you think it didn't?

_____

_____

_____

6. Is there something you can do differently?

_____

_____

7. Go through and do this for every area of your life.

_____

_____

_____

Part 10

Summary and Questions

1. What have you learned about yourself and your codes?

_____

_____

_____

2. What codes are you going to actively change to more positive codes?

_____

_____

_____

_____

_____

_____

3. What is one thing you can do today or this week to impact each area of your life?

_____

_____

_____

4. What's stopping you?

_____

_____

Get started!